Also available at all good book stores

9781785316470

9781785313929

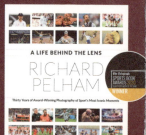

9781785315466

9781785311925

9781909178830

9781909178724

9781905411023

9781905411160

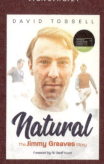

9781785314902

THE
GREATEST
ESCAPE

THE

GREATEST
ESCAPE

The Craziest Season in
West Ham United's History

DANIEL HURLEY

First published by Pitch Publishing, 2021

Pitch Publishing
A2 Yeoman Gate
Yeoman Way
Worthing
Sussex
BN13 3QZ
www.pitchpublishing.co.uk
info@pitchpublishing.co.uk

ISBN 978 1 78531 817 7

Typesetting and origination by Pitch Publishing
Printed and bound in India by Replika Press Pvt. Ltd.

Contents

Acknowledgements

TO KATE, for being my sounding board, editor and best friend through this process. I thank you and I love you, with all my heart.

To Jack and Adam for asking me to tell them a story about West Ham while out walking one day, and then enjoying the story I told them enough to think other people might like it too.

Prologue

'*GOOD GOD almighty, we might actually do this*'. I still remember thinking that to this very day. It was the 90th minute, and we were 3-2 up in the FA Cup Final. Against Liverpool. Liverpool, still the reigning European champions. Surely this couldn't be happening. We'd all been in the same stadium a year prior to this day, but in such different circumstances.

Preston in the 2004/05 Championship play-off final was the biggest game I'd ever been to, the biggest game *most* West Ham fans had ever been to. We'd been an average-to-poor side through most of the season. We somehow ended up scraping sixth in the league but probably weren't even that good in truth.

Then we were the beneficiaries of Ipswich freezing like a deer in the headlights in a blizzard, just to get through to the final in the first place. And if we'd failed to win that game and get back up to the Premier League, we'd have joined Leeds, Sheffield Wednesday and Portsmouth on the list of giants that had fallen from their perches and never made it back to the big time.

But we did win that day. It was nervy, God it was nervy. Goalless at half-time and with not much in it, in the 57th minute Matty Etherington, our most important player at the time in my opinion, made his first successful foray down the left in the whole game, crossed from the byline and there was Bobby Zamora to tuck the ball home and put us 1-0 up, giving us a lead we very comfortably held on to. That's if you call your goalkeeper rupturing his knee ligaments, seven minutes added time, and what felt like 127 crosses into the box and even more shots, comfortable.

But we held on, and West Ham United made it back to the Premier League. As we left that day, emotionally exhausted but elated, we all consoled ourselves in the knowledge that after two consecutive years paying for tickets to ride this emotional rollercoaster (first and only time for that cliché) known as the play-off final, we wouldn't have to go through anything like it for a while, and definitely not the following year.

In fact, as nice as Cardiff is, as much fun before the game as it is, with its streets full of (and I mean full of) bars, which thirsty Hammers fans were more than happy to take full advantage of from as early as we were allowed to do so, I think there was an element of relief that we wouldn't be going back there the following year.

And yet 12 months on from that day, here we all were again in something nobody saw coming when the season began in August. A side that was barely the sixth-best team in the Championship in 2004/05 became one of the better teams in the Premier League the following season, giving the West Ham faithful arguably their most enjoyable season since the famous Cottee/McAvennie-inspired third place in 1985/86.

While this is obviously a book about the season after 2005/06, it would be remiss of me not to briefly mention some of the highlights of that wonderful first season back in the top division, which include the following:

Opening day, things start oddly well: The opening day of a season is always one of the most, if not the most, optimistic days in any football fan's calendar. But as a West Ham fan, before or since 2005, it very rarely stays optimistic for long (as I write this in 2020, we have lost our last three opening games 4-0, 4-0 and 5-0).

This looked to be the case when Andy Todd bundled Blackburn, at this time a Mark Hughes-led established upper-level Premier League team, into a 1-0 lead that they held into the second half. But in front of a raucous crowd who clearly realised the challenges this young team could face over the season, second-half goals from veteran striker Teddy Sheringham, captain Nigel Reo-Coker and Etherington gave us a 3-1 win that set the standard for things to come.

Marlon's big night and an amazing day of sport: This one may be more memorable to me than most people, but hey, it's my book, so I will indulge. For me, Daniel Phillip Henry Hurley, Monday, 10 September 2005 was about as close to sporting perfection as it was possible to get.

PROLOGUE

As well as my passion for West Ham and football in general, I am also a huge cricket fan. This was the day that after spending two summer months watching the 2005 Ashes series, unquestionably the greatest series of cricket ever played, Kevin Pietersen (I imagine making his first-ever appearance in a book about West Ham) smashed Australia around the Oval for 158 and the Ashes came home to England. All this prior to our game at home to Aston Villa that evening.

The win in the cricket, as you can imagine, led to celebrations that involved me and my two best friends and then-university housemates Steve and Chris (even more certainly making their first appearances in a book about West Ham) heading straight to the pub for post-Ashes-winning drinks, pre-football drinks, during football drinks and post-football drinks.

To cut a long story short, Marlon Harewood, our main striker at the time, got over a couple of iffy displays in the first three games to score two goals in the first half hour and a hat-trick in 50 minutes.

The night was then rounded off by Yossi Benayoun, a new signing from Maccabi Haifa, scoring a wonderful fourth goal having twisted and turned Aaron Hughes to the point that he may still struggle with balance to this day.

All in all, it was as perfect a day's sport as it was possible to have, made even better by Chris falling off his chair in the pub shortly after the final whistle. Good times.

'Last team at Highbury': We'll talk about the end to that song later, don't worry. By January, things were going extremely well. We were comfortably mid-table and travelled to Highbury knowing a win would put us only two points behind Arsenal, who were only two seasons removed from the great 'invincibles' season and would end up runners-up in the Champions League to Barcelona four months later.

Fair to say, however, that I wasn't at my most hopeful before the game that night, letting my friends know that I wouldn't be up for our usual Wednesday night out at the erm, world-famous Portsmouth University Student Union nightclub (it's a library now, times have changed). After some gentle nudging by my mates, I agreed that I would come and watch the game with them and then head home for a quiet night. Unless we won, which I really couldn't see happening. I mean, the season had been great, so many of our players were in form and looking Premier League quality, but surely rocking up at Arsenal and beating them was a bridge too far?

It looked as if I was spot on with my pessimism over the first 20 minutes, which if my memory is correct consisted mainly of Henry, Pires and Van Persie kicking the ball to each other in and around our goal line but for some reason not kicking the ball over said line.

This odd tactic was taken up a notch after 25 minutes by Sol Campbell deciding to just not kick the ball full stop, which led to Reo-Coker running clean through on goal for what felt like about five minutes before slotting past Jens Lehmann to give us a 1-0 lead. Ridiculously we doubled this lead shortly after when Campbell, clearly not satisfied with his earlier work, decided to react to Bobby

Zamora cutting back on to his left foot by essentially falling over in front of him; Zamora somehow wasn't put off by this and curled the ball into the far corner of the net, at which point your author nearly passed out.

Mr Henry clearly took this as a wake-up call and scored a goal of his own in first-half injury time, one of what feels like approximately 362 times in my life I have seen West Ham go 2-0 up in the first half of a game only to let a goal in just before the break (the only reason this number isn't true is because we haven't been 2-0 up in the first half 362 times in my time as a fan; if we had been it would be accurate, trust me).

This would obviously then lead to an Arsenal equaliser and winner in the second half, and an expected defeat coming in a way that makes you more upset than you were anticipating. Always fun when that happens; only this time, it didn't. We held on, stayed in the game, kept pushing forward when we could, and then somehow counter-attacked and scored again.

With ten minutes to go, a sweeping move was finished off by Etherington and I began the always glorious football fan ritual of hugging complete strangers while screaming in their faces. Arsenal scored a late consolation but we held on for a win, which led to me going back on my earlier intentions and going out. *Out* out you might say. Good God, I went *out* out that night.

A mix of excitement, Sol Campbell ineptness and out-of-date £1.60 Carling led to one of the drunkest states I have ever been in to this very day. I made it home, which was a minor miracle in itself, but ended the night falling down the stairs at my university house before waking up my good friend Chris (he of the chair incident), who had the misfortune to share a wall with me that night at circa 3am, by playing 'Bubbles' through my speakers. He had an exam at 9am. Sorry again, Chris.

Was a great night, though.

Breaking Tottenham's heart, 'lasagne-gate': And now we come to the game before the FA Cup Final, our last league match of the season and one in which we really didn't have much to play for. We were safe and sound in mid-table, a ninth-place finish all but secure. In those circumstances normally the season-ending game would be a quiet affair, a few players rested and those who are playing doing their best not to get injured, knowing that the biggest game of most of their lives was only six days away.

This last game, however, was a different proposition. This last game was against Tottenham. Not only against Tottenham, but a Tottenham who needed to win to qualify for the Champions League. Suffice to say, this had all the hallmarks of a day to remember for a long time if it went well, or a day we would never hear the end of if it didn't.

In so many instances before or since, this would be a game in which a bigger team would roll us over without too much fuss, but not this season and not against this team. We went 1-0 up early, with a goal from midfielder and definitely-not ex-Harchester United (if you know, you know) player Carl Fletcher, and the Boleyn was rocking.

We then had the double blow of an equaliser from everybody's favourite weasel, Jermain Defoe, and a missed penalty at the other end from Sheringham, which again would knock the stuffing out of a lot of sides. But we rolled our sleeves up, kept fighting and with ten minutes to go won the game with a calmly taken goal from Benayoun.

I am heartbroken to say I wasn't at this game (quite honestly I'm not sure my dad has ever forgiven me), but I was lucky to be in a pub in Portsmouth among what seemed like hundreds of Arsenal fans, all of whom were happy to buy so very many thank-you drinks for me and my fellow university-attending Hammer friend, Owen. A life lesson for everybody there; if you can't be somewhere you want to be, try and be somewhere where you get free beer.

(Oh, and there was something about Spurs players having food poisoning. But who cares about that?)

So back to 4.48pm in Cardiff then …

We really might do this. We're about to go into injury time, not far away now. The throw Scaloni has just conceded to let one of their players be treated, while near our goal, shouldn't be too bad. It might even be quite clever. Four added minutes, I see. The last ten minutes have actually gone quicker than I imagined. Will they throw the ball back to us for a goal kick? No, they've given it to us in our corner; well clear it please, Lionel, as far away as possible. Hmmm, not ideal, straight to Gerrard. Can somebody close him down … oh no.

Both writing and reliving the memory of that goal is still as hard 14 years later as it was that day. My seat, in the top tier of the stadium just to the right of the goal as I looked, was a disgustingly good view to see one of the finest goals in FA Cup Final history bullet into the net.

I clear as day remember saying 'oh, he's scored' out loud before the ball even hit the net. It was just that good. What still hurts most about the game isn't even the goal as such, it's the realisation that without Gerrard, who was nearing the peak of his exceptional powers, we were better than Liverpool that day. Much better.

Dean Ashton, who had signed from Norwich for £7m that January, had arguably the finest game of his career to that point. It is a crying shame that it ended up being the best game of his whole career, but we will get to that. Yossi Benayoun led most of their midfield and defence on a merry dance all afternoon. It is no coincidence in my opinion that two years after this game, he was plying his trade at Anfield. All over the pitch we were very good; Etherington, Harewood, I could go on.

I could list and elaborate upon so many moments of the game and the day. For instance, Reo-Coker hitting the post with 90 seconds to go and the rebound falling to a cramp-stricken Harewood, who on one good leg hit the ball wide when any other player would have tapped it in.

Or Reina's double save from Marlon and Yossi at 2-1 early in the second half. Or the penalties. Or me seeing Chesney Hawkes (he of 'I Am The One And Only' fame) wandering around the concourse before kick-off. I could talk about all of this. But this isn't a book about what happened on that day, it is about what happened after it.

As I am sure you all know, Liverpool beat us 3-1 on penalties after a 3-3 draw. We did ourselves proud and while the agony was oh so real as we filed out of the Millennium Stadium, we could console ourselves with the knowledge that we had a young, bright and hungry team with a manager to match.

There would be money to spend to further improve the squad and European football to come the following season due to a UEFA Cup place secured via the cup final run; Pardew was bullish about our chances in the competition, insisting that we were 'in it to win it'.

Despite the hurt of that day, we all came away feeling like this was the start of something, and that we would be back bigger and stronger. It felt as the new season dawned, that change was coming and it could be a year we would never forget.

How right we were.

Nine months later, we ended the season having signed two world class players, Carlos Tevez and Javier Mascherano out of nowhere, to this very day still one of the most famous and surprising transfers of all time.

Then in classic West Ham style, rather than the success we all thought the signings would bring, we still ended up in a season-long relegation battle capped off with seven wins from nine games, the greatest escape in top division history. Fair to say that on its own would make a season unforgettable.

Let alone going two months without scoring a goal, or suffering through 11 games without a win straight after your new manager has come in. You wouldn't forget that either.

Losing 4-3 to your biggest rivals in a must-win game having been 3-2 up in the 89th minute. Your lead striker breaking his ankle the week before the season begins, and ends up having to retire from the injury. Again, both incidents forever burned into your memory.

How about a season that ends in the courtroom rather than on the football pitch, with all your rivals calling you cheats? Nobody is forgetting that.

Any of these incidents on their own would lead to an unforgettable season. West Ham in 2006/07 had every single scenario listed above happen inside one crazy year, and many more besides …

West Ham United. Tevez. Remembered by anybody who was around to witness it, *The Greatest Escape* is the full story of the highs, lows and controversies that took place in the 2006-07 season …

CHAPTER ONE

May – August (pre-season)

A COUPLE of quiet weeks followed the FA Cup Final. The only news was the England squad for the 2006 World Cup being finalised. It was devoid of any east London representation, which as any Hammers fan knows leaves the national side a minimum of three players short of the required number to win a major tournament.

Somewhat surprisingly after the season we'd had, only Nigel Reo-Coker got anywhere near the squad having been named as an eventually unused standby player. Marlon Harewood (16 goals in the previous season, 14 in the league), Bobby Zamora (ten goals) and Dean Ashton (six goals and man of the match in the cup final) were among the English strikers ignored in favour of 17-year-old new Arsenal signing Theo Walcott, who had made, erm, zero Premier League appearances. While I will no doubt use the benefit of hindsight from time to time during the writing of this book, on this occasion it isn't needed as it seemed as weird a decision then as it does now.

The only West Ham player going to that World Cup was the soon-to-be-released Shaka Hislop, who was going with first-time participants Trinidad & Tobago. The Trinidadians were grouped with England, where Shaka could without a doubt exact his revenge on Mr Gerrard.

Our first signing of the summer window was announced on 8 June, with confirmation that Lee Bowyer would be returning to the club for a second spell from Newcastle. He had joined the Geordies after his initial six-month stint with us ended in 2003, when we had somehow got relegated with a side that quite honestly should have been challenging the top six. The lifelong West Ham fan arrived back in east London no doubt aiming to avoid anything like that happening again.

Bowyer was a curious case. He was clearly blessed with substantial talent, as evidenced by his fantastic spell (on the pitch at least) with Leeds United, where he scored 55 goals in 265 games, consistently challenged at the top end of the league and even played in a Champions League semi-final. This should have translated to England honours but as alluded to above, off-field incidents such as a very public trial for GBH along with then-clubmate Jonathan Woodgate (he was eventually acquitted) played a role in him only earning one cap. By 2006, the midfielder was not the superstar signing he would have been in 2001 and not even the player he was when he first joined in 2003.

He was also still not free from controversy. An on-pitch fight with team-mate Kieron Dyer in 2005 was still fresh in people's memories and is still talked about to this day, mainly because of those cringe-inducing 'funny football moments' programmes that Sky One seem to show on a loop. (Still, now Bowyer had left Newcastle nobody would ever reunite that pair at another club again, right? Right?)

For that reason, it seemed a somewhat odd signing at the time when so much of the 05/06 squad's success had been built on unity. It didn't come across as the wisest of moves to make a signing that requires your manager to tell your official website, 'I will not tolerate any other incidents. He now needs to have a clean bill of health. We had a fantastic disciplinary record last season. One sending-off all year speaks for itself. Lee has to understand they are the standards we have set and I expect him to abide by them.'

Bowyer at least was extremely positive about the move, insisting, 'I loved my time at Newcastle but this is my club. I didn't play well last time. I see this as unfinished business. I want to show the Hammers fans what I can do.' Reports of him taking a wage cut to rejoin the club, so eager was he to prove himself, also seemed like a positive sign, so most fans, myself included, were inclined to give Bowyer a chance and see how this panned out.

Two newsworthy incidents occurred on 15 June 2006; firstly, Steven Gerrard continued his public destruction of Shaka Hislop's self-confidence by volleying a picture-perfect 20-yard effort past him for England's second goal in their 2-0 World Cup group stage win over Shaka's Trinidad & Tobago.

In the 91st minute, of course, just to rub the pain in even further for both the goalkeeper and any West Ham fan with a functioning memory.

Watching the game in a pub in Canary Wharf, I refused to celebrate the goal. Christ knows what difference I thought it would make, but my stance was clear.

The second bit of news on the day was we announced the signing of Manchester United's versatile American-born defender Jonathan Spector. In no way, shape or form signed to justify a trip to America with certain club personnel, Pards was delighted with the capture of the 20-year-old, telling the BBC, 'He has huge potential and we hope that bears fruition at West Ham. He is a player we have been tracking for the past 18 months or so. He is definitely one for the future and, with the UEFA Cup campaign to look forward to, he will add to our defensive capacity. Having developed as a young player at Manchester United, he arrives with a fantastic pedigree. I was also very impressed by his character, which was a big factor in bringing him to the club.'

High praise indeed. Good to know we had sorted out the problematic right-back position so early in the close season as well.

The following day, I was at a friend's house in the evening watching Argentina dismantle Serbia 6-0 in their second World Cup group game. I remember thinking that their young midfielder Mascherano looked a good player and was also interested in a young forward, Carlos something or other, who I hadn't heard of before being brought on before Messi and then scoring their fifth goal with a lovely little finish. I had a brief conversation with my dad on the phone walking home from my friend's that night about how good the Argentina team looked, mentioning those two players as well, and thought no more about it.

1 July was, I dare say, a bittersweet day for most Hammers fans due to events in Gelsenkirchen in the World Cup, where England did what England do in major tournament matches, namely underachieving, getting a man sent off and losing on penalties to a team they should beat. Portugal were the beneficiaries for the second big event in a row, with Wayne Rooney being the man dismissed and Cristiano Ronaldo becoming the pantomime villain for the British public and media. Safe to say, it didn't affect his career too much.

So why would people of a claret and blue persuasion have been cheered by this exactly? Mainly due to the identities of two of the players who missed their penalties, of course. The final pen was missed by apparently our specialist penalty taker, Jamie sodding Carragher, who having never taken a penalty anywhere other than in training, his garden or on a computer game, was for some reason brought on so he could take a penalty in a World Cup quarter-final. He, of course, missed, which as a Liverpool player in 2006 would have cheered up any West Ham fan, despite the sadness of England being eliminated from the tournament.

The main consolation in defeat, however, was the identity of the player who missed the preceding penalty: Shaka Hislop's nemesis, Steven Gerrard. I'm sure Shaka was delirious as Portuguese keeper Ricardo did what he couldn't do that day in Cardiff, or the day in Germany for that matter, and saved a Gerrard attempt on goal from at least ten yards closer in than either of the midfielder's two other efforts.

In fact, as the keeper managed to save penalties from not only two Liverpool players but also perennial villain Frank Lampard, he probably became early favourite for Hammer of the Year that day. Looking back now, what with the fact we were in the market for at least one goalkeeper to replace Hislop, I am genuinely amazed that we didn't try to sign this bloke. It is something we definitely would have done these days. Him then failing to save a penalty in his entire Hammers career would have been spectacular.

My personal story of the game that day was watching it at a 21st birthday party for my then-girlfriend's best friend; I watched the game with a few blokes, various friends of the birthday girl and other halves. None of them knew me particularly well, if at all, so my belly laughing at the three penalty misses, and outright cheering of Gerrard's miss, didn't exactly endear me to the rest of the group. Suffice to say, I am not in touch with any of those people now, nor was I even the following day, which in hindsight is not a surprise.

The following week West Ham were again back in the transfer market with two further additions. Right-back signing number two Tyrone Mears arrived from Preston for £1m to compete with the already signed Spector and young striker Carlton Cole came in from Chelsea for an undisclosed fee.

Mears was a 23-year-old who we signed from the Lilywhites after he had made 70 appearances for them;

this would have been more but he missed the majority of the 04/05 season with a stress fracture. He was a highly rated youngster at the time. Ironically enough, shortly before joining us he was a target of Charlton's to replace Luke Young, who was expected to be leaving shortly to sign for ... West Ham.

We had spent over a month pursuing the England international, who had even handed in a transfer request to force through a move from south to east London. A £4m bid was accepted, only to collapse at the last minute when Young failed a medical. We obviously reacted to this disappointment by moving one name further down the enormous list of available right-backs that seemed to exist in 2006 to Mears' name and signed the player just two days after the Young breakdown.

Cole was oddly not a right-back, but a talented striker who had been a bit-part young player at Chelsea, alternating between the odd sub appearance in the Prem, starts in cup matches and season-long loan spells. Yes, Chelsea were even doing this with their young players back then.

Cole had spent the 2003/04 season at Charlton and the 04/05 campaign at Aston Villa, before a year on the fringes at Stamford Bridge led him to look for new opportunities, and off he ran into Uncle Alan's arms.

Pards was even happier than usual with this signing, enthusing to the club website, 'This is a great coup for West Ham. Several clubs came in for Carlton and it is a great compliment to what we have achieved here that he has signed for us. [He] is a powerful, skilful striker and brings another option to our forward line as we embark on a new season and a European campaign.' High praise and optimism indeed there.

But that was not all from Pardew that day, as promises were afoot as well. 'I am delighted to have Carlton on board, but our search for new players is not over and I want our supporters to know there will be more signings in the coming weeks.'

Excellent news there. Maybe look at a goalkeeper at this point, Alan. We only employed one realistic first-team option (the sometimes injured and sometimes not any good Roy Carroll) as we had released Shaka and sold young keeper Steven Bywater to Derby County. Jimmy Walker, he of the unfortunate injury in the 2004/05 play-off final, was at this point less of a starting option and more of a 'good in the dressing room' squad player. A left-back also seemed a priority, as back-up the previous season Clive Clarke seemed to be on the way out (he would join Sunderland soon enough) and we needed somebody to provide competition to Paul Konchesky.

So we definitely had positions that needed filling, and it was good to know further players would be coming in. Just as long as they weren't strikers (we had five options up front now), and they weren't right-backs. We definitely didn't need any more right-backs. No right-backs.

Three weeks later, right-back John Pantsil was the next signing announced by the club. That's about right.

The former Hapoel Tel Aviv player earned a four-year contract as part of a deal worth up to £1m after impressing in a pre-season trial, having apparently been recommended to Pardew by Yossi Benayoun after the

2006 World Cup, where he had played in the Ghana team that made the last 16.

He also caused controversy when waving the Israeli flag after both Ghanaian goals in a 2-0 win over the Czech Republic. Hard to work out why Yossi may have been a fan of him, then. The question also needs to be asked: if Pantsil had impressed so much during this trial, why did we feel the need to sign Tyrone Mears as well? Particularly when Spector had also been signed earlier in the summer.

At this point, I was beginning to worry. It seemed as if we were signing players for the sake of it rather than adding quality, which looked the far more obvious transfer strategy to pursue after the strong season we were coming off.

I completely understand that there was a long domestic season ahead as well as a possibly lengthy European campaign, which would, of course, create the need for a larger squad. But the club had now employed five strikers and three right-backs.

I know I have joked about the right-back issue a fair bit now but I genuinely can't work out why we needed to sign three players in quick succession for a position where only one would ever be picked. Quite frankly, it occurred to me at the time, and still does now, that Pardew wasn't sure any of them would be quite up to the level required but hoped that if he got three in surely one would be good enough and establish themselves as first choice.

Quantity over quality.

This was a mistake we would make again almost move for move ten years later, whereby after our last season at Upton Park (the only season in my time supporting the club that was better than 2005/06) we prepared for the following campaign looking to build on the previous year's success as well as embark on a European run. Rather than the two or three top-level additions needed, the club decided to sign ten players of varying levels: quantity over quality. We then watched signing after signing fail miserably and went backwards fast. Never accuse West Ham of learning from their mistakes.

At this point, I will fill you in on how pre-season had been coming along on the pitch among all the right-back signings. A tour of Sweden took in three matches in quick succession; up first was a 2-0 win over FC Trollhattan with goals from young Welsh defender (and future Ginger Pele) James Collins and Dean Ashton, which also saw Mears and Cole make their debuts in claret and blue and Lee Bowyer re-debut.

Two days later saw a 2-1 defeat against IFK Gothenburg, where a first-half Zamora strike was cancelled out by two second-half goals by the home side, and the tour was rounded off on the pitch with a 3-1 victory over second division SK Ljungskile, where despite goals from Ashton, Zamora and Benayoun the most noteworthy news item, in the long term at least, was that this match was the first time (but certainly not the last) that the first team were led out by Mark Noble as captain. Noble had impressed throughout the tour and hopes were high that this could be a breakout season for the youngster.

A week later back in England saw a 4-0 win at non-league Cambridge United with goals from Ashton, Noble (not a penalty oddly), Cole and another youth player in left-winger Kyel Reid, before we were back on our travels, this time for a tour of Greece. Clearly Pards had been saving his air miles in preparation for this summer.

Just the two matches on this tour, a 2-2 draw with Aris, where a 2-0 lead with goals from Zamora and Harewood were cancelled out by the hosts, and then a bizarre 2-1 defeat to PAOK Salonikaa, which saw Matty Etherington playing at left-back and the game ending with us having a centre midfield of first-team coach Kevin Keen and soon-to-be-leaving back-up goalkeeper Steven Bywater. It's fair to say teams have taken tours more seriously.

I have no idea why this whistle-stop tour was a good idea or even why it was sanctioned. It seemed to do nothing for anybody other than Greek hoteliers, and I imagine Greek bars, as whoever decided to end a friendly with that centre midfield must have surely been under the influence.

The oddness of the Greek trip was compounded by the traditional final 'marquee' home friendly before the kick-off, where we played the champions of, erm, Greece, Olympiakos, in east London. Having been in Greece earlier that week, I hope the two teams shared a plane back!

The game was drawn 1-1, with another goal from Marvellous Marlon that was cancelled out in the second half by winger Nery Castillo. Many of the fans, me included, hung around at the end of the game waiting for a penalty shoot-out that didn't happen, nor as it turned out was ever scheduled to. Oh for the days of the Betway Cup in future.

So, results-wise, a positive start to pre-season but some worries by the end with no wins from the last three games, but some encouraging performances from Harewood, Zamora, Mullins and Ashton, as well as youngsters Noble and Reid continuing to impress when given opportunities.

Also, we hadn't had too many long-term injuries which is always a positive. Matty Etherington was out for a month with hamstring trouble and Reo-Coker was one of a couple of players who had missed part of pre-season with injury but was fit for the big kick-off. Ashton had gone down injured a couple of times in the Olympiakos match but thankfully was OK. The striker had looked one of the best forwards in the country following his move from Norwich the previous January, the cup final being a true coming-out party for him on a national scale. With a full pre-season behind him, Deano looked leaner, meaner and ready to go this season.

He had even been handed his maiden call-up to the England squad for a friendly at home to Greece, being played somewhat oddly three days before the Premier League kick-off. Still, nice all the same for him to get his first cap, as long as no niggles occurred or anything like that.

Before the final week of pre-season, we added to the squad in an area we actually needed to by paying Sunderland circa £1m for their left-back George McCartney (the fee was reported as £600,000, with Clive Clarke completing his long-rumoured switch to the Black Cats in addition). This looked like a very shrewd capture. McCartney had been the Sunderland captain up until an injury-plagued 2005/06 and joined the Hammers off the back of 157 senior appearances by the age of 25. He was, however, injured for at least another month, still leaving us short at left-back for the start of the season, but overall it appeared a very good long-term signing.

The seventh and final signing before the start of the campaign appeared to be another intelligent one, as Norwich and England international goalkeeper Robert Green moved back to the Premier League on a four-year deal for approximately £2m. Similar to the McCartney deal, this looked like the kind of sensible signing with both the present and future in mind; Green was 26 and had already played 241 first-team matches for the Canaries, including an even-present campaign in the Premier League two years previously. The time seemed right for the stopper to make a career step-up and head to east London.

While this was excellent news and represented a positive week or two in the market, with two important gaps in the squad positions filled with promising players on paper (although it should be noted that like McCartney, Green was injured when signed and wouldn't be available for at least a month), it is fair to say that barely anybody noticed Green's arrival that day. If they did, I highly doubt anybody mustered a smile at the news.

That was because of news that had come out of the England camp the day before, involving a pothole, Shaun Wright-Phillips and Robert Green's former Norwich team-mate.

Without a doubt, the season 2006/07 had many massive moments, ones that affected the club, the fans and the individuals involved. I don't think it can be argued, though, that the biggest single moment for any one individual came on the morning of Tuesday, 15 August.

That morning, Dean Ashton was having a training session with the senior England team, which was basically built around him and how best to utilise his considerable talents on his debut the following evening. This should have been the beginning of the high point of his career. Instead, it was the beginning of the end. Accounts of how the injury happened vary but most accounts say that it was a combination of an errant Wright-Phillips tackle and a piece of uneven ground that led to a badly broken ankle. Initially, it was thought that Ashton would be out for at least 12 weeks. Manager Alan Pardew was understandably gutted but tried to put a brave face on the news. 'We are absolutely devastated,' he told the official club website. 'It's a massive blow for Deano and his family, and for everybody here at West Ham United. We are extremely disappointed by the news but, on a positive note, we still have four quality strikers at this club, which will suppress the blow somewhat. We look forward to a speedy recovery from Deano and hope to see him back in action very soon.'

If the speedy recovery had indeed occurred, we would end the story here and pick things back up later with Ashton as he made his gradual and hopefully successful return. But as we know, that didn't happen. Deano's season ended that day and after a three-year battle with the injury, his career was over as well. After a year of rehab, the striker came back to start the 2007/08 season but he formally retired on 11 December 2009, at the age of just 26. Despite his attempts to recover from the injury, he was never the same player, sadly not even close.

Ashton briefly discussed the rest of the season in an interview in 2017, stating, 'When I broke my ankle, obviously that was huge a disappointment, but I thought I'd come back stronger than ever, but when six or seven months later I had to go in for another operation and it was clear that wasn't going to happen, it was infuriating,' he said. 'Once I knew I needed a second operation, that ruled me out completely – there was no way I could have played a role in the Great Escape. I took myself off into my own bubble, away from the club, so I was quite isolated but that didn't make it any less torturous, watching and knowing I was powerless to help.'

While this was a catastrophic blow for the club and devastating news for the fans, coming as it did only three days before the start of the new season, the real casualties that day were undoubtedly Dean Ashton and his family, as his career had been ripped away from him. To this day, he remains probably the best natural striker I have seen play for us, and I have no doubt that but for that injury he would have been one of the great English forwards of the last 40 years. Without any question, he is one of English football's great lost talents, let alone one of West Ham United's.

CHAPTER TWO

August

EVERYONE AT the club had to quickly dust themselves down after the terrible news regarding Ashton, as the big kick-off was upon us. Just like the season before we started the campaign at home, this time against Charlton Athletic, who at this point had become an established Premier League side, finishing 13th the previous season.

They had, however, lost long-time manager Alan Curbishley, who had decided to take some time away after 15 highly successful years with the Addicks (more about that later); he had been replaced by ex-Hammer Iain Dowie, who himself was coming off the back of a largely successful yet acrimonious stay at Crystal Palace, which took in the unlikeliest of promotions (at West Ham's expense in the play-off final) followed by immediate relegation and return to the Championship, where they had remained following a play-off semi-final defeat to Watford. Dowie's spell there ended with him choosing to leave to take over at the Valley, for which he was being sued for breach of contract by his former chairman Simon Jordan (Jordan would eventually be awarded damages in court). Dowie had come in and signed ex-Chelsea forward Jimmy Floyd Hasselbaink and Scott Carson on loan, who would both make their debuts at the Boleyn Ground.

We also had two debutants in our team, with Tyrone Mears and Lee Bowyer coming in to augment what was a largely settled side. Six of the 11 who lined up in the FA Cup Final were in the team, with the other three changes due to injury and suspension (Carroll and Mullins would have started that day in Cardiff and Ashton would have started here). The full team that lined up on the opening day was as follows:

Starting XI*: Carroll, Mears, Ferdinand, Gabbidon, Konchesky, Bowyer, Mullins, Reo-Coker, Benayoun, Zamora, Harewood*

Subs*: Walker, Pantsil, Collins, Sheringham, Cole*

The game began quietly with both teams feeling each other out in the way teams often do on the opening day, until Danny Gabbidon decided for some reason to try and block Bryan Hughes' cross towards Hasselbaink with his arm. Nigh on the only person who didn't see this was referee Howard Webb; unluckily for us his linesman didn't suffer the same temporary blindness, and a penalty was awarded and duly converted by future Hammers target Darren Bent.

Charlton would hold their one-goal advantage until half-time but would later concede a numerical advantage. Ex-Liverpool defender Djimi Traore (he of the magnificent 'rabona' own goal in a cup match at Burnley that still finds its way into football blooper DVDs now) managed to get booked twice in the blink of an eye, firstly for hacking Bowyer down on the halfway line and then for needlessly sticking out a foot to stop the same player's attempted free kick, leaving Charlton to play with ten men for the remaining 64 minutes.

This led to us getting more on top and the dominance paid off in the second half as satisfyingly as your audacious 37/1 six-match accumulator does once a season, primarily through the intelligent play and passing of one Lee Bowyer. Firstly, his excellent teasing cross was bundled in at the back post by Bobby Zamora, who celebrated by shouting at the fans 'my ****ing team' while looking like he wanted to fight them. He never looked angrier or more aggressive than when he scored and I could never work out why. Then Bowyer's run and pass was finished again by Zamora, his scuffed left-foot shot somehow evading Hreidarsson, the scrambling Carson and El Karkouri on the line when it seemed as if any of the three of them could have simply kicked the ball clear.

The game largely drifted to a conclusion after Bobby and Bowyer's flurry, notable only when Teddy Sheringham became the oldest outfield player to appear in the Premier League at 40 years and 93 days young. Then, in injury time, Carlton Cole came on to become the fourth new Hammer that day and celebrated 90 seconds later by latching on to Bowyer's beautifully chipped through ball, taking his first touch in claret and blue to set himself, and with his second touch lashing in the third and decisive goal of the game, which sealed three points and a second 3-1 opening-day win in succession.

Bowyer was outstanding in the second half, providing three assists in a man-of-the-match display and earning deserved praise from his manager in the post-match press conference. 'He had three assists and hit the post with a fantastic effort. He was an England international on that performance and I think he needed that for the fans. He proved he's going to be a major asset for us.' So, all in all, a highly satisfactory first day's work, and the only way is up, right? Right?

The eagle-eyed amongst you may have noticed that I noted Carlton Cole being the fourth debutant in that game. The third was right-back John Pantsil, who came on at half-time for Tyrone Mears, meaning that we had managed to try two of our right-backs in the first game, which may have been lost in the happiness of victory but in reality was a worrying sign of things to come.

Saturday, 19 August 2006:

West Ham 3 *Zamora (52,66), Cole (90)*

Charlton 1 *Bent pen (15)*

Three days later, the show rolled on to a tricky-looking match at Vicarage Road against newly promoted Watford. These games can often be a banana skin for sides, with teams fresh off a successful campaign in the league below coming up and riding a wave of momentum in their first few games. West Ham had often been a victim in this type of match, so it is fair to say any result that night would have been seen as positive, and a result was just about what we got.

Pardew made two changes to the side from the previous weekend, with half-time sub John Pantsil staying in at the expense of Mears, who didn't make the bench due to injury, and somewhat strangely Yossi Benayoun was left out in favour of James Collins, with the side reverting to a 3-5-2 formation that had barely been seen the previous season.

Pardew rationalised this by saying it was a ploy to deal with the amount of balls coming into our box due to Watford's direct play, which I can understand, but I cannot help but think that by dropping one of our most creative players we played into their hands and made the game easier for them. Watford certainly didn't seem concerned in the first half as they peppered our goal without success, with their talisman Marlon King hitting the post and winger Ashley Young sending an overhead kick just wide.

It seemed as if a goal would come, and sure enough it did early in the second half as King curled in a fantastic strike from at least 20 yards. This seemed as if it would kick the Hornets on but in a most unlike West Ham fashion, rather than crumbling we somewhat oddly went straight up the other end and equalised; a Konchesky cross being bundled in by Zamora for his third goal in the first four days of the season.

The game somewhat petered out after that. It was notable only for Sheringham coming off the bench to make his 700th league appearance, and obviously break his own record as the oldest outfield Premier League player, which shockingly enough he did every time he played during this season, so I won't mention it again.

Our manager's reaction after the game was one of pragmatism and some light patronising for our opponents. 'If I was a neutral, I'd have to say Watford deserved to win. Their endeavour and their organisation and the pressure they put you under, they made it very difficult for us. I thought they deserved to win and that'll bode well for them.' It was very clear that Pards didn't see Watford as a long-term influence on our season.

Tuesday, 22 August 2006:
Watford 1 *King (63)*
West Ham 1 *Zamora (65)*

Four points from the opening two games and third place in the very early table, an encouraging start, particularly with a trip to Anfield next. Before that, we found out our fate in the UEFA Cup as we were handed an extremely difficult tie against Italian side Palermo. The 'Rosenaro' had finished eighth in Serie A the previous season as well as getting to the last 16 of the same competition, so would provide as stern a test as we could have faced at such an early stage.

So on to the trip to Merseyside, where no doubt the always gracious Scouse fans wouldn't rub the events of the day in Cardiff three months earlier in our faces (in the way that some of the idiots did straight after the game as we were leaving the ground). These smiles, however, turned to scowls in the 12th minute, when Bobby Zamora channelled his inner 'cup final Konchesky' and managed to drill a cross from nigh on the touchline inside the near post past the floundering Pepe Reina.

Zamora could do no wrong at this point, something that unfortunately couldn't be said about Marvellous Marlon as he was put clean through shortly after but screwed wide of the goal, sadly an all-too-familiar end result when he was put in that situation.

Now I loved Marlon Harewood more than most West Ham fans did in this era. I would regularly defend him during matches as I believe his power, pace and eye for goal gave us an extra dimension, and even on his bad days (which could be *very* bad sometimes) he always kept defenders occupied and on their toes. With that being said, he may have been one of the poorer strikers I have ever seen when put clean through on goal. It always seemed that having time to think was his biggest enemy and that he would try and be too cute, often dragging his shot wide or hitting it straight at the keeper. When the chance came to be instinctive, however, he could be lethal, which always made Marlon quite the conundrum. For what it's worth, most of the time I preferred him in the team rather than out of it. Most of the time.

Anyway, back to Anfield and our 1-0 lead, which we had held for half an hour and were now very near to half-time against a Liverpool side yet to win this season, so nerves for them would have been growing. We were sat deep in our half watching their young centre-back Daniel Agger, who had never scored for Liverpool, bring the ball out of his half and into ours. Clearly, we were happy to let him bring the ball forward and then deal with some of their more creative players when he passed the ball to them, a strategy that looked utter genius as he smashed the ball from roughly the sodding car park into the top corner.

So our half-time lead had been cancelled out, and we weren't done yet as in injury time Peter Crouch wriggled through our defence after a good pass from Luis Garcia and used his trademark 'good feet for a big man' to round Roy Carroll and put them 2-1 up. Great work all round, lads.

That was the end of the scoring for the day, despite the best efforts of Craig Bellamy and debutant Dirk Kuyt, who both brought good saves from Roy the boy, and also Lee Bowyer for us, as he somehow managed to hit the outside of the post from six yards, a feat that seemed harder to do than at the very least force Reina into a save, if not equalise.

So, a first loss of the season but one we did come away from with credit, as Alan was keen to emphasise in the post-match interview: 'We've come here against one of the real contenders for the title, given a real good account of ourselves and feel aggrieved we haven't come away with anything.'

Saturday, 26 August 2006:
Liverpool 2 *Agger (42), Crouch (45)*
West Ham 1 *Zamora (12)*

The international break was now upon us and all in all it had been an encouraging start; a win, a draw and a loss, four points and sixth place in the table, and by and large some positive team performances. A couple of players, Gabbidon and Harewood in particular, hadn't quite hit the form of the previous season but this had been offset by a massive improvement in Bobby Zamora and a very good start from Lee Bowyer.

The transfer window also had four days still to run after the defeat on Merseyside, so there was still time to add more players to the squad. Fulham midfielder Steed Malbranque looked to be the most likely signing but sometimes surprises can occur in the run-up to the closing of the window, so who knew what could possibly be in store?

What ended up happening would never be forgotten by any football fan who was around to see it.

CHAPTER THREE

31 August and September

ON 31 August 2006, I was just over a month into my first full-time job as a pensions administrator for a financial services company in Chichester, having graduated from university in June. I was still living in Portsmouth with my best mate Steve and his then girlfriend (now wife) Dannii. At this point, though, they were travelling around Australia. So I had the house to myself. Despite this, as I'd just started work I was living a very clean, 'good boy' lifestyle, in bed at 11pm with no midweek nights out.

This changed on Wednesday, 30 August, when at short notice my friend Rikki, at the time assistant manager at a pub/restaurant, told me that due to a surplus of stock all staff could eat there that night with friends for half price, and did I fancy coming along with him and a couple of our other friends? Never one to pass up a (half) free dinner, I cancelled my plan of eating spaghetti bolognese in front of a couple of episodes of *The Office*, and out I went. The dinner turned into a beer, which turned into a few beers, which turned into me dancing on a multi-coloured dancefloor at 1am and going to bed at least an hour later.

As I sat in the loo the following morning at work regretting my own life choices and hoping 5pm would come around really bloody quickly, I received a text message from fellow hammer Owen that changed the tone and tenor of the day somewhat. The following conversation took place, verbatim:

'Mate, we've signed Tevez and Mascherano.'

'Yeah and the cow has jumped over the moon.'

'Check Sky Sports News.'

The last text piqued my interest. If this was a wind-up, as it surely was, why did he just tell me to check the internet and not carry on the joke further? So, I went back to my desk and broke the company's very strict internet browsing rules by clicking on to Sky Sports News. And then my jaw dropped.

'West Ham have pulled off a major coup by signing Argentina World Cup stars Carlos Tevez and Javier Mascherano.' Que? On loan, I wondered? No. 'Striker Tevez, 22, and midfielder Mascherano, 22, join the Hammers from Brazilian side Corinthians on permanent deals for undisclosed fees.' Sorry, what?

I'd read the week before that Tevez was possibly joining Chelsea for around £40m, and Mascherano was regarded as arguably the best defensive midfielder under 25 in the *world*. How exactly had we managed this?

It didn't seem like we were willing to answer these questions, as the official statement said, well, not very much at all: 'The pair have been signed for an undisclosed fee and put pen to paper on permanent contracts with the club this afternoon. All other aspects of the transfers will remain confidential and undisclosed. The transfers represent a massive coup for the Hammers, who have beaten off some of Europe's biggest clubs to secure the services of the duo.'

In hindsight, I do not know why this non-announcement didn't set off more alarm bells. Speaking for myself and I dare say most Hammers fans, I was happy to look past it and wait for it to be explained to me, which did happen to an extent, as I will talk about in a minute. But I have no idea how the wider football community, be that media, other clubs, anybody, didn't question more at the time not only how we had done this, but also why the hell we weren't revealing any real details about it?

By this I mean, football clubs normally like bragging when they pull off a coup, and this looked like the coup to end all coups, so why weren't we crowing about it? Our club record fee at the time was £7.5m for Dean Ashton, both players were valued at considerably more than this, so why in the press release did we not do what every other club has before or since and brag that 'we have broken our transfer record to secure the services of' etc?

And also, what signing announcement ever has not disclosed the length of the contract? They were both 22 years old. Surely you would say that 'the duo have signed four-to-five-year deals', but no, nothing. As we sit here now, we know why this was done; it was because we didn't really own them at all. But how the hell did it take so long for people to work it out, or to even begin questioning it? The probable answer to that is something I doubt many of us would actually want to know.

But anyway, back to happier times, before we worried about all this. I left work at 5pm and walked to Chichester train station in a daze while on the phone to my dad. He was in as much disbelief as me. I had called him briefly when I found out the news and told him, to which he very understandably said, 'What, the blokes who play for Argentina? F*** off!?', and when I spoke to him again seven hours later he was still as baffled. We all were.

While we know how this ended up playing out, God what a day that was. I can honestly say that 31 August was one of the most exciting days I've ever enjoyed as a West Ham fan, one of the few days in my life – and there haven't been many – when I really thought we could win the league.

The conversation with my dad (and several with him and others over the coming days) was how it all felt so exciting, that this could be the start of something. Could top-class players coming to us be a regular thing? A lot of this optimism was centred around the man who was acknowledged to have, at the very least, brokered the deal; a man whose name was becoming more and more prevalent in football in 2006: Kia Joorabchian.

Joorabchian had been the main figurehead of a company called Media Sports Investments (MSI), which had tried to purchase the club from chairman Terry Brown in 2005. Now it seemed that he was back and ready to reaffirm his interest, and had used the two

Argentines as collateral of some sort. This was semi-confirmed by the Israeli in an interview with the now-defunct *News of the World* paper that weekend, in which he stated, 'When you see two players like that joining West Ham then there is no doubt in my mind the club can become massive. It sends out a huge signal that West Ham can now be a buying club, not a selling club. There is massive potential at West Ham. Why? Because the club has such passionate supporters and a fantastic history. What is so impressive is that when they have hit bad times, the passion and loyalty of the fans has seen them stick by the club.' So, it seemed as if this explained how Tevez and Mascherano ended up at West Ham ... sort of.

Naturally, Alan Pardew was delighted with the signings, as you'd bloody hope him to be really, as he enthused in the same newspaper: 'Not only am I excited by the arrivals of Carlos and Javier, but the entire squad is too – and I am sure our supporters feel the same. I have no doubt that this deal will give us a real chance to compete with the very best teams in the Premiership and in Europe. It's a fantastic day for West Ham United Football Club.' In reality, this day would be the beginning of the end of Pards as West Ham manager, but we won't get too ahead of ourselves.

A little more information about the actual players at this point, just in case you are reading this and don't know what all the fuss was about.

Javier Mascherano, 22 years old at the time, had begun his career as a youngster at River Plate, making 46 appearances for the Argentinian giants before joining

Corinthians for $15m in April 2005. He had only made nine appearances for the Brazilian side due to a stress fracture of his foot prior to the 2006 World Cup, where he became a world star by playing every minute of every match in Argentina's run to the quarter-finals (they were eliminated by Germany), having already won a gold medal with his national side in the 2004 Olympic Games.

He was seen at the time of his move to east London as arguably the best young defensive midfielder in the *world*. Typing that now still makes me shake my head, just as I was that day.

Carlos Tevez had started his career at River Plate's great rivals Boca Juniors, playing 75 times for them and scoring 26 goals. One of them came against River Plate and got him sent off as he celebrated the goal by dancing like a chicken (the nickname given to River by Boca fans), which very nearly caused a riot.

Tevez moved to Corinthians for a fee estimated to be in the region of $22m three months before Mascherano did, with comparisons to Diego Maradona regularly being made in the South American media. He scored 25 goals in 38 games for the club prior to departing for West Ham, and like Mascherano had played for Argentina in the World Cup, although in a role that saw him primarily coming off the bench (in fairness, their other forwards at the tournament were Javier Saviola, Hernan Crespo and a youthful Lionel Messi). Tevez was also part of the gold medal-winning Olympic team of 2004, when he was the competition's top scorer with eight goals in six games. Like Mascherano, he was only 22 years old.

So we can all agree, a pretty reasonable couple of signings on paper.

We would have to wait the better part of a fortnight, however, to see the duo in West Ham shirts due to an international break, but luckily enough we wouldn't have to wait that long to see them play in London, as they were both part of the Argentina squad that was playing Brazil in a friendly at Arsenal's new Emirates Stadium on Sunday, 3 September. To say I was excited to watch the game was an understatement, and I spent the Saturday taking a trip to a Portsmouth club shop in the town centre that printed names and numbers on the back of shirts. I persuaded a very dubious person to print 'TEVEZ 32' on the back of my very not-Portsmouth, very-West Ham shirt. He took my request in good spirits and playfully told me that the signing would never work. I laughed and proudly took my shirt home, ready to wear the following day.

The two new Hammers signings clearly took their new club straight to heart, in a joke we all made and laughed at that weekend, by playing for a team that was comfortably beaten 3-0.

In fairness, Tevez was comfortably Argentina's best player before being withdrawn for a young Sergio Aguero on 66 minutes, while Mascherano looked a little rusty having not played since the World Cup and was taken off at half-time. Still, nothing to be overly concerned about, and there was now only a week to go until we played Aston Villa at Upton Park, where the new signings could be unveiled properly.

On the Tuesday in the run-up to the game we held a formal press conference announcing the signings. I recommend anybody reading this to find a video of this presser, as when you watch it back nowadays with hindsight young Carlos and Javier look more confused than any players I have ever seen in this setting.

Uncle Alan was still toeing the company line of saying everything and nothing all in one go. He initially railed against the 'negative press' the club had received over the signings, stating 'People don't like change but let's be honest, the transfer system is changing rapidly and you have to accept this as a coach.' Well, yes you do, and I don't doubt that it was changing, but what changes was he referring to in terms of the norm regarding these transfers? Still nobody had divulged any information on this.

The next set of quotes from the press conference need to be read to be believed. When asked if he was obliged to play the duo whenever available, he said the following, 'Only the press have said it is a temporary measure, they have signed four-year contracts.' Oh well, that's good then Pards, nice and clear. Four-year deals and they're here for the long term, no further questions your honour. Oh, what's that, you're not done? Please continue, always good to get more information and further clarification. 'No matter how long they are here, I have assurances that they will not be going in the next window. So, for a year, let's enjoy their quality and let's see where it takes us.'

Sorry, what? So they've signed four-year contracts, but you've been assured they're not going to leave a few months later? Also, who assured you of this? The chairman? The players themselves? Someone else? And then on to the next sentence, why are we enjoying their quality for a year when they are on four-year contracts? As you've just said? What happens in a year? Why was nobody asking these questions? Sorry Alan, you're still not done?

'At the end of the season, let's review it. Hopefully we can then look at it for two or three years. They have signed four-year contracts – people forget that.'

Alan, what in God's name are you talking about? Who has forgotten it? Nobody knew the contract lengths; the club wouldn't say how long they were when they signed. And if in fact you knew, clearly you forgot one sentence after you initially said it, as you then said you were hopeful that they would stay past January, and maybe even longer than one year.

So, and just to make sure I am clear on this, they are here for four years, but maybe a year, but definitely not just six months, and after a year probably two or three years? Just to be clear.

Again, I am absolutely bewildered how it took as long as it did for anybody to prove something was up with these signings.

We managed to get through the rest of the week with thankfully no further dramas and come Sunday an air of excitement was sweeping around Upton Park, with the fans eager for a first glimpse of their two new heroes in a home game against Martin O'Neill's Aston Villa. I remember deciding not to get the normal train from Portsmouth to London that I would get for a 2pm kick-off, instead getting one an hour earlier, for no reason other than childlike excitement at the day ahead.

This excitement was tempered somewhat by the announcement of the team, with the sensible but somewhat party-pooping decision to start with the Argentines as substitutes. The bench looked stronger than the first team in truth, with the previously injured Robert Green and Matty Etherington joining Tevez and Mascherano. The team, then, lined up as follows:

Starting XI: Carroll, Mears, Ferdinand, Gabbidon, Konchesky, Bowyer, Mullins, Reo-Coker, Benayoun, Harewood, Zamora

Subs: Green, Mascherano, Etherington, Tevez, Cole

Prior to the game, Pardew appeared on the screens around the ground to address the fans via a pre-recorded message in which he explained why he hadn't picked the duo to start, as well as offering a rallying cry to the fans. I will talk about this more later.

To the game, then, and as widely predicted in the week leading up to it, one of the players making their debuts ran the show for their new employer. What wasn't predicted, though, was that player would be Stilian Petrov, Villa's new £6.5m signing from Celtic.

To put it simply, Villa battered us. They took an early lead through former West Ham fan Liam Ridgewell and through the rest of the first half peppered our goal as Petrov, accompanied by youngsters Gabby Agbonlahor (still fast and thin at this point) and Gareth Barry (still pretty good up until retiring 2020) led us on a merry dance. Agbonlahor was getting in behind us at will, and every cross Barry put in seemed to cause blind panic. Juan-Pablo Angel hit the bar twice with headers, every corner created chaos and Carroll in goal had to save well from both Luke Moore and Agbonlahor himself.

Our only real chance of the half was when keeper Thomas Sorenson, I can only presume for something to do, passed the ball straight to Harewood, who with too much time to think scuffed wide from eight yards out, an achievement genuinely harder to accomplish than getting the shot on target from where he was in the area. We were booed off at half-time. Well done everybody.

Somehow, the second half saw us scramble a point through Bobby Zamora's fifth goal in the first four games of the season, a deflection from a Konchesky header past the helpless Sorensen. (As a spoiler, I wondered if I should have described this goal in more detail than that, as it's the last West Ham one I'll get to write about for a while.) This was the end of the scoring for the day, despite Villa continuing to dominate and creating two more glorious chances in particular; an Anton Ferdinand scrambled clearance off the line from an Agbonlahor shot being overshadowed by comfortably the best thing Tyrone Mears ever did in a West Ham shirt, which was a ridiculous overhead kick clearance off the line from a Petrov lob, no more than 30 seconds after Zamora had equalised.

To this day, it may be the best clearance of its type I have ever seen. Mears had to get his foot as high as his actual height, and if that sounds easy please feel free to put this book down and try it yourself, while knowing that you will be looking like a bad Basil Fawlty impersonator.

Tevez did make his debut in the end, coming on for the hapless Harewood in the 61st minute and impressing, with a couple of very lively runs and a dangerous-looking effort straight at the keeper. Mascherano ended the proceedings as an unused sub, so fair to say we hoped for greater days to come, hopefully beginning with the visit to Upton Park of Palermo that coming Thursday, a game that seemed ideal for the pair with their high-level tournament experience.

Sunday, 10 September 2006:
West Ham 1 *Zamora (52)*
Aston Villa 1 *Ridgewell (4)*

Pardew after the game quite rightly described the performance as 'sluggish', while also revealing a slightly odd team talk, to me at least. 'At half-time I said, "Come on, you're the guys who have done everything to get us here."'

Now this to me, in addition to the odd rallying video before the game, really demonstrates why this whole furore around the signings, as well as the signings themselves, was the beginning of the end for Alan Pardew at West Ham. I didn't realise it at the time, I don't think anybody did, but looking at some of the quotes from Pards at the time, as well as knowing what we know now about the man, I really, truly think that the Tevez and Mascherano deal led him to think that he was now at the top table of Premier League managers, when in truth we'd had one truly great season and now needed to work hard to kick on.

Look at the language from that quote, 'You're the guys who have done everything to get us here.' Where had we gotten to exactly? As I have said, 2005/06 was fantastic but in reality, we had come ninth in the league and won nothing, and had then taken five points from four games the following season. We hadn't exactly rearranged the world order, had we? But the praise and media attention was raining down now, justifiably so at the time, it does have to be said, but the true top-table managers can keep a sense of perspective when this is occurring, and I think it is fair to say that throughout Pardew's management career, he has been unable to do that.

One thing throughout Pardew's career, not only at West Ham but in future managerial roles he would occupy, was that when things were going well, you always got the sense that in his mind they were going even better than the reality; that he was untouchable, a Midas-type who could do no wrong.

Dean Ashton revealed in an interview with Talk Sport what Pards' nickname was during his time managing the Hammers, and why. 'He's not short of confidence. His nickname, and what he's fondly known as, is "chocolate" because he would eat himself if he could.' Now this can be both a blessing and a curse, as when things are going well this confidence can definitely keep that momentum going, but when things aren't going well? We shall see.

Four days later, it was time for our first European match in six years as the southern Italians of Palermo rolled into town. Two changes to the side for this game, and you probably wouldn't need to use Google to guess who came into the team. Sure enough, Mascherano and Tevez made their first starts, with Mullins and Harewood dropping to the bench. There was also a change in formation (the third in five games) as Tevez played just off Zamora in a 4-5-1, the idea being that we would look to keep things tight and stifle the opposition.

Early in the game, it was easy to see what the fuss was about with Mascherano. He dictated play and effortlessly ran the midfield. To this day, I can still remember one pinpoint crossfield pass he played to Benayoun that he made look staggeringly easy. Tevez was getting around the pitch well also, belying some comments that had been made in the media about his physique after the Villa game.

Now, in any season, good or bad, I always think there are mini turning points that really shape how a season pans out. Obviously there are glaring ones, a significant injury, a missed penalty, a last-minute winner or loser etc, but smaller moments that also make a critical long-term difference. I honestly believe this game had one of the biggest mini turning points in West Ham's season, if not the biggest of all.

The incident in question took place just before the end of the first half, when Zamora crossed from the left-hand side straight to Tevez, who with a gilt-edged chance in front of goal volleyed too close to the goalkeeper (39-year-old Alberto Fontana), enabling him to make a very good save. It was, however, a save he shouldn't have been able to make. It was a glorious chance for the Argentine to open his West Ham account within the first 45 minutes of his first start, and in a very high-profile match into the bargain.

Had that chance gone in, who knows how the season would have panned out for West Ham and for Tevez in the claret and blue as a whole? The four years, or maybe two or three years but definitely not just six months that he would be with the club could have been a completely different story. Alas the chance was missed, and this was compounded a few minutes later when Andrea Caracciolo guided in Aimo Diana's cross to give the away side the lead, an almost identical chance to the one Carlos had missed at the other end.

We huffed and puffed in the second half but were unable to find an equaliser in the face of some very disciplined, some might say stereotypical Italian defending. The closest we came was when a late snap shot from Harewood (on for Tevez) hit the post, and despite some very good approach play we handed a first-leg advantage to our tough-tackling opponents. A disappointing result, then, and one that could be difficult to turn around in the return leg in Sicily.

Pards, however, was in bullish mood in the press conference after the game. 'In terms of two fighters in the ring, I thought we were evenly matched. The second leg will be an interesting psychological game. With a 1-0 lead, it'll be interesting to see how they approach it tactically. We know how we'll approach it – we'll take the game to them.' Can't say I disagree with that approach. This team were typically at their best when looking to attack and exploit opponents' weaknesses, rather than worrying about ours. A pleasing return to that philosophy, some might say, after a couple of games this season where we had seemed too timid.

Pardew's final noteworthy post-match quote was a fair one, but still concerning. 'We have not really nailed the team down as we would want and we have to do that now.' This isn't uncommon for any side early in a season, and I'm sure people will look at that quote now as much as they did then and decide it was down to Tevez and Mascherano, but I'm not sure the blame can be laid just at their door here. It needs to be remembered that we had added seven other first-team players to the squad (two of whom were injured when they arrived) and only lost a couple of marginal squad players and then our best forward very unexpectedly. Plenty of teams would struggle to know their best 11 so quickly after that level of upheaval, but it was a problem that we needed to rectify and quickly.

Thursday, 14 September 2006:
West Ham 0
Palermo 1 *Caracciolo (45)*

Our next encounter, and third home game in a row, was against Newcastle. The Geordies were coming into the fixture on the back of a successful UEFA Cup result in midweek but two disappointing league defeats prior, a 2-0 loss at Villa and a 2-1 reverse at home to Fulham, so this was a game both sides very much needed a result from even at this early stage of the season. We made just the one change from the defeat to Palermo three days before, with Yossi Benayoun dropping out to enable fit-again Matty Etherington, who had been a key player in the previous season, to come in for his first appearance in this one.

The first half was again a tepid affair as both sides looked a little jaded from their midweek exertions. This was particularly disappointing from our perspective as it was becoming more and more evident that the players and fans needed a jolt after a poor start to the campaign, but one didn't appear forthcoming as we looked noticeably slower and more ponderous on the ball than the previous season. The only chances that came our way in the first 45 were a Tevez free kick that hit the bar and a Lee Bowyer effort from near the halfway line that very nearly caught Shay Given (who always seemed to play well against us) out of his goal.

The break saw Carlitos withdrawn in favour of not-so-marvellous Marlon, which seemed to knock the stuffing out of the crowd (it did for me anyway) somewhat, before Damien Duff compounded the apathy with a low drilled finish past a perennially non-diving Roy Carroll.

Mascherano was then taken off as well for Benayoun halfway through the second half, but it made no difference with Newcastle always looking more likely to add to their lead than us equalise, and they duly did with

15 minutes left through a striker that my dad, with no idea of how to actually pronounce his first name, dubbed 'Overfriendly' (Obafemi) Martins. This goal was an utter shambles to concede, as Bowyer and Danny Gabbidon just stood staring at each other, both wondering what to do with the round, white leather thing on the ground in front of them, which enabled Overfriendly to nip in, fire the ball into the corner and seal a 2-0 win for the away team.

The only other thing worth mentioning about the game was a bizarre incident involving then Newcastle manager and former West Ham manager (somehow) Glenn Roeder. During a lengthy delay in play while Given was receiving treatment after a collision with Harewood, the travelling fans did the quite normal thing of asking their manager to 'give us a wave', to which Roeder obliged, waving back, which nobody batted an eye at initially.

But 15 seconds or so later, Roeder was still waving, with the wave becoming more and more like a 1950s housewife feverishly saying goodbye to her husband for the day. Without a doubt, he was trying to antagonise the home fans, for reasons that are utterly beyond me.

Roeder had been relatively well received by the crowd with a smattering of applause prior to kick-off, but clearly he decided to use this opportunity to get even with the West Ham faithful for having the bare-faced cheek to, erm, have to watch as he 'managed' (pun intended) to get one of the best squads we have ever had relegated four years previously. Yeah, we had that one coming, Glenn.

At 21 years old, while witnessing the strangest wave I had ever seen from a grown man, I remember saying out loud, 'He is just trying to incite people, he needs to grow up,' which says a lot about Roeder's performance. The fans got angrier and angrier over this, and the incident culminated in several people trying to run at the dugout to confront him. I dare say a fair few of the people would have done a better job in the dugout than Mr Roeder did during the relegation season. 'I apologise if I've upset the West Ham crowd this afternoon,' Roeder said later. 'I did nothing more than any manager would do when his supporters are singing his name.'

In fairness, if I was him and had managed to somehow get the bloody Newcastle job after the mess he left our club in, I would probably spend 90 minutes in the dugout dancing while laughing uncontrollably, so maybe a wave wasn't so bad.

Sunday, 17 September 2006:
West Ham 0

Newcastle 2 *Duff (50), Martins (75)*

Three home games in a week, which had seen a solitary goal, two defeats and a wave of optimism nigh on evaporated. We had dropped to 12th in the table, but our next game did offer some hope as we would be travelling to the City of Manchester Stadium (not yet the Etihad) to take on (no UAE money quite yet) Manchester City. We'd had excellent recent memories of this ground, with over 7,000 fans travelling there on a Monday night six months prior to this game to watch us win 2-1 in an FA Cup quarter-final tie, with Dean Ashton announcing himself to West Ham fans and the wider public (the game was live on BBC1) by scoring both goals.

I was at that game myself. I made the trip with my dad, travelling from Portsmouth (I wonder if anybody had made a longer trip than me that night) to London on the Sunday night and then taking up the club's offer of free coach travel to the game, leaving from the ground on Monday lunchtime. It was the first time I'd ever been to City away (and unless I fancy watching a 4-0 defeat will probably be the last) and I would put it very near the top of a list of the nicer grounds I have ever visited. Plus, it had an ASDA right nearby and I got a steak and kidney pudding from a chip shop, which are both wins in my book.

The trip was made all the funnier by a group of lads on our coach who were out to have a good day, let's say. They took the designated coach attendant to their hearts on the trip, a ponytailed, somewhat harmless bloke they christened 'Dave' after David Seaman.

The trip home was quite eventful, as we first had to duck some shoes being thrown at our coach by some angry City fans (who throws a shoe?) then had to run a red light as said fans, I presume, all hopped on one shoe after us.

Then, at our designated rest stop, poor Dave had to beg a couple of the lads not to try to open the locked coach door as they'd forgotten their cigarettes. Suffice to say, Dave was unsuccessful and the door was opened, sadly breaking the lock in the process. The driver was obviously not happy when he returned and wanted an explanation. Breaking what felt like 15 minutes of silence as we all stood round like naughty children in assembly, one of the lads mumbled, 'Dave, I told you to wait till he got back to get your fags.' The rest of the trip home was spent watching awkward looks between the driver and Dave, who had to hold the broken door shut for the last 80 miles or so.

Fair to say that six months later, the people travelling to Manchester wouldn't have done so with the optimism that we all had that night. Even less so when they saw the team, which featured Christian Dailly making a first appearance of the season as emergency right-back, as all three right-backs signed in the summer (Mears, Pantsil and Spector) were injured. See, told you we hadn't signed enough right-backs.

Tevez was dropped to the bench along with Bowyer, an odd decision as most people felt he had been our best-performing midfielder thus far. The changes saw Benayoun and Harewood come back into the side, which meant that Mascherano was the only member of the 11 who hadn't been with us the season before, indicating that Pards had gone to the 'go with what you know' plan to get us out of the rut we were in.

The injuries in defence continued to mount up as Anton Ferdinand went off injured after 22 minutes. This saw Dailly move to centre-half and central midfielder Hayden Mullins come on as an emergency right-back, the fourth player we had used in that position in the opening seven games.

Two second-half goals from Greek striker Georgios Samaras won the game for City, the second of which saw him comfortably lift the ball over Roy Carroll as the keeper advanced from his line seemingly in slow motion. Carroll's form was becoming a real concern, as if there weren't enough other problems to worry about.

At this point, I would normally run through a couple of events in the game or chances that we'd had, but I can't do that for this one. Reason? We didn't have any. Not one single shot on target against a team that at kick-off were one place outside the bottom three and had only scored three goals in their first five games. Midweek, they had even been knocked out of the League Cup by Chesterfield, who coincidentally we had drawn in the third round.

What had begun as a concerning start was fast becoming a crisis. We'd now dropped to 15th, having not won a match since the opening day, and had not scored in three games. Talking to Sky after the game, Pards explained that he believed that Anton's injury was a key factor in the defeat. 'That was a blow to us and I thought it was the difference really. Unfortunately for us, we keep conceding the first goal. We're searching for a win and we need to get one whichever way it comes. We have a squad that's big and well balanced, but we need to get back to what we are about.'

Can't say I disagree with any of that. Could definitely do with not conceding the first goal in every game as well, couldn't agree more with him there. Particularly in games when you don't have a shot on target.

Saturday, 23 September 2006:

Manchester City 2 *Samaras (50,63)*

West Ham 0

BOTTOM 6: (23/09/2006)

	P	Pts	GD
WEST HAM	6	5	-3
Middlesbrough	6	5	-5
Tottenham	6	4	-6
Watford	6	*3*	*-3*
Charlton	6	*3*	*-7*
Sheffield United	6	*2*	*-7*

The following midweek, we were off to Italy for the second leg of our UEFA Cup tie against Palermo. Some of our fans reportedly took the Godfather movies literally, with reports of 'about 500 West Ham fans [parading] down the city's main shopping street, skirmishing with locals'. This would turn out to be as much danger as any Italian was in that day.

This game saw five changes in personnel as well as yet another formation change. Spector was in at right-back for his debut, James Collins replaced the injured Anton, Bowyer and Tevez returned to the 11 and bizarrely Zamora, responsible for 80 per cent of the goals we had scored up to that point, was benched in favour of Carlton Cole, making his first start for the club. We lined up in a 4-3-3 formation, with Tevez and Harewood charged with playing either side of the former Chelsea man.

In fairness, this was a match that by and large we played very well in. The front trio all missed good early chances, with Tevez first seeing a volley saved by Fontana, who also saved well from a Harewood overhead kick and then made a ridiculously good stop when turning away a Cole header.

This was how it was going for us at this point, though. Simply nothing would go in even when we were playing well. This was an issue our opponents that night didn't have, with a low shot from Fabio Simplicio somehow getting through a crowded penalty area and sneaking past Carroll, who in fairness had been injured earlier in the game but still really should have done better. That made the already-uphill task even more difficult, and early in the second half it became insurmountable as Simplicio was put clean through and showed a calmness and poise that nobody in our team was capable of at that point by simply lifting the ball over our (again too slowly) on-rushing keeper for the hosts' second goal on the night and third of the tie.

Not long after, future Hammers loanee David Di Michele sealed the game beyond all doubt with a clinical finish, and we were left to rue a 3-0 defeat and an exit at the earliest possible stage of the UEFA Cup.

Let's not forget, we had gone for quantity over quality with some of the summer transfer window signings with a lengthy run in this tournament in mind; winning this tie would have put us in a group stage with a minimum of six more matches even if we hadn't qualified for the later stages.

This now meant we had a 'bloated squad', as Pardew had said previously, and still no idea of our best team, with just the domestic competitions to focus on. One positive at least was with the European adventure now over, this increased focus could hopefully lead to that form turning around.

The manager echoed these sentiments in interviews after the game, while also pointing to what was an improved performance. 'We had great chances and their keeper made fantastic saves. 1-0 down from the first leg, if we'd scored the first, everyone knew it was game on. There were not four goals between the sides. The difference was quality in forward areas, which is down to confidence. But we're big enough to stand up for errors and now we have to focus on improving our Premiership position.'

So, a dark and disappointing September after the most positive of beginnings. October needed to be better, much better. Scoring a goal would have been a start.

Thursday, 28 September 2006:
Palermo 3 *Simplicio (35,62), Di Michele (68)*
West Ham 0
(agg: 4-0)

CHAPTER FOUR

October

OUR FIRST game of October was on the first day of the month, an intriguing task against a newly promoted side enjoying a very similar campaign to ourselves 12 months earlier: Steve Coppell's Reading.

They had swept all before them in the Championship the year before, losing only two games all season (one of them on the opening day) and finishing with 106 points, 16 clear of Sheffield United and 25 points clear of Watford in third place.

They'd carried on this form in their first-ever season of top-flight football; on the opening day, they overcame a two-goal deficit to beat Middlesbrough 3-2 and they made the relatively short trip from Berkshire to London having taken seven points from their last three games, with a 1-0 victory at home to Manchester City and a 2-1 win at Sheffield United preceding an extremely creditable 1-1 draw against Manchester United, who needed a Cristiano Ronaldo goal 15 minutes from time to earn a point. So, while on paper Reading at home may have seemed a good chance for us to get our season back on track, this was by no means an easy task against an in-form side. In fact, this was precisely the sort of game that we, in Reading's position last year, were turning up and getting a result in.

For me personally, this was a bigger game than it was for the vast majority of other Hammers, due to the little-known fact that the student base of the University of Portsmouth from 2003–2006 seemed to be almost entirely made up of people from Reading and the surrounding areas. I'd gone from being an 18-year-old living in London who had never met anybody from Berkshire to someone who now, at 21, knew not only Reading but most of the suburbs around it as well. As well as people from Reading, I seemed to know people from Aldershot, Bracknell, Didcot, Yateley, Winnersh and Taplow.

So, for me, this was now my equivalent to a game against Arsenal or Tottenham for most West Ham fans. A win would put me on cloud nine, a defeat would see me have to endure endless mockery. As long as it wasn't a defeat so bad that it would still be brought up nearly 15 years later, I'm sure I could cope. No chance it could be that bad.

This was our final game to be played on a Sunday due to European commitments what with the Palermo defeat, and we went into it with four changes to the side that lost in Italy three days prior, two forced and two unforced.

Collins and Bowyer dropped out injured (Bowyer would need a minor operation on a groin injury) and were replaced by Dailly and Etherington. Benayoun came in for Harewood and in a change that would end up leading to ridicule for those involved to this day, Javier Mascherano, at this point a regular in the Argentina team and a player who would end up with 147 caps for the national side, one of which was in a World Cup Final, as well as winning five La Liga titles and two Champions League medals among many other accolades, was dropped in favour of ex-Crystal Palace midfielder Hayden Mullins.

Now obviously a lot of this is said in jest and with the benefit of hindsight, but even then it looked an odd call. Mascherano was gradually coming to terms with English football and leaving him out for Mullins seemed like a change for change's sake. This was compounded by the complete lack of form displayed by the other central midfielder, captain Nigel Reo-Coker.

A *tour de force* in the previous campaign, at this point Reo-Coker seemed to be regressing on an almost weekly basis, with rumours of a big-money move to Arsenal still hanging around and reports in the media of a growing ego in the previously humble skipper. It did seem even then that if a change was to be made, he should have been the one to step out for a rest and potential reinvigoration rather than the Argentine. Another formation change was made as well, as Tevez and Cole led the line in a return to 4-4-2.

Anyway, on to the game. A fast start was desperately needed here, as was the need to do as the manager had previously asked and not concede the first goal. Two minutes in, as Reading won a free kick not far in our half, this didn't seem too much of an immediate issue. South Korean forward Seol Ki-Hyeon had other ideas, though. As the ball was squared to him about 57 yards (in my mind anyway) from goal, he hit a shot so sweetly that if it hadn't hit the net it may still be travelling through the air now.

While I joke about 'the plan' not to concede the first goal, all of us know as fans when you are on a horror run how important the opening goal is confidence-wise, and this game was a textbook example of that. We had 58 per cent of the ball and 17 shots to Reading's three, but never really threatened to equalise.

Spector, Tevez and Mullins had shots on target from long range but we created nothing of note until injury time, when Benayoun lifted the ball over Reading's American keeper Hahnemann. We were all ready to remember what scoring a goal felt like when my fellow ginger, Steve Sidwell, let the side down and got back to hook off the line. It wasn't quite Mears-esque but impressive nonetheless.

We also ended the game with another forward combination as Zamora, Harewood and Sheringham were all on the pitch, with Cole and Tevez having been replaced, along with the struggling Reo-Coker.

Another loss, then, which made it five defeats in 14 days and still no goals. Tottenham's 2-1 win over Portsmouth meant that we had dropped to 16th in the league after seven games, four of them at home.

Sunday, 1 October 2006:

West Ham 0

Reading 1 *Ki-Hyeon (2)*

The relegation zone didn't look too far away and we were now nearing full-on crisis mode. Pardew decided in an interview with the media after the game that the reason for us losing every week and not scoring any goals was because of, erm, the injuries we'd had in defence. 'We have had some issues that affected the team. The back four; we must try and get a settled back four because the rhythm of passing was affected today. I just look at the team and the rhythm of our passing and I think that until I get a settled back four, I don't think we're really going to be at full speed but in terms of what we had out today, it was a really good performance, albeit a bad result.'

Now I'm not saying he's wrong, of course he isn't; a settled defence will be a help to any side. But to decide this was the reason for the run we were on is bizarre. While we did have several defenders out injured at this point, three of the back five, Carroll, Gabbidon and Konchesky, had started every game thus far. And the argument could also be made that a settled midfield and attack could be just as useful, and we were chopping and changing those areas every game. Here is a list of the forward combinations we started with in the eight games from Aston Villa at home to Tottenham away (jumping ahead a couple of games, I know, but I doubt you're reading this and hoping to avoid spoilers).

Changes in bold:

Villa (h): Zamora, Harewood

Palermo (h): Zamora, **Tevez**

Newcastle (h): Zamora, Tevez

Man City (a): Zamora, **Harewood**

Palermo (a): **Cole**, Harewood, **Tevez**

Reading (h): Cole, Tevez

Portsmouth (a): **Zamora, Sheringham**

Tottenham (a): Zamora, **Harewood**

Only once was the same forward line in the same combination picked in consecutive matches. I know we weren't scoring and that, of course, leads to changes, but I struggle to see how continuity was crucial at one end and not needed at the other.

I think, sadly, this was the other main issue Pardew had as a manager, namely that when his team were on a bad run, he didn't ever really have a plan as to how it could be turned around. During this run, we never really seemed to try and grind a game out, or even go more gung-ho/devil may care. All that happened was he was just changing various combinations around and hoping something stuck.

And as we have seen, things were sticking about as well as a 12-day-old plaster at this point. At least we now had a fortnight's break before the next match due to an international break. Hopefully, over this time we could find a formula that would turn things round, or at the very worst explain to the team what that big rectangular thing with white posts and a net inside it was that seemed to be at the end of every pitch they played on.

The main source of entertainment over the break involved various updates with the ongoing takeover of the club. A couple of days after the Reading loss, the board met to discuss the potential interest of Joorabchian's group, which for one reason or another had gone quiet since the initial hoopla of the Tevez and Mascherano signings. This reportedly was partly due to Joorabchian taking time away from business due to the death of his father, but very little else was being said about any concrete bid save the odd headline in the papers, one of which said that Pardew had offered to resign due to the takeover uncertainty, a claim swiftly denied by both the manager and chairman.

It was reported following the board meeting that it had been decided to give the Israeli more time to secure the funds needed for the purchase, as his potential backers had been slow to confirm interest. If they were getting cold feet on the deal, I can only assume one investment they had made at that time was a Sky Sports subscription.

Later that week, however, things took an interesting turn with the report of a second interested party. *The Independent* reported that a spokesman for the mystery consortium had contacted the paper to inform them that they intended to challenge the Kia Joorabchian-led group for control of the club. The group wanted to remain anonymous apparently, a plan that lasted for all of five days when the frontman was revealed as Icelandic businessman Eggert Magnusson.

Magnusson was a 59-year-old with vast experience in football administration. At the time, he was head of the Icelandic FA and worked on UEFA's executive committee. It seemed odd initially how those credentials led him to have the money to buy a Premier League club (his personal wealth was reported at around £40m at the time), but this made more sense the following day with reports of the bid being primarily funded by billionaire businessman Bjorgolfur Gudmundsson.

'BG', as he was mostly known during his time with the club, initially made his money in alcohol, selling various breweries to Heineken and Pepsi among others, and at this point had a major stake in Landsbanki Bank, at the time the second biggest bank in Iceland, as well as owning four of Iceland's top ten businesses. He was Iceland's first-ever billionaire and was ranked 350th on the Forbes 2006 list of wealthiest people, up from 488th the year before. At that point, his estimated personal fortune would have made him the third richest football club owner in Europe.

So, that was nice. Things progressed quite quickly over the coming days and it was formally announced to the stock exchange that the Icelandics had entered 'initial discussions' regarding the purchase of the club on 12 October.

The other newsworthy item came from the manager in his pre-match press conference prior to the trip to Portsmouth, which contained confirmation that the widely reported enquiry/bid for captain Nigel Reo-Coker had indeed taken place.

While not outright naming the club, which as already mentioned was believed to have been Arsenal, Pardew revealed, 'There was an enquiry for Nigel but I said what should happen and that is what did happen. He stayed here as a West Ham player.'

This fanned the flames of suspicion for West Ham fans, who believed that the skipper was the latest in a long line of players over the years that we'd seen have his head turned for possible bigger opportunities (and paydays) elsewhere. But according to Pards, this was not the case: 'Subconsciously, things affect you, and I'm not going to say it hasn't affected him. But I don't think it has affected him in a negative way. The games just haven't unfolded very well for him. He perhaps has not been in the greatest of form, but I am not worried about him.' Hopefully, this public show of support would lead to a big performance from the skipper as the players and fans made the short trip south to Fratton Park.

For me personally this was the easiest trip of the season. As I've mentioned, at the time I lived (and still do live) in central Portsmouth, and Fratton Park was only a 15/20-minute walk for me. My dad got tickets for the game too, so travelled down to join me along with his mate Barry, a lovely bloke but the sort of guy you imagine looked 50 even when he was 14, as well as also being the most nervous man I have ever seen at a football match.

We all want our teams to win and are frightened of losing, I completely get that, but Barry took it to the next level. My favourite memory of him was at the 04/05 play-off final against Preston, a day that, as I said at the very start of this book, saw probably the biggest game any of us had ever been to and a game we absolutely had to win for the future of the club. We were all nervous but it turns out we didn't need to be. It turned out the whole game rested on one thing and one thing only.

Which was that we would win the match and secure promotion as long as Barry didn't take off or unbutton his coat.

Christ knows why he thought this made a difference, although I don't mind superstitions. During a long batting partnership for England in a Test match or one-day international, I've been known not to move seats for an extended period, that kind of thing. But I honestly to this day cannot work out why he decided his coat was the difference-maker. How long had he not taken it off for? Since the semi-final win at Ipswich? The things we do for our club. It was boiling that day as well. Anyway, dad and Barry drove down to meet me in Portsmouth and in one of the stranger/stupider things that have happened to me, we decided to go for a drink at a local pub a street and a half away from where I lived at the time. We were refused entry as it was 'home fans only'. I repeat, I lived within five minutes' walk of the pub.

To this very day, I walk past the pub at least twice a day as I go to work and back. I had been in that pub earlier that very week and knew several of the bar staff by name. But in the ridiculous world that football fans must inhabit compared to fans of other sports, that day if I had gone into the pub down the road from where I lived, I would have smashed it up because I happened not to support Portsmouth. I definitely wouldn't have ordered a drink and quietly had a chat while sat at a table, which I had done all the other hundreds of times I had been in there, when I also didn't support Portsmouth.

But as I say, at times being a football fan is a strange existence. Don't forget we are the only group of fans who aren't allowed to take an alcoholic drink to their seats when watching outdoor sport; cricket and rugby fans can drink to their hearts' content while watching the action and even make 'beer snakes' out of God knows how many plastic glasses. But football fans, as we know, would lose all control of their senses if they ever saw blades of grass while drinking £5.40 pints of weak lager. But anyway, I digress.

We got to Fratton Park (sober as judges, of course) to find that we had made another three changes to the side that lost to Reading; Anton Ferdinand was fit and returned to partner Gabbidon, and both strikers changed again as Tevez dropped out through injury and Cole dropped to the bench, to be replaced by Zamora and 40-year-old Teddy Sheringham, who made his first start of the season. No real reason that I can see for this other than Pardew thinking he had tried everybody else, so why not Teddy? He would be marked by Sol Campbell that day in what almost seemed like an old episode of *Premier League Years* that was happening inside an actual football match.

In this Groundhog Day-like run, the changes made little or no difference. The first half saw us again fail to muster a shot on target and again give away the first goal, Kanu nudging Ferdinand aside and heading past Carroll, who for some reason was more concerned at appealing for a foul/handball than trying to save the effort. We came close early in the second half as attempts from Konchesky and Etherington were well saved by ex-Hammers keeper David James, in between chants of 'Will we ever score a goal?' from the away end.

With 20 minutes remaining, both forwards were again substituted as Zamora and Sheringham were replaced by Harewood and Cole, as the ongoing striker hokey cokey continued. As we poured forward chasing an equaliser, another goal seemed likely. It came but sadly for us it was via Teddy's former Manchester United nemesis Andy Cole, who until I started researching this book I had no memory of ever playing for Portsmouth despite my seeing this goal live with my own eyes.

He took a pass from Matt Taylor, held off Spector presumably while reminding him that he was nearly old enough to be his father, and slotted the ball into the corner. The game petered out to a 2-0 loss and we had now gone 578 minutes (nine hours 38 minutes) without scoring a goal. The bad news kept coming with a win for Middlesbrough and a draw for Sheffield United seeing us drop into the bottom three for the first time that season, behind Wigan on goal difference.

A reasonable display but no cutting edge again saw Pardew clinging to the positives in TV interviews after the game. 'I think the important thing for the team is just to keep believing that it's going to come right. It wasn't a performance that leaves you scratching your head and thinking that nothing is going to come from that West Ham team. There's talent in that team and talent in the dressing room. I think we've got a good spirit and I think that if we're going to have a [bad] run, let's get it out of the way now, regroup, and attack the rest of the season. We've obviously got that but we've had it at the start of the season – and there's plenty of time to put it right.'

Saturday, 14 October 2006:
Portsmouth 2 *Kanu (24), Cole (82)*
West Ham 0

Assistant manager Peter Grant had left to join Norwich as their manager the week prior to the loss at Fratton Park, and his replacement was confirmed early the following week as coach Keith Peacock stepped up to fill the role. Peacock's first game as Pardew's number two would be at White Hart Lane against our old friends Tottenham.

Martin Jol's side had also had a bad start, seemingly still struggling to get over their disappointment of not making the Champions League the previous season. What a shame. They had, however, picked up in their last two games, which had yielded four points, but we still went into the game knowing that a win would take us above them, which would be quite the filip after such a bad run.

We made the now-almost standard four changes to the side. John Pantsil returned after injury and replaced Spector, Matty Etherington missed out with a knock which saw Mascherano come back in and Reo-Coker move to the left wing (a position he had never played in before), Harewood replaced Sheringham and thankfully a change was made in goal as a fully fit Rob Green replaced the almost immobile Roy Carroll.

I was at this game as well, my first and only trip to Spurs away. Quite honestly, it's a ground I've never really thought much of. We never seemed to win there and I couldn't stand the thought of giving them my money. Going there didn't change my mind, either, I thought it was an average ground inhabited by horrible people. Having abuse shouted at me and my dad as we committed the heinous crime of walking back to his car after the game only reinforced that opinion.

Looking back, I also wonder at my own sanity. This is the first and only time I have ever attended back-to-back away games and it was during a run in which we hadn't scored in two months. Then again, I have written a book about this season rather than the few good ones I've seen us have, so clearly I haven't changed much in the last 15 years or so!

On to the match. I always think there are certain players who, as a fan, you are more afraid of than fans at other clubs, mainly because they always seem to play well and look a threat against your team. Players who come to mind for me include Romelu Lukaku, Theo Walcott, Olivier Giroud and Anthony Martial. Well, on this day Aaron Lennon made that list.

He absolutely destroyed Paul Konchesky, seemingly using a jet engine to speed past him time and again. He laid a couple of chances on a plate for Defoe early on, one of which was fantastically saved by Green, a novel experience as I hadn't seen a keeper make an above-average save for us in about nine months. As I write this, Lennon is an ageing occasional winger for Burnley, but if he came on against us now I would still be terrified.

We gradually came into the half and Harewood forced a good stop from then-England keeper Paul Robinson, and just as we started to grow in confidence we predictably conceded. Mido (again a future Hammer, Jesus it feels like every footballer ever has played for us at one point) collected a good pass from Edgar Davids, turned Anton and fired into the corner. He celebrated by taking his shirt off and running towards our fans in the corner, presumably mocking us in advance for the absolute state he would have looked shirtless during his brief but still not brief enough spell with West Ham four years later.

The other noteworthy event in the first half was Mascherano being bitten (yes, bitten) by Jermain Defoe. Javier had brought him down with a crude challenge, so obviously Defoe did the only thing a rational human would do and bit him on the shoulder. For reasons still beyond me now, nothing at all was done about this. I assume because Defoe was a young English forward and Mascherano a South American, there must have been some sort of misunderstanding.

The BBC report of the game indicated as much, bizarrely stating, 'The England striker seemed to bite his opponent's arm but the Argentine hardly helped the situation by attempting to outdo Robert De Niro in the acting stakes as he hit the ground like a felled tree.' So Mascherano was apparently at fault for reacting to being bitten then? A very strange take. But stereotypes won out, Defoe wasn't sent off and nothing more was ever made of it.

I've tried not to repeat myself too often in this run, but I'll be honest, I've run out of ways to write 'we were losing at half-time and tried really hard but didn't score'. So that's all I'll say this time. We were losing at half-time and tried really hard but didn't score. A Dailly header cleared off the line in injury time was as near as we got.

The 1-0 loss saw us drop to 19th, below a Watford side that hadn't won a game yet, and the goalless run now stood at seven games or 668 minutes. Eleven hours of football without a sodding goal.

Pardew was pragmatic yet realistic in his post-match press conference. 'I have to look at the group, and the effort we put in today certainly deserved something. You couldn't fault our spirit and commitment to the cause. We're trying to turn this horrible run around. For sure, we lacked a little bit of quality in the final third but that comes with confidence, a win and a goal. But I think that anybody that was here today – and the West Ham fans that travelled here – would have seen that you couldn't fault our commitment to try and win the game.'

Cannot say I really disagree with that, and it does have to be said that as bad as this run had been, the worst thing you could fault the players for up to this point were poor performances rather than a lack of effort or interest. That would come later.

Sunday, 22 October 2006:

Tottenham 1 *Mido (45)*

West Ham 0

Only two days later, we had the treat of playing again, this time away at League One Chesterfield in the League Cup third round. The nice people at Sky Sports had decided to show the match live for the justifiable reason that an upset could be on the cards.

We went into the game on the back of some good news at least, as Carlos Tevez had done an interview with an Argentinian newspaper saying how much he was enjoying his time in London. 'Here, everyone is very nice. West Ham helped us to get to know London and to look for an apartment. The people get ten out of ten. It is wonderful. The stadium is full, the people are near us and there are no barriers. It is impossible to imagine that in Argentina. The supporters do not bother you here. I go out and I am calm. If they are in the stadium, they are fervent. But day by day they are not like the South Americans.' How nice of him to say. A few goals sooner rather than later would help pay all the fans back with interest. Hell, just one goal would have done at this point.

For the game at Saltergate, we only made three changes, clearly seeking to avoid the ever-so-obvious 'giant killing'. Christian Dailly oddly came into central midfield with Mascherano rested, and there were first starts of the season down the left-hand side for George McCartney and young winger Kyel Reid.

Only two minutes into the game, striker Colin Larkin (no, me neither) had only Robert Green to beat but the keeper saved well to his left. Then a couple of minutes after that, it happened. A long clearance downfield from Green was headed to the edge of the area and Marlon Harewood volleyed a shot into the net. *We had scored an actual bloody goal.* I dare say a group of Premier League fans have never cheered an away goal at Chesterfield so enthusiastically. The players remembered how to celebrate and everything!

We'd even scored the first goal in a game; Pardew's plan was all coming together. The only issue was that for most of the next 86 minutes, Chesterfield absolutely battered us.

Shots from Larkin and Downes went inches wide, and Downes had an effort well saved by Green. With a centre midfield of Mullins and Dailly shockingly failing to provide much going forward we had no outlet, and ten minutes into the second half the Spireites got the goal they deserved, and our resistance was broken. Against Chesterfield. Our resistance against Chesterfield. God what a pleasing sentence that is.

Future Hull striker Caleb Folan's shot was turned on to the post and Larkin fired home. Zamora missed two great chances to win the game for us in the last ten minutes, and then oh so predictably Folan poked the ball under Green as we failed to properly clear a lumped free kick into the area, despite having three centre halves and two other defenders on the field.

Despite the scoring of the mythical unobtainable goal, a new season low had been achieved. To be not only beaten and knocked out of the cup by Chesterfield but comprehensively outplayed by them was terrifying, let alone worrying. Keep in mind, eight of the players who started the game had been deemed good enough to start at Tottenham. Admittedly, there had only been 48 hours between the games but tiredness shouldn't have led to such a disparity in class between the two sides.

In his interview with Sky after the game, Pardew at least acknowledged that this was the case, and the positivity that he had still been trying to show had been replaced by one of outright anger. 'I'm getting to the level where I'm looking at individual players and maybe at taking out one or two who are not performing at the level they should be. Players have to look at themselves and ask if their displays are good enough for West Ham United. We've been beaten fair and square, and that's not acceptable for me, for the team or for the club. We need to show the same intensity on Sunday that Chesterfield showed tonight.'

Tuesday, 24 October 2006:
Chesterfield 2 *Larkin (54), Folan (87)*
West Ham 1 *Harewood (4)*

Pardew's position was now under intense pressure. At this point, we had broken our own club record for consecutive games without scoring and were one defeat away from equalling the unwanted club record of nine consecutive defeats, which had been set in 1932. Jose Mourinho once made the point that no manager could ever survive ten straight losses no matter how well they had done beforehand or how popular they were, and Pards was on the verge of testing this theory to its fullest.

He did, however, retain the support of the fans, which we will get to shortly, and of the still-incumbent chairman Terry Brown. In a rare interview for the website, Brown said, 'I went down the tunnel [after the Chesterfield game] to make sure that Alan was OK. Nothing negative or critical was said, I put my arm around him and told him that everything would be fine. It is disappointing that one or two sections of the media have made such suggestions but they will not distract us from working hard to turn around the team's current situation.' The dreaded vote of confidence but in as soft a manner as could be delivered, it would seem.

The next match at home to Blackburn was now pivotal for Pardew, though. There could be no doubt about that. For all the 'OK' displays, we were 19th in the league and hadn't won a game for two months.

The three games after the visit of Mark Hughes' side were against Arsenal, Middlesbrough and Chelsea. If defeat to Blackburn didn't spell doom for Pardew, the likely further adverse results in that run of difficult fixtures would surely see his position become untenable. A story doing the rounds a couple of days before the match suggested that should Kia Joorabchian be successful with his takeover bid, Pardew would find himself replaced by Sven-Goran Eriksson, who at that time was available having recently left his role as England manager. This was strenuously denied by Athole Still, Eriksson's agent.

The other noteworthy story prior to the weekend involved reports of a training ground bust-up between Harewood and Reo-Coker, which was rubbished by Marlon in an interview with Five Live Sport. 'I don't know where the media got that from. It's just them trying to stir up trouble. We've got such a great atmosphere at West Ham.' No need to speculate on player power or disunity inside the camp, then. Yet.

The side showed four changes from the team that lost the last league game at White Hart Lane. Both full-backs changed as Spector and McCartney replaced Pantsil and Konchesky, Etherington came in for Mascherano and Teddy Sheringham, who was without a goal for West Ham since turning 40 six months earlier, replaced Harewood, who was somewhat harshly dropped having become the only player other than Zamora to have scored since the opening day in the Chesterfield defeat. Tevez was still out injured and Lee Bowyer was fit enough to return to the bench. The full squad for that day (as I haven't showed this for a few matches) was as follows:

Starting XI: *Green, Spector, Ferdinand, Gabbidon, McCartney, Benayoun, Mullins, Reo-Coker, Etherington, Sheringham, Zamora*

Subs: *Carroll, Dailly, Mascherano, Bowyer, Harewood*

The atmosphere before the match was raucous, with the home crowd realising how much the team and the manager would need them that day. In hindsight, Blackburn visiting Upton Park in recent years had often proved catalysts for us to have good seasons or runs. The previous three games against them had seen a 2-1 league win to finally give us a long-awaited first home victory of the relegation campaign on 31 January 2003 (I couldn't bring myself to write a book about that season), a 3-1 win on the opening day of the previous season that I've already written about, and then a 4-2 win in the fourth round of the FA Cup on our way to the final.

This, in addition to the desire to get a result and show support to the boss, led to the crowd chanting 'Alan Pardew's claret and blue army' and 'There's only one Alan Pardew' for several minutes prior to kick-off and then also in the early minutes of the match. This seemed to really galvanise the team, as we began playing at a pace which hadn't been seen in recent weeks. Etherington was getting in behind the Blackburn right-back Lucas Neill, who he had terrorised at home twice the previous season, and Benayoun was teasing and probing as he had done so often during the previous campaign when at his best.

An opening goal seemed a likelihood rather than a far-off wish for the first time in a while, and it duly came in the 21st minute when Yossi's deft cross was emphatically nodded home by Sheringham from 12 yards out. We continued to press but couldn't find a second goal before half-time. We also defended well when required and found ourselves leading at the break for the first time all season in the Premier League. Blackburn improved in the second half, with Green needing to make a superb save from Neill's snap shot, but we still seemed by and large in control of the situation, which any Hammers fan will tell you almost always guarantees an imminent equaliser.

Not on this day, though. We missed a fantastic chance when Zamora, clean through on goal, decided not to square to Harewood for a tap-in but shoot himself and saw Friedel make a good save. The killer second goal arrived from the resulting corner, Etherington's delivery missing everyone at the near post and being touched in by Hayden Mullins. I assume this goal was shown at length in the coming days to Mascherano to coach him as to what he was doing wrong.

A 2-0 lead we fully deserved, but we still had to do the classic West Ham thing of giving away a goal at the death, David Bentley tapping in after Benni McCarthy (two more future Hammers) had a shot spilled by Green. We held on for the last couple of minutes of injury time for a huge, huge win, one that moved us above Newcastle, Watford and Sheffield United and out of the relegation zone.

Pardew spoke in his press conference after the game about the support the fans had shown both him and the team. 'The fans were special today, they showed the quality that some grounds can't get. I'm not the most emotional of people but I was a little bit choked at the start with the way they backed me and I thank them for that.'

He also felt that this could be the start of a better period for the team, even with Arsenal being the next opponents. 'So we've set ourselves up nicely for Arsenal; instead of going in and maybe suffering the majority of possession that they're going to have, we can enjoy it. We had great results against them last year, so go and enjoy Arsenal – our fans are going to be up for it and it'll be a good game, I think.'

Sunday, 29 October 2006:
West Ham 2 *Sheringham (21), Mullins (80)*
Blackburn 1 *Bentley (90)*

CHAPTER FIVE

Early November

AS THE month of November began, the proposed takeover was still rumbling on; Joorabchian's bid seemed to be on the rocks for a variety of reasons. They included disputes over payment schedules, not wanting to take on the liability for the money still owed to Norwich for the Ashton transfer and worries over being unable to further develop the ground should the preferred move to Stratford not materialise.

There also still seemed to be long-term concerns over the funds involved; all of these made it look more and more likely that we would end up going to Iceland. No worries over the pre-match lunch buffets in that case, vol au vents all round. Whoever the preferred bidder ended up being, it looked as if the saga would drag on for a couple more weeks yet.

The next engagement with Arsenal came around soon enough, no bad thing for a side looking to build on the excellent display a week prior. This was a game that had an edge to it even before kick-off, as it was fair to say that the two managers, Pards and Monsieur Wenger, didn't see eye to eye.

There had been an issue the year before, with Pardew taking exception in a pre-match press conference to the lack of English players in Arsenal's team, commenting that he had seen 'a headline saying they [Arsenal] are flying the flag for Britain. Then I wondered where that British involvement actually was when I looked at the team, which is a shame.'

Wenger responded with fury and not without subtle accusation. 'It's really disappointing. First, we kick racism out of football and racism starts there. When you are a manager, you want to accept a technical opinion but not that kind of remark. I think it is very, very disappointing to hear that because it is a regressive way of thinking.'

He also had a friendly reminder for Pardew regarding a loan deal we had struck with Arsenal the previous season. 'When Alan Pardew calls me at the beginning of the season and asks for [French striker] Jérémie Aliadière on loan, he didn't check if he was English or not – he just checked if he was good or not.' Nowadays, I think that is known as being owned. So yes, fair to say they weren't on each other's Christmas card lists.

We made two changes for the game, with Konchesky returning at left-back and interestingly Bowyer coming back into the team at the expense of Sheringham, with the side lining up in a 4-5-1 formation designed to shackle some of the Gunners' more creative players. Tevez returned to the bench, but Mascherano was nowhere to be seen.

Arsenal were at full strength, with Fabregas in midfield and Thierry Henry (my personal favourite all-time non-West Ham player) and Van Persie up front. Wenger was understandably reluctant to rest any of his players for an important London derby despite a trip to Moscow for a Champions League match only three days earlier.

The game began with us knowing that a result, however difficult it would be, was very much needed, what with wins for Watford against Middlesbrough (their first all season) and Sheffield United at Newcastle the previous day putting us back into the drop zone prior to kick-off.

The change in formation and plan worked well in the first half; Reo-Coker stuck to Fabregas throughout in an attempt to stifle the midfielder's creativity, while Zamora up front kept running the centre-halves into channels with the idea of winning us throw-ins and set plays further up the pitch. This shackled Arsenal to the extent they only had one clear-cut chance in the first 45 minutes, with Rosicky hitting wide in a one-on-one situation from which he should have scored. Other than that, Green made saves that he would have been expected to make from long-range efforts by Van Persie and Henry (these were the only shots on target Arsenal had that day), and half-time arrived with the two teams scoreless.

We came more and more into the game in the early part of the second half, with attempts from Etherington and Zamora going narrowly wide. The players and management seemed dialled into the task at hand, with Wenger realising the need for change by bringing Adebayor on for Van Persie (who had disappointingly been struck by a coin thrown from the crowd in the first half – for which the club were deservedly fined) and going to a straight 4-4-2. What the Arsenal manager wouldn't have expected is that we almost immediately brought Sheringham and Harewood on for Bowyer and Zamora and matched up with a 4-4-2 of our own; it seemed as if some of Pardew's belief and swagger was coming back.

The game at this point became less attritional and more two sides trading blows; Hleb really should have won a penalty when brought down by Spector but was bafflingly told to get up by referee Rob Styles and Kolo Toure fired inches wide from about 35 yards out, whereas at the other end Clichy made a fantastic goal-saving tackle as Teddy was about to tap in for his second goal in two games, and Marlon, put clean through, again, took too long to make up his mind, again, and saw his shot saved, again.

The game looked as if it was heading for a stalemate, still a very creditable point against one of the league's top sides, but then, as we headed into injury time, Sheringham and Etherington combined down the left-hand side, a couple of one-twos led to Matty getting clear down the left, and his low cross was swept into the net first time by Marvellous Marlon Harewood. The ground went absolutely mental.

One of the loudest eruptions I have heard at Upton Park followed, my dad and I jumped on each other and were joined by several other delirious Hammers fans in an impromptu human pile-on. The very best of moments.

Marlon helped whip up the excitement by running up to the corner where I sat, taking his shirt off and throwing it into the crowd before being engulfed by almost every one of his team-mates. Everybody knew the significance of the goal and the moment, not least the manager, who celebrated a last-minute winning goal the way anybody in his position would, by cheering, leaping for joy and celebrating with his staff. This for some reason wasn't to the taste of Professeur Arsene, who initially shouted abuse at the Hammers manager then walked up to him and pushed him a couple of times, before the two were pulled apart by officials and various coaches (the primary separator being coach/popular general helper Jimmy Frith, who as well as working at West Ham since seemingly the dawn of time, also taught me football at secondary school when I was in Year 8 in 1997. Fair to say, I would probably have been one of his poorer students).

Being honest, I still don't understand what Pardew did wrong. We have seen him do some very questionable celebrations over the years, the shuffle when Harewood scored in the FA Cup semi-final and the bizarre reggae-style dad dance he did (I still see this all the time on Twitter and am still hypnotised by it when it comes up) when Palace took the lead in the FA Cup Final in 2016 being the examples that spring to mind, but on this occasion he just celebrated a goal with his staff, with no antagonising behaviour whatsoever towards the Arsenal bench.

I think it would have come from the previous beef Arsene had with him, plus the Frenchman was never too gracious with people who got results against him (Jose Mourinho anyone?) and Pardew now had two wins and a draw over him in three meetings, along with two clean sheets. The sulking Frenchman sloped off at full time without shaking Pardew's hand, and shunned post-match interviews.

Our manager was more than happy to speak to the assembled media after the game, though, (as he had done after all the defeats as well, in fairness to him) and was obviously delighted, as well as contrite regarding the touchline shenanigans. 'Tactically, we had a game plan. We loaded the bench with strikers with a view to getting ourselves in a position where we could bring them on. Bobby Zamora worked incredibly hard and got us into that position so that Teddy and Marlon could come on and grab the headlines. I realise that that's not what the headlines will be about but that was the plan!' Regarding Wenger, Pardew added, 'Well, if I was over-zealous in celebrating, I apologise. Ludo nearly killed me when we were celebrating! I hope I can iron things out with Wenger before he leaves. I have great respect for him. Did I say anything I regret? No, I told him I was just celebrating. Did he say anything to me? He said a number of things.'

Both managers were charged by the FA that week for 'alleged aggressive and confrontational behaviour'. Wenger continued to stay quiet, while in a statement on our website club MD Paul Aldridge quite rightly stood by our man. 'West Ham United are astonished by this charge. We believe Alan Pardew did no more than celebrate in a passionate manner following a crucial goal in a London derby. Alan Pardew has the full backing of the board with regards to this charge, which will be defended vigorously.' For what it's worth, I don't think the charge against Pardew was ever heard, the reasons for which we will get to in a while.

Sunday, 5 November 2006:
West Ham 1 *Harewood (90)*
Arsenal 0

The week between the Arsenal victory and the trip to Middlesbrough largely passed without incident. The only real news that occurred were further reports that Messrs Magnusson and Gudmundsson were forging ahead in the battle to take the club over in front of Joorabchian, as their willingness to accept conditions the Israeli was still haggling over and being able to provide clear and direct proof of the necessary funds seemed to be marking them as clear front runners.

I broke my mighty run, of well, two, consecutive away games by deciding to do what it seems most Middlesbrough fans do: not attend a Middlesbrough home match. Jokes aside, being an entry level pensions administrator straight out of university, as I was at the time, doesn't lend itself to being able to afford travelling from one end of the country to the other too often. Not that I would have wanted to go anyway; I'd had one experience of travel to a game in the North East and that was more than enough for me, even though it was a successful one.

The game in question was one that many of our fans would remember and no doubt attended as well; our FA Cup fifth-round tie away at Sunderland in 2001, coming hot on the heels of the magnificent 1-0 win at Old Trafford in the previous round (I'm talking about that game later, never fear).

Still a bit giddy from that game, me and some mates decided we would travel to whatever game we were drawn at in the following round. None of them were season ticket holders, a couple of them weren't even West Ham fans, but a load of 16-year-olds would never pass up a day trip if one was on offer. It was easy back in those days to take advantage of the 'page from your season ticket book' scheme, so my dad and I asked some of the guys who sat near us who weren't going if we could take their pages. They obliged and off we went.

The one slight complication was the good people at Sky deciding on a 12.30pm kick-off on a Saturday lunchtime. How nice and courteous of them. This meant we all had to leave London at 4.30am to get to the game on time, all on coaches graciously provided by the club free of charge to transport the 5,500-strong contingent of tired yet happy Hammers.

I remember me and my mates being pretty much the only sober people on the coach. It hadn't occurred to us naïve types that this could have been a good opportunity to have a drink or three then head straight to the game.

By the time we had passed Watford, however, we were the only people awake on the coach, as the previously excitable 'lads lads lads', as they would be known nowadays, were having a sleep and recharging before they woke up somewhere near Birmingham to get the party started again.

After what felt like about six weeks of travelling, we got to Sunderland to see that most of the back gardens had broken glass on the tops of the walls to stop unwanted intruders, which was reassuring. If Sunderland had been a potential university destination for me before this visit, it wouldn't have been afterwards. Ironically, a trip to a sunny Southampton for an away game the following season, where my friends had a very pleasant afternoon seeing some of the local ladies walking around the town centre before kick-off, actually made Portsmouth a much more attractive uni option. Not Southampton itself, though. They rejected my application. Scummers.

My mate Patrick decided to take the local 'hospitality' as a challenge rather than a warning and spent the last 20 minutes of the journey with his backside hanging out of the window. It got the reaction you would expect. The trip was made well worth it with a 1-0 win due to a goal from Freddie Kanoute, who randomly I was on speaking terms with at the time. I worked as a checkout operator at ASDA while at college and he would come in every Monday night to do his weekly shop. So the day was a success in the end, but by the time we had got home at 9pm that night I remember thinking that it would take a significant game to ever tempt me to travel that far again, and a trip to 'Boro for a league match in November was not the one.

We made three injury-enforced changes for the game at the Riverside, as Ferdinand, Bowyer and Zamora dropped out and were replaced by James Collins, Sheringham and Harewood. The lesser spotted Mascherano also returned to the bench alongside Tevez. This was a big game for us in the quest to move further away from trouble. Gareth Southgate's side were below us on goal difference after consecutive defeats without scoring, so a result was both needed and looked possible.

At this point, I would love to write about the game in detail and talk about a great performance in which we built on the back-to-back wins earned at home. But I can't do that because there wasn't a great performance. From either side. In fact, next to nothing happened, as we oddly seemed nervous and completely devoid of confidence rather than a side getting back to the heights of the previous season, as fans were hoping would be the case. We mustered only two shots on target and one corner throughout the 90 minutes, and were beaten by Massimo Maccarone's goal 15 minutes from time. We dropped back below Middlesbrough to 16th and had to reflect on an opportunity missed with a trip to the defending champions Chelsea to follow.

Saturday, 11 November 2006:
Middlesbrough 1 *Maccarone (74)*
West Ham 0

BOTTOM 6: (23/09/2006)

	P	Pts	GD
Blackburn	12	12	-6
WEST HAM	12	11	-6
Sheffield United	12	10	-9
Newcastle	*12*	*9*	*-7*
Watford	*12*	*9*	*-8*
Charlton	*12*	*8*	*-9*

That week, we had the first significant rumblings of discontent of an Argentine nature, with Mascherano's agent, Walter Tamer, revealing in an interview for a South American website that the midfielder didn't want to return to South America, but that a move within Europe could be on the cards. 'The possibility of Mascherano signing for Flamengo or any Brazilian club is zero,' he said. 'He elected to go to Europe, and that is where is he likely to stay.' I can only presume Pardew was baffled by any potential speculation, what with the iron-clad six-month/three-year/possibly two-year contract he had signed.

Jokes aside, at this point it seemed almost certain that Javier would be moving on at some point very soon. While Mascherano being dropped for Mullins has always been somewhat of a punchline, the truth was having been given an opportunity to re-establish himself in the team the ex-Palace midfielder had been one of our better players. Added to this was the fact it seemed the other spot in central midfield was sewn up, as Reo-Coker had seemingly been deemed undroppable by the manager despite below-par displays throughout the season so far.

Thus, it was hard to imagine that a player good enough to play every minute for Argentina in a World Cup six months previously was going to be happy to stick around and sit on the bench for a side fighting against relegation to the second tier of English football. It was unclear if this was also the case for Tevez. His people had been silent on the matter to this point and first-team chances also seemed more readily available to him, despite Tevez still not having scored for the club. Hopefully, that stat would change sooner rather than later.

We made the short trip across London to Stamford Bridge on Saturday, 18 November in the knowledge that the club would imminently be under new ownership. It had emerged that morning that an offer of £75m from the Icelandic consortium had been accepted, and Eggert Magnusson would be formally announced as chairman that week.

Tevez returned to the first team for this game, his first start since the Reading loss seven weeks prior. The Argentine was one of four changes to the side, as Anton, Bowyer and Zamora all returned from injury, with Collins, Benayoun, Harewood and Sheringham all making way. Tevez would line up on the right-hand side, with a return to the 4-5-1 formation that had worked so well against Arsenal.

It was relatively successful in this match as well as we held our own to an extent in an entertaining, but ultimately fruitless encounter. We created chances,

Etherington volleying just wide and Reo-Coker seeing a goal-bound shot blocked by Ashley Cole (I swear Cole made blocks like that at least once a game through his career), but ultimately we were beaten by a perfectly struck free kick from Geremi.

The goal caused Matt le Tissier on *Soccer Saturday* to burst out laughing as it went in, due to him thinking Drogba and not the Cameroonian would take the set play. Always appreciated seeing people laugh on TV when your team concedes. We made changes through the second half in search of an equaliser and ended the game with Tevez, Sheringham and Harewood all up front, but ultimately failed to register a shot on target, again, and went *another* game without a goal.

The overall run now stood at four goals in 12 games, which was clearly far from good enough and couldn't go on for much longer.

Pardew's positivity in the face of defeat was back in his post-match presser, with an absolutely baffling boast in the bargain. 'There was no luck about their win but we pushed them all the way and are starting to show that we can match even the best sides.'

So off the back of beating Arsenal and losing narrowly to Chelsea, we were now matching the best sides, were we Alan? God knows how good he thought Reading, Portsmouth, Manchester City, Newcastle and sodding Chesterfield were, then. Probably start with working out how to beat or even score a goal against any of those sides before you brag about us pushing the top teams.

We remained 16th in the league due to all our rivals losing that weekend, except Newcastle, who got a very credible draw with Arsenal at the Emirates, where no away side had won yet.

Saturday, 18 November 2006:

Chelsea 1 *Geremi (22)*

West Ham 0

CHAPTER SIX

Late November

ON TUESDAY, 21 November, West Ham United entered into foreign ownership for the first time in their 111-year history as Eggert Magnusson was formally confirmed as the new chairman of the club.

A short statement on the official website read, 'West Ham United is delighted to announce that the takeover bid from a consortium led by Icelandic businessman Eggert Magnusson has been successfully completed this morning. Following the finalisation of necessary paperwork and formalities between lawyers acting on behalf of the two parties on Monday evening, a statement was released to the London Stock Exchange today, confirming acceptance from the major shareholders of an £85 million offer.'

My thoughts, and I am sure the thoughts of all West Ham fans when this was finally agreed once and for all, was now what? What long-term plans for the club did they have? In the situation the club they had purchased found themselves, the short term was arguably more important.

There were six weeks until the start of the January transfer window, when it seemed apparent that reinforcements would be required and clearly of greater quality than most of those brought in during the summer window. Also, what of the manager?

When the takeover talks first started after the Villa game, any thought of Pardew being replaced by new owners would have been deeply unpopular with the supporters. While the Blackburn game had shown the relationship still had some strength, nine league games later, with only six points and three goals to show, in addition to exits from two cup competitions at the first hurdle and the seeming failure to fully integrate the two Argentinians into the squad, had led to this being a far less thorny issue for any new owner than it would have initially appeared.

Magnusson did his best to answer these queries in an initial interview with the BBC, firstly stating, 'We can now end the uncertainty of recent weeks and move forward into the next phase of development of this great club, with Alan Pardew leading our efforts on the pitch. I will be continuing talks with Alan Pardew on how he sees the future on the playing side. This is very much his domain and he has my full confidence and support. He already knows that funds will be made available for the January transfer window but we need to discuss his needs and the investment that might be required to strengthen the squad.'

Nicely cleared up early doors, Eggert. Pards is the man to move forward, barring any major catastrophes, of course, and he will be backed in January, I presume with a 'war chest', as the media like to say.

'War chest' is one of my favourite football sayings, as I love the thought of any chairman bringing a massive pirate-style treasure chest into the bemused manager's office the day before a transfer window, telling him, 'Here you go, see who you can get with this' and then leaving.

Off topic, but another one I've always enjoyed, is when a club is placed on 'red alert' by a player they supposedly want to sign doing an interview in which he vaguely says he might want to leave his current club. In this instance, I've often imagined Arsene Wenger sat quietly at his desk before a flashing siren goes off beyond him, as Edinson Cavani tells Foreign TV he would like to play in England one day.

The Egg man was also happy to give details of some of his long-term plans for the club in an interview with the club's in-house online channel WHUTV, which I will include here but, you know, probably not bring up again too much. 'This club has so much to be proud of and I want everyone who loves and supports the club to bring their pride and passion to help build this next stage of West Ham's future. The main financial supporter of our bid, Mr Gudmundsson, [his] commitment to the club is vital and he also believes that we can build something very special here at West Ham. There is a genuine excitement in the club about what we can achieve together, which I hope the fans will share.'

Great stuff, Eggert. Let's just hope nobody involved goes completely and utterly bankrupt two years later or anything.

One of the first issues that would have landed on the new chairman's desk, and probably one of the first bills to pay as well, was that goalkeeper Roy Carroll had checked in to rehab for alcohol and gambling-related issues. The media reported 48-hour drinking binges that again called into question the culture, behaviour and attitude of the players, not for the first time that season.

The club brought in Gabor Kiraly in an emergency loan deal from Crystal Palace to cover for Carroll. You may not remember his name unless you are told that he was the bloke who played in goal in grey tracksuit bottoms. You probably remember now.

Prior to the visit of Sheffield United the coming weekend, there were reports of an interview that Tevez had done in the South American media about his time with the club so far. The interview was, somewhat surprisingly, very positive.

Tevez acknowledged some of the difficulties he'd had adapting to the Premier League. 'English football is very physical and you have to be very quick. I knew it would be different but not this much. You don't see much dribbling here, you only get one touch otherwise they eat your legs. There aren't any small defenders, they're all big.'

No complaining or getting the agent to discuss moves across Europe, then, which was very heartening to see, particularly with what was potentially the first 'six-pointer' of the season on the horizon against the Blades.

Sheffield United had arrived back in the Premier League that season, their first campaign in the big time since 1993/94, and were scrapping away somewhat creditably to that point, defying their pre-season prediction of no-hopers with a couple of decent results. Before travelling to Upton Park, they had narrowly lost 2-1 at home to Manchester United, with a late Wayne Rooney strike sealing victory, and had also won 2-0 at Newcastle in their most recent away trip.

Managed by the then widely disliked and nowadays oddly popular Neil Warnock, they were a combative, no-frills outfit very much in the guise of their manager and didn't look like they were a team who would drift towards relegation quietly. Indeed, the reason for the aforementioned 'six-pointer' tag was because the teams went into the game separated by only a point, with Sheffield United in 18th place with ten points, two places behind the Hammers, who had 11.

For the first time all season, we named an unchanged starting 11. Seeing as the game was taking place in late November, this stat shows the level of uncertainty about what our best side had been or could be, as well as the injuries and general rubbishness that had festered throughout. To celebrate the milestone, let's look at what the team for the day was:

Starting XI: *Green, Spector, Ferdinand, Gabbidon, Konchesky, Bowyer, Reo-Coker, Mullins, Etherington, Tevez, Zamora*

Subs: *Kiraly, McCartney, Benayoun, Sheringham, Harewood*

On paper, a pretty decent first 11 with a strong bench. I haven't mentioned the right-back situation for a while, you may have noticed, but at this stage young Jonathan Spector, bought for the future rather than the present, had usurped Pantsil and Mears to become first choice due to some tidy displays that had left the other more experienced options in the wilderness.

Prior to kick-off we welcomed Eggert formally, with the new chairman wearing the obligatory claret and blue scarf and waving to all corners of the ground, while holding his baffled-looking two-year-old grandson (I would hazard a guess that this match was the young man's only ever visit to the Boleyn Ground).

The game was the scrappy encounter we expected it to be; we thought Tevez had finally broken his duck with an effort that from our view in the West Stand looked as if it had burst the net, but sadly it had smashed into the side netting. The noise that the 'goal' from the Argentine created, though, did give an indication of things to come, however.

We made the breakthrough just after the half-hour mark, as a corner was flicked on by Ferdinand at the near post and bundled in by Hayden Mullins, his second goal in three home games no less, not bad for someone with three goals in 121 appearances in the three seasons prior. Clearly, Mascherano coming in had inspired him to find this aspect of his game!

Mullins' goal had gone in in front of the Bobby Moore Stand, which was the end of the ground furthest away from me, with my seat in the Lower Tier of the West

Stand being in the corner near what would go on to be known as the Trevor Brooking Stand. Our control of the first half meant the fans in our part of the ground saw very little action in front of them, and the Blades' domination of the second half meant we saw next to none then either.

This led to one of the funnier periods of my time going to matches, particularly during such a tense game, where the lower tiers in my corner, along with the guys opposite us in the East Stand and our part of the Centenary, mercilessly taunted their keeper Paddy Kenny. The Irish stopper had found himself having some very public marital issues the week prior, and the lack of action led to some very cruel yet darkly hilarious chants being levelled at him. As the half went on, it led to the keeper moving further and further from his goal, presumably to avoid hearing the chants quite as clearly, until he was only ever standing in his area when we threatened to attack, and barely so then.

As already touched on, we rarely did attack that half, though, as the opposition pelted our goal with attacks. Efforts from Nade and Quinn came close, and their winger Nicky Law managed to screw a shot wide from eight yards out, which was harder to do than put the ball into the almost unguarded net.

This all paled by comparison, though, to what seemed to be a 94th-minute leveller for the away side as Green came for a cross but could only parry it into the air, and the ball was then nodded in by defender Robert Kozluk. The devastation in the crowd was quickly replaced by elation, however, as it transpired that the goal had been disallowed by Mike Riley for, erm, reasons.

The only way I can describe it is that it was one of those goals that are ruled out because a player had jumped near a goalkeeper, who then made a mistake. Any of us who watch football know what that type of 'goal' is, and we also know those goals should always be given as keepers are massively overprotected in these scenarios, and can also, you know, use their hands. But they never are.

At least on this occasion, we were on the right side of the error. The final bit of comedy of the afternoon was when Kenny saw the ball hit the net and ran towards us to celebrate, looking to get his own back on his tormentors in the crowd. The only issue was it was a good ten seconds before he realised the goal hadn't been given, so all the poor sod had done was add insult to injury. The final whistle went seconds later, and the 1-0 win took us four points clear of United, who remained in 18th. Our third home win in a row moved us into 15th place, with hopefully better times ahead under the new ownership. Fingers crossed it would be the last we'd hear from Warnock and Sheffield United that season.

Saturday, 25 November 2006:
West Ham 1 *Mullins (36)*
Sheffield United 0

As well as the positive result, two other newsworthy items came out of that game. Firstly, our main centre-half and reigning player of the year Danny Gabbidon was ruled out for six weeks due to a hamstring injury sustained when blocking a shot from Nade. The Welshman had started the season poorly but improved to something near his best form in recent weeks, so this was a massive blow.

Also, young Carlos had got himself into trouble. Pardew revealed that after being taken off for Teddy Sheringham with 25 minutes to go, the Argentine had not only gone straight down the tunnel, he had gone straight home.

Pardew gave his reasons for the change in his interview after the game, as well as making it clear Tevez would be read the riot act. 'We lost Gabbidon and suddenly looked a very little team. I brought Teddy on to defend set plays – that's where we were today. If I felt we'd been in control of the game, Tevez would have carried on – that was the only reason I took him off. We looked small. I needed two big strikers on to defend. I'll have to listen to Carlitos' explanation. I'm sure it's just disappointment but that's no excuse – he has an explanation to give to me on Monday morning.'

Tevez was fined a week's wages and apologised for his actions early the following week on the club website. 'I would just like to say that I left the ground in anger on Saturday; it was a spur-of-the-moment decision which I regretted almost straight away. I know I did very wrong in going, and I have made it clear to the manager and my team-mates that I in no way meant to disrespect them.'

Not the finest episode for the striker, particularly at a time when he had got back into the team after a spell on the sidelines, and poor timing also as in the two games that he'd been back he had looked more like the player we had seen play for Argentina than at any other time in his spell so far.

The fans were clearly with him as his aforementioned withdrawal against Sheffield United saw mass booing in the stadium. While there hadn't been a goal to speak of yet, West Ham fans have always been knowledgeable in terms of knowing when a player is giving his all and 'dialled in' to the club, and that was clear to see in Tevez. His style of play was that of an all-action bulldog-type. He clearly didn't know any other way to play the game other than full commitment to the cause and the fans in the stadium were responding to that. While it hadn't quite clicked for him on the pitch yet, a bond between player and supporter was forming at a rapid pace.

It was only a couple of days before Tevez was in the media again, with Eggert voicing his opinion on the signings of him and Mascherano in the most negative of fashions, which made its way into several national newspapers. 'No way would I reach such an agreement. I think the club should have total rights over their players. I am not happy with agents or consortiums owning players. That's not the way to move forward. Now I can choose myself as chairman how we go about that. I want to keep them until the summer but after the summer, it is not up to us.'

Yet again, these quotes are the club almost literally hiding in plain sight. To jump ahead slightly, the rules on third-party ownership in that era specifically forbade an investor from attempting to 'influence club playing and selection decisions, or transfers, or indeed any other major club policy'.

Magnusson actually said in the interview above that it wasn't up to us if they stayed past the summer or not. He said this, in an interview with the media! And still, nobody questioned it, or posed a question as to whether we had broken any rules. How the Premier League as a governing body hadn't seen or heard enough evidence to at least look into the two transfers by this point, Lord only knows. If they had, it may have saved them a fair few problems later in the season.

It was also becoming apparent that Magnusson was going to be quite the opposite of the previous chairman Terry Brown, who was nigh on a mute when it came to the media, whereas the Icelandic was producing more quotes than a builder on a new housing development. It appeared that things certainly weren't going to be dull in east London as December rolled round.

CHAPTER SEVEN

December

DECEMBER WOULD begin with three crucial games in a week for Pardew's men, with a midweek home game against Wigan Athletic the buffer between two away games, firstly at Goodison Park against David Moyes' Everton and latterly at the Reebok Stadium against Sam Allardyce's Bolton. While performances had been better over the previous five league games, we were still very much in trouble and these games were opportunities to pick up some points, score some goals and move into mid-table comfort before the expected influx of players in January due to that sweet, sweet Icelandic money.

The three games were definitely not cakewalks, all against competent, well-drilled and smartly managed sides from the North West, but a haul of at least four, possibly six points would not have been beyond any Hammers fan's wildest dreams. Everton, in particular, we seemed to be playing at the right time. They were in the middle of a crippling injury crisis and would have to put out a back four composed entirely of centre-halves against us, as well as losing key players such as Mikel Arteta and Phil Neville.

We, on the other hand, were largely at full strength, only Gabbidon and Benayoun of the players we were actively considering picking at that point being injured. Mears, Pantsil and Cole may have been injured but I don't think anybody would have noticed at this point, in another ringing endorsement of the summer transfer strategy. Wigan were also on a bad run, with only one point and a solitary goal from their last three games, including a 4-0 spanking at home to Liverpool the day before we travelled to the Reds' near neighbours.

So, some opportunities for definite, ahead of what appeared to be a pivotal six days for West Ham and Alan Pardew in particular. Pards at this point still largely had the fans' backing, the goodwill that had been built up from getting the club back into the Premier League and the fantastic 2005/06 season still evident. There seemed more of a consensus among most supporters that the downswing in results wasn't due to Pardew losing his magic touch, it was more due to the players themselves.

Without a doubt, several established first-teamers hadn't played to the level they had the year before. This list included Paul Konchesky, Anton Ferdinand, Marlon Harewood, Bobby Zamora (who after the five early-season goals was now without a goal in three months) and most notably captain Nigel Reo-Coker, about whom rumours of an inflated ego and issues in the dressing room wouldn't go away. It seemed for some of the players and the manager, this week could prove to be a make-

or-break situation, where some of the above would either have to shape up, or face shipping out.

Everton first, then, managed by the (at the time) up-and-coming and highly rated David Moyes (whatever became of him?). At this point, they were an upper mid-table side, the sort of team we were no doubt expecting to be competing with at the start of the season, but one that went into this match seven points and seven places ahead of us. A victory there, though, as we had managed the previous season (2-1 via a Zamora winner) and we could possibly work our way back into Mr Moyes' rear-view mirror.

We just made one change to the starting 11, with Collins coming in for the stricken Gabbidon, while as already mentioned Everton had a patched-up side, with centre-halves playing in both full-back positions and winger Andy van der Meyde starting his first game for eight months.

The *ad hoc* nature of the hosts' set-up was evident in the first half, in which we were by far the better side in all areas. Tevez teased and tormented the Toffees' backline, forcing a good save from Tim Howard with a crisply driven shot and also laying a sitter on a plate for Lee Bowyer, who managed to side-foot the chance against the goalkeeper from no more than six yards out. It wasn't the first time Bowyer had done that in claret and blue; indeed over two spells and more than 20 games, he still hadn't scored his first goal for the Irons. I imagine him and Tevez got along particularly well at this point.

It had been a first half of domination, in which we created several chances and forced 12 corners no less, but guess what? No goals.

Again, no goals, just as it had been in away games at Manchester City, Portsmouth, Tottenham, Middlesbrough and Chelsea, as well as Palermo in the UEFA Cup. We had scored three goals away from home all season, Zamora's header at Watford, one at Chesterfield in a loss and one from a shanked Bobby Zamora cross at Anfield.

It seemed whether our performance away from Upton Park was good, bad or indifferent, we just couldn't score a goal. And if you can't score a goal in a game of football, you tend not to win too often. Case in point, Leon Osman cutely lifted the ball over Green six minutes into the second half and their young striker James Vaughan sealed the game in injury time, clinching a 2-0 win for Moyes' men.

Overall, we had nearly 57 per cent of the ball, forced 18 shots and had 14 corners, to Everton's three. But they scored two goals and we did not, and despite what people who play computer games all day or post pictures to various sites that have the word 'bible' at the end of them say, that is the only statistic in football that really matters.

The loss meant we dropped to 17th, one point above Newcastle, who had a game in hand. Sheffield United had instantly made up the points lost at Upton Park with consecutive wins against Watford and Charlton, meaning they had now gone two points above us.

Pardew wasn't panicking in his interview with Sky after the game (still), and took lots of positives (obviously) while hoping for a change of luck. 'It's frustrating because in terms of our penetration and control of the game, it was good right up to the finish. We just need a break, really. One moment's inspiration or a bit of luck. David Moyes almost apologised to me at the end. He must have felt as if he got a victory out of nothing today.' I'm sure he was all right, Alan, I wouldn't worry about it.

One final footnote of the defeat on Merseyside was the second Everton goal came courtesy of Javier Mascherano, on as an 87th-minute sub, trying to dribble the ball out of defence and being dispossessed. It would be the final thing he would do in a claret and blue shirt (unless you deem Barcelona's kit to be claret and not purple. He did a lot of things in that shirt).

Sunday, 3 December 2006:
Everton 2 *Osman (51), Vaughan (90)*
West Ham 0

Eggert was back in the papers the next day, in bullish mood about the prospect of relegation. 'I am not worried about going down. The players and manager are far too good. I realise the situation we are in at the moment, but I think we will move out, sooner rather than later.'

However, in stark contrast to the full backing Pardew received when he took over the club, it was made clear that for his sake it definitely needed to be 'sooner'. 'The manager is responsible for the team. I have told Alan,

"It is your team, it is not for me to tell you which players to buy. You are going to be judged by how the team performs. It is your throat that is going to be cut if you do not produce results in the long run.'" The thought of the cartoon-looking Magnusson as a throat slasher is quite the visual, I'm sure you'll agree.

Only three days later saw the visit of Wigan in what had now become an absolute must-win fixture. As it was a midweek match and I lived 100 miles away, I wasn't in attendance for this game. Quite frankly, if I lived *one* mile away I'm not sure I would have gone to this one, as home games against Paul Jewell's side in this era never seemed to go well.

The previous year saw a 2-0 home defeat three days after Christmas, when Wigan battered us to the point that we took off midfielder Carl Fletcher after 25 minutes to change formation, so overrun were we.

The year before that was somehow even worse, for me personally if not for everybody else. We were playing the Latics in a Championship fixture early on a Sunday afternoon in August in a match I had oddly decided I had to attend. I say oddly as I had spent the previous day, evening and night in Wokingham, where my then-girlfriend was hosting a party that was attended by a mix of her local friends and some of our mates from uni.

The party had started on the Saturday afternoon and ended some time the following Tuesday by my estimation. At least that's how it felt when I woke up the next morning. I think I went to bed at what I assume was about 5am. I remember the sun was coming up anyway. When my alarm went off at 9am for me to get up and travel into London to go to the game, every fibre of my being said to go back to sleep. For reasons not even known to myself, I didn't. I got up and went to the game, while ignoring the sleeping bodies dotted around the house and the weeping from several of my internal organs. But I made it because I'm a true fan, damn it. Or an idiot, one or the other.

Now I think a lot of fans nowadays laugh at the attendance figures given out at matches, where clearly half-empty (or half-full depending on your life perspective, I guess) stadiums are announced as being nigh on at capacity. The Emirates, the Etihad and ahem, the London Stadium spring to mind. Well, I can tell you now, dear reader, no bigger lie regarding capacity has ever been told than the figure of 23,271 fans apparently in attendance to watch West Ham lose 3-1 to Wigan on Sunday, 15 August 2004. I swear to you there was about half that amount in the ground, in my mind anyway. Even Wigan only brought half of their normal number of fans – two carloads rather than four.

Part of the reason I'm so sure of this is because it is the only game of football I have ever attended in a stadium where I watched the game lying down. I was laid across four seats watching Wigan dismantle us and wondering if any of the other people at the party had woken up yet. My girlfriend was still asleep when I rang her after the match to tell her what the score was. She hadn't even realised I'd left. She's the hero in that story, not me.

So yes, home games with Wigan were not traditionally happy occasions for West Ham. But this one desperately needed to be. Pardew made a couple of changes to the team beaten at Everton, with Benayoun returning in place of Bowyer and Harewood being the lucky winner of that week's striker lottery, coming in for Zamora. We desperately needed a fast start to get the crowd bouncing and behind us, so obviously Wigan hit the post from a free kick after 45 seconds. Winger Kevin Kilbane was the unlucky taker, he had another great chance 15 minutes later but fired straight at Green with only the keeper to beat, then shortly after the other winger David Cotterill fired inches wide. I'm sure the crowd was on fire at this point.

We did have our own chances as well in fairness. Marlon sent two shots just wide and Tevez was inches away from connecting with a corner that flashed across the six-yard box, but we went in at half-time without a goal, again. At this point, we had scored three goals in the first half in 16 matches. Relegation struggles come from statistics like that.

The turning point of the game, and the beginning of the end of Alan Pardew's time as West Ham manager, came across 120 seconds in the second half. On 50 minutes, Carlos Tevez collected a pass from Benayoun, dribbled past a couple of Wigan defenders and curled a shot across keeper Chris Kirkland and against the inside of the post, and out again. Wigan got the ball and broke straight up the other end, Kilbane turned James Collins inside out and crossed for Cotterill, who curled the ball into the top corner of the net.

Upon seeing news of the goal while sat in my living room, I remember burying my head in my hands. At this point, we didn't seem capable of overturning a lead, and all hope looked lost. Seven minutes later, a shot from Leighton Baines deflected off Spector and past a helpless Green, and another defeat was confirmed. We offered next to nothing in terms of chances on goal after the double strike. If anything, Wigan could and should have added to their tally, and boos rained down at full time from the fans brave enough to stomach the beating until the bitter end. Newcastle won 3-2 at Reading and sent us back into the bottom three, two points from safety.

Wednesday, 6 December 2006:

West Ham 0

Wigan 2 *Cotterill (51), Spector og (58)*

Pardew offered no excuses after the game. 'On behalf of the players I apologise to the fans, who have paid good money tonight. Their status as Premier League players is under threat and we have to stand up and be counted. They had better realise it. When they get home tonight and see the league table, it will soon sink in. It's no good facing it in two months' time – "Ah, okay, we're in a bit of trouble here." We *are* in trouble. We need to dig deep, show the sort of character we showed in the Championship to turn this situation round quickly.'

For the first time, Pardew had admitted relegation was on the agenda, quite the turnaround from the smiling manager metaphorically patting little Watford on the head back in August. This game was also the first match attended by Bjorgolfur Gudmundsson, which may help explain what was to come.

BG hung around in England to make the trip to the North West for the Saturday evening live televised game at Bolton, the third of the critical, pivotal three games in six days that I discussed earlier. At this stage, they had been a disaster. It didn't, at least on paper, look to be the worst time to be playing Sam Allardyce's side, though. They went into this encounter having won only one game in their last seven (an admittedly impressive 3-1 win over Arsenal) and had lost four of these matches 1-0. That fact, allied to the, erm, agricultural style of football Allardyce could play at times, as well as our absolute refusal to ever score a goal, gave the impression that this would be a tight affair and one that probably shouldn't have been selected for live broadcast. God, I wish it hadn't been.

We again made two changes to the 11 swept aside by Wigan, with left-back George McCartney coming in to play at centre-half in place of the injured Ferdinand and centre-half/sometimes right-back Christian Dailly replacing Benayoun to play in holding midfield, rather than centre-half. We picked the left-back to play there.

We also didn't bother taking world-class holding midfielder Javier Mascherano to Bolton. He was at home (I can only assume not) watching this on TV. We took Christian Dailly to play there instead. His compatriot Tevez, who despite the lack of goals had been comfortably our best striker over the last four games, was at least in the team. But rather than playing up front, he was on the right wing.

So just to clarify, a left-back was at centre-half, a centre-half was in midfield and our best striker was on the right wing. I think it might be fair to say that Pardew had lost it at this point.

I'm not going to offer any commentary on this game, as if you are reading this book I dare say you remember this night. If you're reading this book and you don't remember this night, you are lucky. The summary is that we were beaten 4-0, with two goals from Kevin Davies and one each from El-Hadji Diouf and Nicolas Anelka. It could have been more. Campo hit the post and Nolan missed at least two great chances, but if it had been 4-0, 5-0, 6-0 or whatever, it was immaterial.

In games up until this point, we had largely been competitive and there had been the sense the players were still fighting, still giving their best and trying to change things around. This didn't look quite as much the case against Wigan, and in this match it was gone, all gone. It wasn't a team now in the slightest, it was 11 individuals strolling around the pitch watching a far more unified and committed team kick their backsides.

And it didn't seem like any of them could have cared less about it. Bolton were first to every ball, had more skill, more heart, more determination. We had a group of players who we knew had the capability to match teams, to raise their intensity, their will to win and their fight, because we had seen them do this before with our own eyes while they were wearing our shirt, but had zero interest in doing so.

As a fan of a team at West Ham's level, you know that bad performances and bad defeats will happen sometimes; you don't want them to but they do. As I write this, I have been a fan attending matches for nearly 27 years. In that time, I have seen us lose 5-0 and 7-1 in consecutive games (to Everton and Blackburn, for God's sake), I've seen us lose 4-0 three times in a week, I've seen us lose 5-1 at home while having three players sent off, hell I've seen Glenn Murray make a career out of scoring against us twice a year.

But not too often, even in the bad defeats and the bad runs, do you see a complete team look utterly disinterested in what is going on during a match. I've always thought in games like the Bolton one, where a team is being outplayed, that the reaction of the players on the pitch when the opposition scores is a tell-tale sign. Do they look angry? Is there any gesticulating or pointing to other team-mates, any clear signs of emotion that show they're dialled into the match still and showing professional pride? With each goal here, the players within shot just stopped, turned around and started to walk back to the centre circle. No anger, no interest, no anything.

In those 27 years, out of all the bad performances and all the hammerings (pun intended), this Bolton game is still without a doubt in my top ten of the very worst all-round displays I have seen from West Ham. As you can probably guess, it's not the only entry from this season.

I watched the debacle at my then-girlfriend's house in Eastbourne. She watched the first half with me, then left the room at half-time as I was in such a mood she thought it better I be left alone. We were supposed to be going out that night after the game had finished. It was decided that a night in would be better due to what bad company I would be. I try to not let games of football influence my actual life too often, but this was a special occasion.

Saturday, 9 December 2006:
Bolton 4 *Davies (17,52), Diouf (77), Anelka (78)*
West Ham 0

At lunchtime on Monday, 11 December 2006, it was announced that Alan Pardew had been sacked by West Ham United. The club's official statement read, 'Alan has made an important contribution since joining as manager in September 2003 but this season's results have been disappointing and have left the club in a very difficult position.

The chairman, Mr Eggert Magnusson, and the board have been concerned by the performances of recent weeks and feel that it is the right time to make a change in the best interests of the club. Mr Magnusson and the board would like to place on the record their thanks to Alan Pardew for his hard work and commitment and to wish him well for the future.

'The search for a successor is now underway in order that a new manager can be in place ahead of the January transfer window. First-team coach Kevin Keen will take temporary charge of team affairs until a new appointment has been made. No further statements on this matter will be made by the club before that time.'

Obviously I am only guessing, but I don't think a 'regulation' defeat at Bolton would have led to this decision being made so quickly. It is worth remembering that it was only three weeks prior to this that Magnusson had publicly backed Pardew upon his arrival at the club. But the capitulation at the Reebok Stadium, the complete lack of motivation all round, added to the awful, awful week the team had just been through, forced the chairman's hand.

Magnusson said this as much later that week in a press conference unveiling Pardew's replacement. 'I was really shocked after those two games, first against Wigan and then Bolton. It was not the results but more the way the team was playing, the lack of motivation. It's a very important time; we have five matches until New Year's Day, we have the January window coming up and I know that I had to make a very difficult decision. I took that decision, and it was very tough as it always is in matters like this, but I did it in the best interests of this club, and that is the result.'

In my opinion, it was probably the right decision. I was a fan of Pardew until the end, and to this day I am still grateful for the good he did for us; as I said right at the start of this book, the promotion in 2004/05 was pivotal for the future of West Ham to this very day, and 2005/06 is my second favourite season ever as a fan, behind the final season at Upton Park in 2015/16. But the stats and facts of the campaign to this point really did not leave much room to argue a case for his retention.

We were 18th in the league, with 14 points from 17 games. In our last 16 games, we had scored only five goals. *Five* goals in 16 games. We hadn't won away since the previous April and hadn't scored a goal away from home in over three months. We'd only scored three times in the first half of games. We had lost 14 times in 20 matches in all competitions. This wasn't a bad run, this was a downward spiral.

Up until the Bolton game, there was still widespread belief it could be turned around, but after that it seemed that the players had given up too, and any hope that Pardew could motivate them and turn things around had evaporated. In my opinion, the only hope we had to stay up was to make a change and see if new ideas and fresh faces could make a difference.

Early runners and riders for Pardew's replacement included Sven-Goran Eriksson, Iain Dowie and Wigan boss Paul Jewell, but the clear and nigh on unbackable favourite was ex-Charlton manager Alan Curbishley.

'Curbs' was out of work after an extremely successful 15-year spell managing the Addicks. He became joint manager with Steve Gritt in 1991 and then took sole charge from 1995. When Curbishley took over initially, Charlton were a mid-table second tier club without a permanent home, ground sharing with Crystal Palace. By the time he left, Charlton were an established Premier League side, having been promoted to the big time twice (in 1998 and 2000) and finished seventh, 11th and 13th over the previous three seasons. In 2004/05, they were even in the running for a Champions League place until a late drop in form, mainly attributed to the sale of Scott Parker, widely considered their best player, to Chelsea.

He had left the club six months prior to Pardew being sacked to 'take a break' from the game after such a long spell in the hotseat, and judging from comments he made in his newspaper column the day after Pards was given the boot, he was ready to end that break and speak to Dr Eggman ASAP. 'I have to admit that watching Chelsea and Arsenal made me realise how much I miss the drama and theatre of Premiership football. I found myself caught up in it. The excitement of such matches is something that affects anybody in love with the game. Having the chance to manage [West Ham], five years after they were allegedly seeking me to replace Harry Redknapp, is a massive honour.

'Once you are brought up in a background like West Ham, the affection you have for the club never goes away. West Ham are my club. I come from Canning Town, grew up as a trainee, became a first-team regular and sat at the feet of the incomparable Bobby Moore. I can easily tap into the fans' passion for the club, what they want and what they stand for. I suspect we will get together over the next day or so when the dust has settled.'

As he stated himself in his column/sales pitch, not only had Curbishley been a successful manager, he was also an ex-West Ham player, having made 85 appearances from 1975 to 1979 after joining the club as an apprentice. The chance for Magnusson to bring in 'one of our own', as well as the job Curbs had done at Charlton, primarily in terms of steering them away from any relegation trouble, made him the obvious candidate.

Later that day, it was reported he was in talks at Upton Park and 24 hours after that, on Wednesday, 13 December, Alan Curbishley was formally announced as the 11th permanent manager of West Ham United on an initial three-year contract. His long-time assistant at Charlton and fellow former West Ham player Mervyn Day, a respected goalkeeper during his playing days and then a coach, joined as assistant manager.

Eggert shockingly was straight back into the media to articulate his delight at the new appointments, with a statement on the club website … 'I am absolutely delighted that Alan has agreed to join us. He is a manager with a proven track record and a real love for this club. He did a fantastic job at Charlton and I know how highly regarded he is throughout the football world. We are also delighted that Mervyn Day has joined the club as assistant manager, and I'm aware of how much this club means to him. This is indeed a great day for West Ham United and I'm sure that we now have the right management team in place to take the club forward.'

Curbs' first press conference came later that day, when he discussed a wide variety of topics, starting with his pride at taking the job and hopes for the immediate future. 'If you could have said to me when I was 16 joining the club as an apprentice that one day I'd be the manager, I would have thought it was impossible. I'm deeply, deeply delighted and obviously looking forward to the challenge. I'm delighted to have come, and I'm looking forward to lifting us out of the position we're in at the moment so we can all enjoy the rest of the season, if we can.'

He was also asked about the escalating reports of dressing room unrest. Shortly after Curbishley's arrival, Reo-Coker had again been in the headlines over a possible move away from the club. There were also stories questioning his attitude and partly blaming the midfielder's poor performances over the season for Pardew's demise.

Curbishley was as non-committal regarding the furore as it was possible to be, a sensible move for any manager looking not to alienate his captain on day one of a new job. 'Dressing room disharmony? Obviously I don't know anything about reports. I think I'll have to assess it when I get in there. When teams are perhaps not having the best of times, all these sorts of things come out. Obviously I've seen from afar and read things, seen the situation. I'm not in a position where I can do without the services of players, I've got to go in there and we've got to hit the ground running, so everyone's got a clean slate.'

Somewhat by the book in terms of any manager press conference, but good to hear nonetheless. Would this be the end of the questions about players' attitudes?

Curbishley's first game as head honcho couldn't have been any more difficult, coming against the only club playing in the Premier League that season that he had never beaten, Manchester United. Ferguson's men were sweeping all before them this season as they looked to reclaim their title from Chelsea. Before the fixture against us, they sat on top of the table five points clear of the Blues, with 44 points and 14 wins from 17 games. To put into context the difficulty of the challenge we were facing, United had won four more league games than we had scored goals to that point.

The game was picked for live TV broadcast by Sky, so would be played on Sunday, and no doubt Curbs would have had his Saturday ruined the same as many other Hammers by Sheffield United and Blackburn. The two teams who were 16th and 17th before kick-off both won away from home, 2-1 at Reading and 1-0 at Wigan respectively. This took them clear of us and meant that even in the unlikely event that we were victorious on the Sunday, we wouldn't have been able to climb out of the bottom three. The new manager clearly had his work cut out for him.

Curbishley's first starting 11 was a conscious decision by the new man to go back to what worked the previous year, or as close to it as he possibly could anyway. Eight of the players picked had been mainstays in the 2005/06 campaign, with Green, Spector and Bowyer the only 'new boys'. The full 16 was as follows, with Reo-Coker retained as captain:

Starting XI: *Green, Spector, Ferdinand, Collins, Konchesky, Bowyer, Reo-Coker, Mullins, Etherington, Harewood, Zamora*

Subs: *Carroll, McCartney, Benayoun, Sheringham, Tevez*

The new management team were given the predictable but always welcome round of applause prior to kick-off, and then saw those cheers almost turn into tears two minutes into the game as Spector somehow cleared a Ryan Giggs cross from the path of an awaiting Wayne Rooney. This was largely the pattern of the first half, as United controlled the play as would be expected, but were met with hard work and resolute defending, two descriptions that couldn't have been used to describe our players in the weeks previous.

Saha had some reasonable attempts from range saved by Green, but the best chance of the half was for us, as Zamora, clean through on goal having shrugged off Rio Ferdinand, could only shoot straight at Van der Sar with the goal at his mercy. His personal goal drought was now past the three-month mark.

The second half saw United turn up the heat early on, with Giggs blazing over the top shortly after Cristiano Ronaldo had forced a ridiculous save from Green, a fiercely struck right-footed shot being somehow turned around the post by the goalkeeper's wrist. Normal people would have had their arm in plaster due to the ferocity of the low effort. (As an aside, my eight-year-old son is bewildered that West Ham ever managed to beat a team with 'CR7' in it. Come to think of it, so am I.)

The game was starting to look as if it was drifting to a scoreless conclusion, much the same as the Arsenal game six weeks prior, but then with 15 minutes to go, just as happened against the Gunners, we scored. Sheringham (on for Zamora) and Harewood combined in the area,

Marlon managed to turn away from Rio and squared for Reo-Coker to tap the ball into the net.

The West Ham captain decided that scoring this goal entitled him to 'answer his critics' as the media often put it, and rather than celebrating the goal with any joy he decided to cup his ear to the fans behind the goal, presumably indicating that he had showed them the error of their ways.

If anything for me personally, this did more to confirm the rumours of a bad attitude and ego than it did to dispel them. Bar a smattering of boos before the game and some people complaining on message boards (pre-widespread social media, let's not forget), Reo-Coker hadn't been subjected to any abuse or vocal criticism by the fans on any sustained level. The stories that had been doing the rounds had been in the media, which as best I know isn't controlled by West Ham fans directly (although having said that I know a fair percentage of the football media are Hammers!), so the critics he was supposedly answering, as best I could see, weren't sat in the Bobby Moore Lower Stand.

The celebration also seemed to indicate that he believed himself to be completely on the right side of the argument, which is curious to me. Even if the stories were fabricated, Reo-Coker was still the captain of a side having a terrible season and in the relegation zone. He had played every game of this season and before this point had contributed zero goals or assists, all the while earning largely widespread poor reviews for his performances across all platforms. While it is possible that he wasn't as at fault for the poor season and sacking of Pardew as had been speculated, he certainly hadn't helped the situation, so as club captain discretion on this matter would surely have been the correct decision.

We held on pretty comfortably for the remaining 15 minutes plus 'Fergie time' for a crucial 1-0 win. I remember being impressed with Curbishley's management of the time remaining, in particular a shrewd substitution that saw George McCartney come on for Etherington to double up with two left-backs in the face of an onslaught from Giggs, Ronaldo and Rooney on the United right. The win saw us move back into contention with the sides above us, and revel in some rare optimism for the season ahead. Little did we know this would be the last time we would win in the Premier League for three months.

Sunday, 17 December 2006:
West Ham 1 *Reo-Coker (75)*
Man Utd 0

Curbs was buoyant in his press conference after the game, well as much as he could ever bring himself to be. 'I've been out for six months but those last five minutes reminded me what it was all about! It was a terrific result. We said to the 11 that were picked "Go out and give it everything you've got" and they did. The noise when we scored – what a noise! I said on Wednesday that last year the fans galvanised the players and the players galvanised the fans, and they had such a good season. I think that this year the fans have still been galvanising the players but they haven't delivered. We need to get back to that. Coming to Upton Park should be difficult.'

Not an insane wish there. A busy Christmas period would see two home games in four days against Portsmouth and Manchester City. If the players could do as the new manager asked and galvanise the crowd with two more strong performances, there was ample opportunity to get a run going at home that would no doubt help the club rise up the table.

Before that, however, came a trip to Craven Cottage, where the travelling fans carried the hope that with Fulham's ground only being 13 miles from Upton Park, it might con our players into thinking they weren't playing an away game and, you know, score a goal. The goalless run in the league away from home now stood at over seven games, or 708 minutes to be exact, since Zamora's goal at Anfield back in August. Every one of those seven games, plus the one at Liverpool, had been lost. That's a lot of miles travelled by the most loyal fans for zero reward.

We made just one change to the squad that had performed miracles against United six days before, which was Christian Dailly coming into the side at centre-half rather than defensive midfield (Pardew must have been baffled) in place of the injured James Collins. As for the Argentinians, Tevez was only on the bench again and Mascherano had completely stopped being mentioned by anybody at the club. Suffice to say, this wasn't how we saw it going with these two players that heady day in August.

The game was an entertaining affair, with us looking relatively secure in defence and just as reasonable in attack. This was also the case for Chris Coleman's Fulham, however, which ultimately led to a stalemate. As it was West Ham playing an away game, the only possible scoreline that could lead to a draw was 0-0, what with our policy not to score goals away from home and all.

We had our chances. An Etherington header looped on to the crossbar and was probably handled on the line by a Fulham defender as the ball dropped, which sadly for us went unseen by referee Chris Foy, and Harewood also hit the post and had an under-hit effort smuggled off the line by Liam Rosenior.

Fulham did have opportunities themselves, though. Green made smart saves from strikers Brian McBride and Heidar Helguson, so in the end a draw was probably the fairest result. Four points from two games and clean sheets in consecutive matches so far, then, for the new regime, a satisfactory start all round. We remained in the bottom three due to Middlesbrough beating Charlton 2-0, a point behind Blackburn, who had played a game less, and two behind Sheffield United, Boro and Manchester City.

Saturday, 23 December 2006:

Fulham 0

West Ham 0

BOTTOM 7: (23/12/2006)

	P	Pts	GD
Middlesbrough	19	20	-7
Manchester City	19	20	-9
Sheffield United	19	20	-10
Blackburn	18	19	-10
WEST HAM	*19*	*18*	*-13*
Charlton	*19*	*12*	*-20*
Watford	*18*	*11*	*-13*

The only black marks from the day, other than the run of not scoring away continuing, was a harsh red card given to Paul Konchesky for a professional foul that provoked fury from the player and his team-mates. He had clearly played the ball rather than taken out winger Wayne Routledge, and there was also some anger from the away support at Tevez being an unused substitute for the second game in a row while Teddy Sheringham saw minutes again instead.

The main worry for fans at the Curbishley appointment was that he may be the 'safe' option, and the decision not to utilise the Argentine thus far did cause alarm bells. Keep in mind in the games leading up to Pardew's sacking, Tevez had been comfortably our best player and seemed to be fully getting up to speed with the Premier League. Persisting with Zamora instead, who looked utterly bereft of confidence having gone 15 games without a goal, just because he was more familiar with him would only give those doubters more ammunition.

The following day was Christmas Eve, which saw Alan Pardew receiving an early present in the form of a new managerial position, as fellow strugglers Charlton came calling for their former player and appointed him as their new boss, replacing Les Reed, who in turn had replaced Iain Dowie. Seven points adrift from safety, our ex-boss had quite the job on his hands to keep the south London side up, potentially at the expense of ourselves, which I am convinced every West Ham fan upon hearing this news was immediately 100 per cent certain would end up happening. I know I was.

Pardew had a quick mention for his former employers in his initial interview when being presented as the Addicks boss. 'I felt aggrieved at West Ham because I thought it was too early [to be sacked],' he said. 'I feel that there was no situation in which they were going to get relegated and I still don't.' Pards would have a chance at revenge in February when we were due to visit the Valley, but we will talk more about that later.

As I briefly mentioned earlier, the fixture list had been relatively kind to us on paper over the Christmas period, with the trip to Fulham followed by back-to-back home games against Portsmouth and Manchester City. So minimal travel for the players allied to two fixtures where it appeared points could be earned.

The team that I lived most local to were having a triffic season under Harry Redknapp, which I know first-hand was delighting the Pompey faithful. They would visit us while sitting in sixth position in the league, a fantastic achievement and one that is all the more notable when you weigh up what has happened to them since. Clearly, this would be a difficult game but it still didn't appear to be one that we couldn't get a result out of.

Manchester City seemed the easier game and also the more important one. They were far nearer to us in the league, only two points clear on Christmas morning, and were struggling for goals almost as much as we were, having only notched 15 in their 19 games. Much like I said earlier regarding the three games in a week with Everton, Wigan and Bolton, a haul of four points didn't look out of reach, and it was crucial that this was achieved to help us keep pace with our relegation rivals.

For the visit of Pompey (I didn't travel down with the away support as I was in London already for Christmas), we made two changes to the team. There was good news as Gabbidon was fit again and replaced Dailly, and Bowyer was dropped from the team and not even named on the bench as Benayoun came in for his first start under the new boss.

Now one of the big positives so far under Curbishley and one of the reasons that the fans had an increased level of optimism for these two home games was the better defensive capability the side was showing. Two clean sheets, including the first one away from home all season, had led us to feel confident that even if we were continuing not to score too often or weren't looking much of a threat going forward, we would at the very least stay in games by being solid at the back.

Fair to say, that optimism died in this match. In the first half of the game against Portsmouth, we were a complete and utter shambles.

Every corner, every free kick that got put into our box caused blind panic. It was like the team had never met before or been given instructions on how to mark a different set of players. Sixteen minutes in and their centre-half Linvoy Primus, who had gone two years to the day without a goal, pushed off a limp challenge from Harewood and nodded the away side into the lead.

Shortly after that, Sean Davis, a 5ft 11in central midfielder no less, managed to bury a header past Green only for it to be hacked off the line by Mullins, the rebound being somehow skied over the bar by Sol Campbell. Pedro Mendes whistled an effort wide from a set play we actually managed to scramble clear, and then from a free kick given due to a handball by Spector, Primus, who at this point had gone 22 minutes without a goal, brushed aside Mullins and doubled Pompey's tally.

The crowd's mood during this battering went from indifference to annoyance to full-on anger at the ineptness of the display. Every passing moment had the air of the old 'one step forward, two steps back' saying, as we witnessed a display every bit as bad as the defeat against Wigan, if not quite in the rarefied Bolton territory.

The fact it was Primus, to everybody outside Portsmouth a random footballer unlikely to create too many memories during or after his career, doing the damage only seemed to exacerbate the crowd. I can tell you via local knowledge, however, that inside Portsmouth

Primus is quite a celebrity. I and many other people know him as the unofficial 'Mayor of Portsmouth', as if you are opening a shop, a school or an envelope he will be there, smiling and with scissors to cut a ribbon if necessary. I didn't know until I researched him for this book that he was born and brought up in east London as well, which wins him the coveted 'Daniel's favourite player to score against West Ham' award for this season. He would at least definitely turn up to collect said award.

We made a double change at half-time, which is always an indicator of how well things are going, with Sheringham replacing Harewood and Tevez making his first appearance under Curbishley, coming on for Etherington and playing on the left wing. We improved marginally in the second half. Sheringham scored with nine minutes to go with a tidy finish from an acute angle to get us back in the game, but in truth Redknapp's side always kept us at arm's length and duly held on for a 2-1 victory that they fully deserved.

The Boxing Day results were not kind to the Hammers either, with three of the five teams above us that could be considered in trouble at this point all recording positive results: Middlesbrough got a creditable 0-0 draw at Everton, Blackburn beat Liverpool 1-0 in the sort of result that only ever seems to happen when it's your team in the bottom three, and Manchester City warmed up for their trip to the Boleyn with a 1-0 win in a big game at Sheffield United. This took them five points clear of the relegation zone and meant that a win against them four days after the Pompey debacle was essential to keep them as a side we could realistically look at catching. Our gap from safety had extended from one point to two, with Sheffield United now the side nearest to us.

In his press conference after the game, Curbishley conceded that the first half had been poor, but then showed uncharacteristic Pardew-like optimism/denial about the overall 90 minutes of the game. 'I was really disappointed with the first half and there is a lot to work on. The attitude and steel we showed against Manchester United and Fulham was not there. We let in two soft goals, particularly the second one. I'm not taking anything away from Portsmouth but I can't really remember anything else [bar the goals]. When you're getting beat 2-0 or 2-1 at home and you've been opened up three or four times, or [there's been] goalmouth scrambles etc etc, but there was none of that.'

Maybe the odour of Pards' aftershave was still knocking around in the manager's office and clouding his brain as there were at least two 'goalmouth scrambles' from set plays that weren't conceded. Also, a manager of the experience of Curbishley should know that when you look like scoring from every set play you win, you do not really need to do a lot more than win set plays. The win took Portsmouth up to fifth, above Liverpool crazily, and they would finish the season comfortably in ninth.

Tuesday, 26 December 2006:
West Ham 1 *Sheringham (81)*
Portsmouth 2 *Primus (16, 38)*

Our final game of 2006 came four days later, when former Hammers player and future assistant manager Stuart Pearce brought Manchester City to town. As I said earlier, the good people of the UAE hadn't yet come calling for the Citizens, so it was a very stripped-down City side in comparison to nowadays that visited east London.

Personally, looking back at City during these times as a perennial mid to lower table Premier League side feels so odd now. I can only imagine how it must be for their fans who are around my age or older. My eight-year-old son Adam still thinks I'm joking when I tell him I have seen City relegated from the Premier League twice in my lifetime, let alone that they even went down to the third tier. To this day, my 15-year-old son Jack's favourite ever game that he has attended is a 0-0 draw with City in November 2012 after we had been promoted back to the Premier League.

Even though he saw us beat City the following season, the draw the year before is still his favourite, as at seven years old he couldn't believe he was seeing Aguero, Balotelli, Tevez (yep him again) etc in the flesh. The fact that we got a result from the game still blows his mind even today. If you are reading this and do not have kids, trust me when I tell you that whatever we think of the modern-day incarnation of City, to English football fans under 16 they are the Manchester United of my era, or the Liverpool of the era before. Which, as I say, makes this version even stranger to look back at.

They weren't even at full strength for this visit, with key players Joey Barton, Dietmar Hamann and ex-Hammer of the Year runner-up Trevor Sinclair all missing due to injury. To use a popular phrase, City were down to the 'bare bones', so this was without a doubt an opportunity for us to be on the front foot in a game and take advantage. We'd had opportunities like that during this season, though, and not made the most of it (Everton, for example). This needed to change and quickly.

Our team showed three changes from the Portsmouth game, all enforced as Konchesky and Reo-Coker were serving one-match bans and Zamora was injured, so Dailly came in with Spector moving from right-back to left-back (George McCartney was injured as well), and Bowyer and Sheringham returned to central midfield and up front respectively.

Tevez was again on the bench, left out for a player legitimately old enough to be his father. You may also notice that neither Pantsil nor Mears, our other two right-back acquisitions, were considered to, erm, play right-back. Mears was on his way out of the club – he had reportedly been touted to Championship clubs on either a loan or permanent deal – and quite honestly I have not been able to find any record of where Pantsil was at this point. We'll be kind and assume injured. So Christian Dailly, a 33-year-old centre-back who had been with the club for seven years at this point, was now playing right-back for us. Suffice to say, we would be looking for someone with experience of playing in that position, as well as ability, in January. We should have done that in July.

In any season when your team is struggling against relegation, as well as the spectacularly bad defeats, there are the bad defeats in even worse games, and these in my opinion are the ones that end up sending a team down. The scrappy losses against teams no better or even worse than you, that in a season that goes well you nick 1-0 or get a draw in, you narrowly lose due to a defensive error or one bit of uncharacteristic brilliance.

These are the matches for teams outside the top six that can define a season one way or the other. Win most of these and you can find yourself seventh or eighth, and your manager is fielding questions on how did it all go right? (Burnley are probably the best modern-day proponents of this.) Lose most of these and you can find yourself 17th or 18th, and your manager is fielding questions on how did it all go wrong? This game was the latter for West Ham.

City were terrible. There for the taking, barely able to string three passes together. Luckily for them, we were every bit as bad. The game was played in driving rain, because why wouldn't it be? All games of this 'quality' should be in conditions befitting the standard. Sheringham had a shot deflected wide, Green made a decent stop from Vassell and, erm, that's about it.

But at least a dreary 0-0 draw would be *something* to build on. We had brought Tevez on to try and create some magic with half an hour to go. Playing on the wing again, just because. City reacted by bringing on winger DaMarcus Beasley, an American on loan from PSV, to try and do similar. And lo and behold, one of the players provided said magic, scoring his long-awaited first goal for his new club by cutting in from the wing and dancing through with a jinking run, beating a couple of defenders and slotting past the keeper to win the match and leave his fans delighted.

Beasley would only score two more goals in his loan spell at City and was playing for Glasgow Rangers the year after.

The 1-0 loss was an absolute hammer blow to the club. It was the same old story as so many of the defeats that season; 18 shots, six corners, but no goals and no real threat of a goal. Reasonable approach play and a shot from distance or a poor attempt on goal, but never any conviction or genuine threat to score.

The only player who looked like scoring at this point was Tevez and he had been consigned to the bench or the wing, something that was mystifying fans who could see the threat he was offering and improvement from the first couple of months. All that was stopping him was bad luck, which couldn't be said of the other forwards.

Curbishley referenced the supporter discourse in his interview after the game. 'The fans? Well, they're calling for Tevez but he's not scored a goal. I don't know how many games he's started but he hasn't scored. Harewood hasn't scored, Zamora hasn't scored. Teddy Sheringham has a couple. I can understand their frustration and they're calling for certain players, but I've been here for two weeks. You have to assess what you've got. I can understand them calling for someone because they've seen no goals.'

So, if I am correct, because Tevez hadn't scored we wouldn't pick him, we would pick the other people who hadn't scored instead. Right. It was becoming clearer for all to see that Curbishley wasn't aware of what he had got himself into.

If he didn't know that yet, it would become abundantly clear to him 48 hours later.

Saturday, 30 December 2006:
West Ham 0
Man City 1 *Beasley (83)*

CHAPTER EIGHT

January

THE SECOND home loss in a week meant the table was starting to make for deeply concerning reading. Blackburn capitalised fully on our defeat to City by beating Middlesbrough 2-1, moving seven points clear of us and in all likelihood away from trouble. What was even more galling was Arsenal managing to lose 1-0 to Sheffield United, who played the last 28 minutes with centre-back Phil Jagielka in goal. Arsenal had stuffed us a few times in the past when we had been struggling (2-0 up against Bolton only to draw 2-2 and losing 3-2 at home to Leeds in the 2002/03 relegation season), but this was taking the biscuit. They barely even looked like scoring against Jagielka, for God's sake. Sheffield United moved five points clear of us with the unlikely win, and now only Middlesbrough were within three points of us.

Charlton had also had the new manager bounce that we were hoping for but hadn't got, as one Alan Pardew had got them moving with four points in two games, a 2-1 win over Villa following on from a 2-2 draw against Fulham. They were only two points behind us now and seemed to have momentum, while we had nothing of the sort.

BOTTOM 7: (30/12/2006)

	P	Pts	GD
Blackburn	20	25	-8
Sheffield United	21	23	-10
Wigan	20	22	-6
Middlesbrough	21	21	-8
WEST HAM	*21*	*18*	*-15*
Charlton	*21*	*16*	*-19*
Watford	*19*	*11*	*-14*

We still had 17 games left to turn this round, but we were running out of chances and fast. The three games in a week at the start of December where we needed at least four points had yielded zero. The two home games straight after Christmas; four points needed, again zero acquired. This couldn't carry on much longer.

We'd had chances against teams who were stricken by injuries, such as Everton, Manchester City and Middlesbrough, and lost them all. We had also played teams who were woefully out of form such as Wigan and Portsmouth, and again we hadn't made the most of the chance. We had played them back into form rather than capitalised. This had to stop, and we had an opportunity to do just that on New Year's Day 2007, when we made the short trip from London to Berkshire to play Steve Coppell's Reading.

They had beaten us somewhat fortuitously back in October at Upton Park in what could have been described as a 'bad day to play them', a phrase often used by fans. Back then, they were bang in form and full of confidence, but when it came time for the reverse fixture, they were anything but. They had gone from sixth in the Premier League in early December with 25 points from 15 games to ninth at the end of the month, having only taken a further two points from the preceding six matches.

This included their last two home games, disappointing defeats against Blackburn (2-1) and Everton (2-0), sides that could be perceived as at a relatively similar level to ourselves, so there was understandable hope that we could continue that run and keep Reading's slump going. Indeed, a victory at the Madejski would take us to within just six points of the Royals, and possibly get them to start looking over their shoulder. This was still their first season back in the big time, so who was to know that panic wouldn't set in?

We made three changes to the starting 11 beaten by City two days prior; Sheringham and Etherington dropped out and weren't involved in the squad at all, and Reo-Coker, Zamora and Konchesky all returned, with the latter replacing Spector rather than Dailly, who bewilderingly remained in the side at right-back. I assume this may have been to deal with set plays on the day, what with Dailly being a centre-half by trade.

Also returning to the bench for the first time all season was Shaun Newton, a winger signed in the promotion season and a bit-part player in the season prior, who had served a seven-month ban for failing a drug test.

Let's recap the full team for this game, just to make sure we know the guilty parties:

Starting XI: *Green, Dailly, Ferdinand, Gabbidon, Konchesky, Bowyer, Reo-Coker, Mullins, Benayoun, Harewood, Zamora*

Subs: *Carroll, Spector, Newton, Cole, Tevez*

I'll be honest, when I decided to write this book, the afternoon of Monday, 1 January 2007 was second on the list of games I was dreading writing about (you can probably guess what made number one on that list), but here we are.

We actually started the game well, Bowyer and Reo-Coker having good chances within the first ten minutes, and that right there is all the positive I have to write about this game.

As I mentioned, we had retained Dailly at right-back over the far more athletic Spector, I presume to deal better with set plays, what with Portsmouth causing us so many problems with them a few days prior. So, when Reading won their first dangerous-looking free kick about 35 yards from goal around the 10-minute mark, we had picked a team to deal with these situations, particularly when you add the height the two forwards provided.

Nicky Shorey clipped the ball into the area, a perfectly straightforward ball to deal with, and midfielder Brynjar Gunnarson rose, unchallenged, to score his first-ever

Premier League goal. He was Icelandic as well, just like our owners! Oh how we laughed. We managed to drag ourselves back into shape for the kick-off and restarted the match. And then, quite frankly, most of the players may as well have walked off, for the amount of heart, desire and professional pride they showed.

Three minutes later, Steve Sidwell got in behind us on the left-hand side, completely untracked by Reo-Coker, and crossed for Stephen Hunt, who headed in unchallenged to also score his first-ever Premier League goal. What gracious and accommodating visitors we were.

Hunt somehow had nobody within five yards of him when slotting home. It was like we had been done on the counter-attack when in reality we hadn't been out of our half for nearly a minute. Dailly was stood next to the centre-backs, which would have been fine had he not been picked in the team as a right-back.

Shortly after the second goal, Lee Bowyer dislocated his shoulder and was substituted for Shaun Newton, who I presume spent most of the match as near to the big white lines on the side of the pitch as he could to try and cheer himself up.

On the half-hour mark, Reading won a free kick on their right-hand side when Leroy Lita 'Cruyff-turned' Gabbidon, who hauled him down. The set play was whipped in by Shorey, again, but this time one of our defenders managed to get his head to the ball, so ha, the joke was on Reading. Sure, Anton Ferdinand headed the ball in blind panic past Green to make it 3-0, but there was progress at least; we won a header from a free kick. Take the positives where you can, I guess.

Four minutes later Shorey, bored of just assisting goals from free kicks, decided to get the ball, dance through our pathetic excuse for a central midfield, dribble past whoever the bloke was impersonating Paul Konchesky (it can't have been the tough-tackling, hungry player from the year before) and pass to James Harper, a midfielder actually making a purposeful run, which must have baffled his claret and blue counterparts. Harper squared the ball to Kevin Doyle, who unchallenged (have you noticed the theme?) tapped the ball past Green.

4-0 at half-time, then.

As a supporter, you often hope in this situation that the break would at least see the manager tear into the players for the shambles of a display they had just produced. You maybe hope of stories emerging of arguments in the dressing room and this resulting in a bit more fire and maybe a goal or two to get back some respectability. Hell, maybe even a red card or two would be acceptable to the fans sometimes after a half when they've just seen such a complete lack of passion and desire. Curbishley responded by taking Harewood off and bringing Spector on to go five at the back so, as he admitted after the game, 'it wouldn't end up 8-0'. Move over Winston Churchill.

Leroy Lita made it 5-0 in short order, and with 12 minutes to go a Shorey corner was headed in, unchallenged, *again*, by Doyle for his second goal and Reading's sixth. That was thankfully where they declared. I'm pretty sure now in a book about West Ham

I have described more goals assisted by Nicky Shorey than any other player, which shows how well things had gone through this disaster of a season.

My poor dad went to this game. He was gutted when I spoke to him later that night, crestfallen even, but undeterred, a couple of days later he bought tickets to Charlton away. The optimistic idiot.

I turned my phone off for a day or so to ignore the various Reading fans I knew. Not sure why I bothered, as the game gets brought up every now and then to this very day. In their defence, it's the biggest top division win in their history.

Monday, 1 January 2007:

Reading 6 *Gunnarsson (12), Hunt (15), Ferdinand og (30), Doyle (36, 78), Lita (53)*

West Ham 0

Curbishley savaged the players to any and all media after the game, justifiably so. 'I don't want to hear how good they were last year. It's nonsense. Last year is last year. It's a different season. Everyone keeps telling me about last year, and I don't want to hear it any more. If Reading finish ninth this year, they won't go on an open-top bus ride. To keep going back to last year is nonsense. We're in this year now.'

The 'open-top bus ride' comment was in relation to the players doing just that after the previous season, which while a cute line was in relation to the FA Cup Final appearance rather than finishing ninth. But I think he can be excused for getting a couple of digs in after a result and performance the like of which he had just witnessed.

The next criticism, though, was one that would turn the focus of the English football media on to West Ham's players, as well as coining a phrase that is still used today to describe players perceived to be underperforming and overpaid. 'That has been coming, the players have shown me why they're down there. Today, Reading had everything we didn't: enthusiasm, pace, shape, aggression and, above all, hunger. They want to be in the Premiership, they want to drive a Baby Bentley.'

And with that, the 'Baby Bentley' generation of footballers was born.

The players were roasted in the media over the following days, with the running theme being that this group had done nothing significant in football but had been given all the rewards as if they had. Papers ran lists of the players and the cars they owned, while pointing out that it looked like those cars would be visiting Coventry and Colchester next season. It seemed like every columnist in every paper and website had their two cents to add, and sympathy for the 'guilty' parties was hard to find.

Reo-Coker and Anton Ferdinand were at the forefront of the accusations, and both defended themselves publicly, the captain in particular when speaking to Sky Sports. 'I've heard the criticism so many times about players not being hungry because of the financial rewards we get, but I don't know where the information comes from. I have no fat contract. I'm still on the same deal that I was when we were promoted. Other players have had improvements and if I wanted to be a problem I could have gone in and demanded this and that all the time. I haven't done that.' In interviews years later, both players would still reference how much the comment bothered and upset them.

Curbishley had without doubt rolled the dice here with such public criticism. Whether there were issues in the dressing room, overconfidence, lack of motivation etc, to air those issues in a public forum and not in house smacked to me of him not realising what he was taking over when he took the job initially.

At this point, he had been in charge for 20 days and five games. I don't know what the record would be for a manager publicly steamrollering players but this must have been close. In my opinion, Curbs saw a talented squad and assumed that for them a change would be as good as a rest. He misjudged the amount of confidence that had been eroded over the season and perhaps the loyalty that a lot of the group still had to Pardew.

I believe this was coupled with the manager for the first time not being the biggest fish in a small pond. With all due respect, West Ham are a different animal to Charlton, then, now and previously, and the increased scrutiny over bad displays must have been a shock to him; in his previous role, any defeat or bad run could be partially excused by 'it's only Charlton, they're overachieving'. Not so here.

Also Curbishley had deservedly built up tolerance for any bad result or one-off hammering over his 15-year reign at the Valley, but he was starting afresh here and hadn't created any goodwill to live off. I think the comment was possibly born out of some frustration or panic at any or all of these factors. He had never taken over a Premier League club and therefore a Premier League dressing room before; he had created them. These players had no loyalty or gratitude to him in the way many of his players at Charlton would have for giving them their big chance. The group he inherited at West Ham were already at the top level, Baby Bentley in tow, with or without him. Maybe this frustration caused the comment to come out, so quickly and so publicly.

It could also be argued that if all the rumours were true, that the players had all become unmotivated and disinterested, as manager his job was to turn that around, rather than publicly flog them. Was the comment a motivational tactic? Maybe, but if it was, Curbishley had never said anything remotely close to it before in his managerial career, nor would he ever do so again.

One way or another, the comment was going to stick and/or linger for all involved, for the rest of the season and beyond. Whether it was to be remembered as the moment the tide turned, or the moment the club imploded in upon itself, remained to be seen.

The one positive that came from the day of 1 January 2007 was that it was the first day of the January transfer window, and it was clear as day that this window was going to be a busy one, what with that heady cocktail of new owner money, a new manager and an existing team that can't win a raffle, let alone a game of football.

To that end, it should be mentioned that among all the falling debris following the Reading defeat was that Middlesbrough beat Sheffield United 3-1 on the same day, which had caused the gap to safety to increase to four points behind Wigan, who were now in 17th. Jewell's side also had a game in hand on us; any result gained in that game would stretch the margin further to at least five points.

It became clear early on regarding potential transfers that the beleaguered boss was looking to experience to help us get out of the situation. The first two names strongly linked were both wide players, Chelsea winger Shaun Wright-Phillips and Fulham left-sided midfielder Luis Boa Morte. Reports emerged of a £10m bid for SWP, while their west London rivals were offered in the region of £5.5m for LBM. Chris Coleman's side were a lot more agreeable than their blue counterparts, and within 48 hours of the interest being reported, Boa Morte was a West Ham player.

Aged 29 at the time, 'Boa' was a Portuguese international who'd had a pretty successful career in England. Signed by Arsenal from Sporting Lisbon in 1997, he had been a bit-part player in what was, in fairness, a supremely strong Arsenal side. A disappointing spell at Southampton followed but it was with Fulham that he had found his best form. He played a major role in them winning promotion in 2001 with 18 league goals, and in the Premier League he'd had over five years in which he had successfully established himself as a key man in their ranks; indeed, at the time of joining us he had been club captain for over two years. In all competitions, he made 249 appearances and scored 56 goals for the Whites, and all in all looked a very sensible signing. He'd also at this point represented his national team on 25 occasions. In theory, this was an established Premier League player joining us for what traditionally would be classed as his prime years. Hopes were high that he could come in and establish himself quickly as a leader on the pitch, as well as chipping in with some badly needed goals and assists.

The Portugeezer was delighted with the move despite the troubles we had been in on the pitch, which he enthused on the club website. 'I'm delighted to have signed for West Ham United. Alan Curbishley has given me the opportunity to join what I consider to be one of the biggest clubs in the country, and I am really happy to be here. Yes, I considered the fact that West Ham United are currently in the bottom three of the Premiership but even with that, I quickly decided that the opportunity was too good to turn down.'

Curbs was equally happy along with making it clear that we were far from done with our month's work. 'I'm very pleased that we have been able to get the deal done so quickly,' he said. 'Luis is versatile and experienced, which is something I think we need and have been endeavouring to bring in. We are currently juggling a lot of balls in terms of the players we have targeted in this transfer window, and they haven't all come down yet, but this is a good start and I am sure Luis will make a big impact for us.'

Boa Morte wouldn't have to wait long for his first-team debut as he was put straight into the side for an FA Cup third-round tie at home to Brighton, who at the time were a mid-table League One outfit, and presented a chance to help restore some confidence. Or help assist with the slide into the abyss. One or the other.

He was one of six changes from the Reading debacle. I won't list them all, but the notable ones included Boa's debut, Tevez making his first start since Pardew left and a first appearance of the season for young Mark Noble. 'Nobes' had come back from a productive loan spell with Ipswich in the first half of the season, and now seemed set to make the break into the first team full time, having had a role in the promotion season two years' prior and a couple of starts in the previous campaign. Indeed, this start would be his 28th appearance in claret and blue, so he was no first-team novice, and at 19 years old, now seemed the time for him to move up the ranks.

The day was a largely positive one for Hammers fans, a rarity during this season. The first half was admittedly a lot closer than it should have been given the disparity between the sides (41 league places at the time the game kicked off), but in the second half the Premier League experience shone through and we won comfortably by three goals to nil, with a late strike from Mullins adding to Carlton Cole's first goal since the opening day, and a first-ever goal in claret and blue for Noble, a low drive in the 49th minute delighting the crowd who saw possibly a shining light in the gloom that the winter of 2006/07 had provided.

Here seemed something we could possibly build on, a young player, West Ham through and through (I think he was anyway, it's not like anybody has ever mentioned that since) and maybe something a little different to what we'd had so far that season, some passion allied with skill that could get the crowd right behind him, and by proxy the rest of the team as well. You could even argue that his entrance into the first team set-up was like a new signing, meaning there was no real need to sign any central midfielders during the window.

Tevez was also excellent, setting up Noble's goal and generally looking the class above that we all knew he was. The elusive goal would surely come soon.

The only person who didn't seem happy after the game was the manager, who used his post-match press conference as an opportunity to rail against the press for their criticism of Reo-Coker in particular, criticism that he had, y'know, partly caused. 'I've been here four weeks and I've been outraged at the criticism that Nigel Reo-Coker has received since I've been here, as if it's his fault that we're in the bottom three. That's total nonsense and I'd like everyone connected with West Ham to leave him alone. He's a young boy and it's not his fault. It's easy to pick on people and he's been picked on.'

I'll assume the captain had replaced his car with a Ford Escort that week or something. We were drawn at home to the Premier League's bottom club Watford in round four, and with the Hornets having beaten only one top division side in 20 attempts so far that season, a possible cup run looked on the cards.

Saturday, 6 January 2007:

West Ham 3 *Noble (49), Cole (58), Mullins (90)*
Brighton 0

We continued to press ahead in the search for new recruits in the week that followed the Brighton victory. Rumours of us signing Tal Ben-Haim from Bolton and Freddie Ljungberg from Arsenal were rebuffed by Eggert (I assume not forgotten, though, as they both ended up here in the end) and there were widespread reports that Wright-Phillips had decided to remain with Chelsea, a decision that quite honestly looked as sensible then as it does now.

A second signing was made that week, however, as central midfielder Nigel Quashie joined from West Bromwich Albion. Two days after Noble's performance against Brighton, he had been pushed a notch further down the list.

But what of the player who had done the pushing? He signed from West Brom, who had been relegated from the Premier League the previous season, having joined them from Southampton who had, erm, been relegated from the Premier League the season before that. How very encouraging.

Curbs, however, saw sense in the signing, even if nobody else did, as he explained in full on the club website. 'We've signed Nigel because he is an experienced player who will add competition to our central midfield positions. He comes in knowing full well the position we are in, and he is confident and convinced that we will be able to get out of the bottom three. I have not promised him anything in terms of first-team football – he will have to earn it like the rest of the players – but he brings vast experience to the club and has shown me that he is eager and hungry to do everything he can to help us.'

Quashie could best be described as a 'journeyman' midfielder. As well as the two clubs mentioned above that he had been relegated with, he had also played for QPR, Nottingham Forest and Portsmouth.

His spell on the blue side of the south coast endeared him to me somewhat more than most West Ham fans, due to a night out in my second year of university in the hallowed halls of Tiger Tiger. I was out with my usual group of mates but at a point during the night found myself stood next to the then-Pompey midfielder at the bar. We had a brief chat while waiting to be served and ended up speaking for half an hour or so. He was very down to earth and seemed like a really nice bloke, out with team-mate Lomana LuaLua, who in truth wasn't as chatty. My good mate 'Nige' further endeared himself to me by the end of the night when he encouraged a young lady who I had been speaking to through the night to leave with me. What a guy.

West Ham fans who he hadn't helped get laid weren't quite as enthusiastic, though. In truth, it seemed like the definition of a mediocre, needless and uninspired signing. We were in desperate trouble at this point, so quite who thought the solution was bringing in a 30-year-old midfielder who was in and out of a team in the league below, and whose only Premier League experience in the previous two years had been to be relegated from it, probably needs their head tested.

To make this signing as well when Noble had made such a successful appearance just two days prior was utterly bizarre. It just looked like a signing that wouldn't work, would add next to nothing and would end up leading to us paying him for at least a year to do very little in terms of appearances. And that is exactly how it turned out.

Further players linked that week included right-backs Lauren, Luke Young and Lucas Neill, who sadly for us looked Liverpool-bound, but there were no further additions to the playing staff before Fulham came across London not only to glare angrily at Boa Morte, but also to play us in a game of football.

Their manager Chris Coleman had recognised the trouble we were in and decided to use his pre-match press conference to let the football world know – as if nobody else was aware. 'Everyone is waiting for West Ham to get out of it; they're a big club with good players. But it does not always happen. Regardless of what Alan has to spend in the [transfer] window, he knows he has a big job on his hands. He will have to call on all his experience to get them out of trouble. There are 16 games to go and I think they need to win eight of those to give themselves a chance – and that is not easy.'

Thanks for that, Chris. I hope you didn't say all this because you were bitter and twisted about your captain leaving you to join us. Oh what's that, you're not done? 'I am not being bitter and twisted, but I don't think we will be weakened by [Boa Morte's] departure. If you have someone at a club who doesn't want to be there, it will show in their performances.' How wonderfully catty of you, Chris. Let's hope you never end up being sacked in a documentary available on a streaming service for all to see.

The line-up for the meeting with the Whites showed seven changes from the Reading game 12 days prior, which had been our most recent league fixture. The squad is listed in full below:

Starting XI: *Carroll, Dailly, Collins, Gabbidon, McCartney, Benayoun, Reo-Coker, Quashie, Boa Morte, Cole, Tevez*

Subs: *Green, Spector, Mullins, Newton, Zamora*

So, being as brief as I can here, Cole and Tevez retained their places following good outings in the Brighton game, as did Roy Carroll, which was a fair bit more perplexing. I know Green had conceded six at Reading but I don't think anybody was singling him out for specific blame. Anybody with eyes could see that he was the superior keeper of the two and it really felt like making a change for change's sake, which we had done enough of already during this season.

Ferdinand and Bowyer were injured so dropped out, Konchesky and Harewood were ditched and didn't even make the bench, and the two new signings were straight into the team, meaning that Hayden Mullins, having seen off the challenge of Liverpool-bound Javier Mascherano, was then back on the bench because we had signed Nigel

Quashie. Oh, and Christian Dailly was still at right-back. Of course he was.

I mentioned earlier that there are certain types of games a team on course for relegation or a relegation struggle typically go through during a season. We had knocked out two of these types in our two previous league games; the scrappy game that you shouldn't lose but do, and the absolute shellacking. Well, this game saw another type of game: the one where you play well, do a lot of good things but *everything* goes wrong.

We started positively, passing the ball around well. The two new players looked understandably keen and motivated to get on the ball and make a difference, and Cole and Tevez were linking up well and, dare I say it, showing signs of a partnership. That was the first ten minutes. Six minutes later, we were 1-0 down and two players had gone off injured.

Collins was first to go off, pulling up with an injury, and wouldn't be seen again for some time. He was replaced by Spector, with Dailly shifting to centre-back. Then, two minutes later, Tevez was injured too. He was replaced by Zamora, meaning the promising strike partnership would play 13 minutes together up front and barely see each other again.

Shockingly enough, Fulham's goal shortly after came from a corner, Helguson's header hitting Tomas Radzinski and diverting in past Carroll. That was now six goals conceded in three-and-a-bit games from set plays, this from a manager who had previously been lauded for his organisational skills.

Typically, this would be the point where I have to write something along the lines of 'we threatened to score a couple of times but didn't and lost', and in this scenario there would be some mitigating circumstances in fairness. To lose two players in key positions that early in a game would be difficult for any team. But on this occasion, that wasn't the case. On 28 minutes, a long ball was flicked on by Carlton Cole and Bobby Zamora picked the ball up, drove into the area and slotted past Lastuvka. An equaliser! In the first half no less! What is this sorcery? It was Bobby's first goal for 19 games and three months. We got into the break level and with no further injuries, and a massive second half lay ahead.

A positive start and an early goal would have been just what the doctor ordered, but then we could have said that about almost all the other games that season and it hadn't happened in any of those, so why would it today? Well, maybe it would happen because the Yossi Benayoun of 2005/06 decided to turn up and turn up in style. Within 30 seconds of the resumption no less, the Israeli took a pass from Zamora, looked up and with his left foot from outside the area, sumptuously chipped Lastuvka in the Fulham goal.

It was a mirror image of a wonderful goal Yossi had scored against the same opposition the previous year, at the same end of Upton Park, but with his right foot instead. The crowd, some of whom were still returning to their seats (I was just about to sit back down when Yossi got the ball) roared with joy, but also some belief; if Yossi was back to top form, we had a real-life creative outlet again, for the first time in a long time.

Fulham obviously equalised 13 minutes later because times of hope during runs like this can never last for long. The American international striker Brian McBride was the lucky recipient of our 'no marking strikers from crosses' policy on this occasion, nodding past the helpless Carroll. The most frustrating thing about the goal was that we were legitimately playing well, we had been passing the ball with more of a zip than we had for a long time and hadn't even gone into our shells after taking the lead, as you might expect.

Pleasingly, we kept this up after the equaliser, and only five minutes after being pegged back, we went and scored for the *third* time in one match. That's right, in 36 minutes we had scored the same amount of goals that we had scored in the previous 11 games put together. Benayoun it was again, profiting from some indecision in the Fulham backline. He nicked the ball, ran through, rounded the keeper and as defenders were getting back on the line, he somehow threaded the ball between them to put us 3-2 in front.

Boa Morte missed a great chance to silence the boos of his former fans (and manager, probably) not long after. Not to worry, though, I was sure the goals would start flying in from the £5.5m man soon enough. We held the lead relatively comfortably until the last quarter of an hour, when the wheels came off in almost comedic fashion.

First, Zamora, adrenaline pumping after winning a 50/50 challenge moments earlier, slid into a challenge with Bocanegra. It was a full-blooded tackle, may have got the ball but quite possibly didn't, and referee Graham Poll showed the forward his second yellow card in ten minutes and sent him off. Just our luck that he was counting the cards correctly that day.

Shortly after that Gabbidon went off injured, to be replaced by Shaun Newton. So, we had now lost both centre-halves and our best forward to injury, in addition to another forward having his first good game for three months being sent off. We would have to hang on for the last ten minutes with a man less, a winger at right-back and Spector and Dailly in the centre of defence. (If you're keeping count, Newton became the sixth different right-back used in the season so far.)

It was now one-way traffic, with the Whites pouring forward and our rag-tag line-up hanging on for dear life. Boa Morte went down injured soon after but stayed on, so we were practically at nine-and-a-half men now.

We made it to injury time somehow, five minutes to be played. Fulham won a corner. Christ, we may as well have lined up for the kick-off to save time. The corner was played in, met by Queudrue and Fulham equ… hang on, Yossi cleared it off the line! We were going to do it, weren't we! This is the turning point! Yossi and his band of men are going to lead us to salvation, in the biggest miracle ever pulled off involving anything to do with Israel!

Just get the ball away now, for Christ's sake … and we almost did. We smuggled it to our left-back area, Fulham blocked a couple of clearances and worked the ball back to the edge of our box, Dailly lost a header, Reo-Coker I want to say lost a header but the truth is barely challenged for it, and the ball fell to their centre-half Christanval, who lashed it into the ****ing net. There were about 45 seconds of injury time left.

The noise in the ground as the ball went in was a mix of guttural shouting, swearing and that sound only football fans know of seats being kicked or smashed back into their upright position. We had played well, really genuinely well, for the first time in months. And still we couldn't get over the line. However well we played, we just couldn't win a goddamn game. It was hard to see us coming back for a while from the heartbreak of this one. Five games now without a win, and only one point gained from home games against Portsmouth, Manchester City and Fulham. And if you don't get points from those games, you know what happens.

The misery was compounded by everyone around us losing bar Middlesbrough, who won 3-1 at Pardew's Charlton. This was a real chance to get ourselves right back in the mix and we had blown it at the death. The gap closed only slightly to three points to 17th-placed Wigan, who still had a game in hand. Of the injured players Tevez wouldn't be seen for a month, Collins for two months, and Gabbidon wouldn't play again that season.

Saturday, 13 January 2007:
West Ham 3 *Zamora (28), Benayoun (46, 64)*
Fulham 3 *Radzinski (16), McBride (59),*
Christanval (90)

JANUARY

BOTTOM 6: (13/01/2007)

	P	Pts	GD
Aston Villa	23	26	-4
Sheffield United	23	24	-12
Wigan	22	22	-13
WEST HAM	*23*	*19*	*-21*
Charlton	*23*	*16*	*-25*
Watford	*21*	*12*	*-17*

The mounting injury list meant getting further quality through the door was even more imperative. The club pressed on with their search in the days following the Fulham game. A move for Arsenal right-back Lauren failed to materialise, and then-Watford winger Ashley Young fell at the first hurdle when he declined to even meet with us after a £10m bid had been accepted, and moved to Villa a few days later. Charlton striker Darren Bent was also linked for the second transfer window in a row (he would be linked for about the next seven after this one as well), but it was at the other end of the pitch that immediate reinforcements were needed after the injuries picked up that weekend. This saw a move for centre-back Calum Davenport materialise quickly. He was signed from Tottenham for £3m within 48 hours of the link initially being reported.

Davenport was a 24-year-old who had started his career at Coventry, making 75 appearances for the Sky Blues before moving to White Hart Lane in 2004. He only played 15 times for Spurs, however, while being farmed out on loan to a few clubs, one of which was ourselves during our first season in the Championship after the relegation season of 2002/03. He made ten appearances in that spell to mainly positive reviews, so the hope was that he could settle back in quickly, as obviously time to bed in wasn't a luxury we could afford right now, as Curbishley emphasised on the club site after the signing was announced. 'We are delighted to sign Calum. After Saturday, we faced another set of problems with injuries to Gabbidon and Collins, so it was important that we brought someone in. He is fully fit and has been playing regularly, so he is up to speed and will be able to hit the ground running with us.'

The right-back conundrum that had plagued us throughout the season (and every few pages in this book) finally looked to have been solved as well, as somehow we had persuaded Blackburn right-back Lucas Neill to reject Liverpool and ply his trade in the east side of the capital instead. People were perplexed at what Neill's reason would have been to turn down a side that had won the Champions League 18 months prior (and would be appearing in the final again at the end of the season), until it transpired there were about 50,000 reasons. Per week.

Neill, however, rejected this as his motive, stating in an interview with Australian TV prior to the signing being formally announced that his reasons were purely football based. 'It wasn't about cash – that didn't come into it. It was about being wanted. West Ham were knocking down the door to get me. People who have raised their eyebrows at me for making this decision are in for a surprise because West Ham have a shopping list of players which almost blew me away.' Who knew Neill was such a big Nigel Quashie fan?

Jokes aside, this was a fantastic coup for the club. Neill was a top-class and vastly experienced Premier League right-back, exactly the type of player we should have been looking to sign in the summer when we went for quantity instead.

Aged 29 at the time, Neill had started his English career with Millwall, making 152 appearances for them before joining Blackburn in 2001. He'd had a highly successful five-and-a-half-years with Rovers, playing 188 times, and was regarded as possibly the best full-back outside the 'big four' (was only four back then, not the 'big six' we have now), so to get a player of his quality and experience was a massive boost to our hopes of finally turning the ship around.

Neill didn't sign in time to be involved in our next fixture, which was a trip up north to St James' Park to play Newcastle. Eleventh at the time, the Geordies were coming into the game with ourselves on the back of two very impressive results in the league, a 3-2 win at Tottenham following up a 2-2 draw with Manchester United on New Year's Day. They had, however, just been pounded 5-1 by Championship side Birmingham in the FA Cup three days previously, so there was a possible lack of defensive confidence that we could look to exploit. As the goalless run away from home had now stretched to over four months, we would need all the hope we could get.

The only changes made to the team were injury enforced, with the centre-backs and Tevez being replaced by Davenport, a fit-again Ferdinand and Harewood. Dailly was still at right-back.

Eighteen minutes into the game, it happened – after 140 days, 906 minutes or 15 hours and six minutes of football. If you were one of the poor people who had been to every game, you had travelled circa 2,765 miles since you had last seen it. That is the equivalent of driving from London to Tehran. But it was all worth it. Because at 3.18pm on 20 January 2007, West Ham United finally scored an away goal.

A corner from Benayoun was headed across by the giant Davenport and volleyed in by Carlton Cole. It was all so simple, yet so wonderful. We had scored. And we were 1-0 up. This was momentous.

Four minutes later, we went and bloody did it again.

McCartney played the ball into Harewood, who was being marked by their centre-half Peter Ramage. Ramage had committed the cardinal sin of marking Harewood 'touch tight', as coaches say. When a defender did this to Marlon, it only ever resulted in one thing. Marlon would use his immense strength to roll past the defender and run clear of them. One such example would be the first goal in the fantastic 2-0 win at Ipswich in the play-off semi-final, when the 'roll' was done to their left-back Matt Richards and led to the Marvellous one squaring for a tap-in for Zamora. On this day, the roll put him clear on goal, and a toe-poked finish past Shay Given put us 2-0 in front. So, we were now scoring away goals every four minutes, then. This tactic was a big improvement in my opinion on the previous, non-scoring strategy.

The only fly in the ointment was that there were still 68 minutes of the match to go. The next 23 of those minutes went by with us largely untroubled, however. The two Nigels in centre midfield were playing well together and Newcastle didn't create much of note, other than a cross-shot from James Milner that went in but was correctly flagged offside as Scott Parker, who was past the last defender by at least two yards, jumped over the ball, and allowed it to go through his legs, obscuring Roy Carroll's view as the ball nestled in the far corner.

No drama there, then. Except the match referee Uriah Rennie having spoken to his linesman and for reasons best known to himself, decided to allow the goal …

We were quite rightly apoplectic at the goal being given. Ferdinand and Carroll were immediately booked for their protests, which to me always shows the ref knows he has made a mistake. If he knew he was right, he would explain the decision to the players rather than stand there in silence holding up a card.

Rather than being booed off by their fans for being 2-0 down to a team in the bottom three, the Newcastle players were roared off at the interval just to emphasise how pivotal the moment was. Eight minutes into the second half, Boa Morte slipped when trying to clear a free kick and clearly handled the ball. Solano dispatched the resulting penalty to equalise.

One positive, though, was that after the score went to 2-2, we didn't cave in as may have been expected. Roeder's side had chances, including Overfriendly Martins hitting the post, but we held on for a point, and nearly won it at the end as Marlon forced a good save, as well as Davenport having a headed goal ruled out for a somewhat questionable push. If only we'd had somebody standing two yards offside, it would have been given, I assume.

Saturday, 20 January 2007:
Newcastle 2 *Milner (45), Solano (53)*
West Ham 2 *Cole (18), Harewood (22)*

The draw took us a point closer to Wigan, who were beaten 2-0 by Everton the following day, but Aston Villa's win over Watford took them clear of any trouble, meaning that we were now nine points behind Fulham in 15th. The gap was widening and the number of clubs we could conceivably catch was shortening with every passing week. The only two clubs still below us were managing to pick up wins as well now. On the same day we drew on Tyneside, Charlton were at the opposite end of the country winning 1-0 at Portsmouth, and three days later Watford got their second victory of the season, beating Blackburn 2-1 to move to within five points of ourselves. Since Pardew had taken over at the Valley, he had taken seven points from five games, cutting the gap to us from six points to one in a matter of weeks, with a fixture against us coming up on the horizon as well.

BOTTOM 7: (13/01/2007)

	P	Pts	GD
Aston Villa	24	29	-2
Fulham	24	29	-10
Sheffield United	24	24	-14
Wigan	23	22	-15
WEST HAM	*24*	*20*	*-21*
Charlton	*24*	*19*	*-24*
Watford	*23*	*15*	*-18*

The Neill signing was officially announced on the Monday after the Newcastle game. In addition, a second signing that day was also announced as Spanish striker Kepa Blanco arrived on a six-month loan deal from Sevilla with a view to a permanent move. Blanco would end up a solid West Ham pub quiz answer as he became the first Spanish player to ever play for the club, and arrived having scored six goals in nine games for Los Palanganas. He had been kept out of their team mainly by former Hammers striker (and my friend) Freddie Kanoute, who was incredibly on his way to ending the La Liga season as the third-highest scorer, level with Ronaldinho and above Torres, Villa and Messi. So you can see why Kepa couldn't get a game.

With Tevez injured and it being accepted at this point that it was unlikely we would see Ashton again before the end of the season, a short-term move for a striker made sense. Kepa would be thrust into the squad immediately before then obviously not staying past the end of the season in the tradition of all strikers West Ham ever sign on loan in January (I won't list any of the other players as I wouldn't want to bring you out in a cold sweat).

Reports also continued of us making bids for Birmingham defender Matthew Upson. An initial £4.5m bid had been rebuffed and a £6m bid was then also reportedly rejected. It was assumed that we would try again prior to the window closing the following week, but Blues boss Steve Bruce had publicly stated that he didn't need to sell his captain and that it would take a 'top dollar' offer for him to consider changing his mind. Upson had been quiet throughout the saga and hadn't been in the media agitating for the move, so either he was a loyal professional or wasn't overly bothered about playing for us either way. I wasn't sure then and, in truth, I'm still not sure 14 years later.

The next encounter was a break from the league but not from Premier League opposition, as the bottom club Watford made the short trip for an FA Cup fourth-round tie, the first of two trips they would be making to east London in three weekends as the league game at the Boleyn was scheduled for a fortnight later.

Despite a league game at home to Liverpool being only 72 hours away, Curbishley resisted the urge to make wholesale changes; Ferdinand (again) and Benayoun were injured, Davenport cup tied and Harewood suspended, which meant Neill came in for his debut along with Spector, Newton and Zamora.

(As a side note, why to this day are rounds of Premier League games always scheduled in the midweek after early-round FA Cup games? So often knowing a league game is around the corner makes managers make more changes than they would otherwise, which leads to hundreds of 'the

Cup is dead/no magic etc' stories, when there are so many other midweeks during a season that they can be played? Feel free to add your own conspiracy theories.)

This was Watford's 24th game against top-flight opposition that season. They had won two of the previous 23, and none of the 11 games they had played away from Vicarage Road. As far as opportunities came for us to get a credible win against a Premier League outfit on the board, it didn't come much better than this, and that was emphasised by a Zamora header hitting the bar in the opening minute. A display anywhere near the level of the Fulham or Newcastle games would have been enough to get a victory and a place in the last 16 of a cup that we had been two minutes away from winning the season prior. But yet again, yet again, yet again, when there was a chance to take one step forward, we took two steps back.

We controlled the first half, with Quashie and Newton drawing good saves from Foster and Dailly having a header cleared off the line by young defender Jordan Stewart, but as had happened so often through this season, we couldn't convert good play into goals. And then as sure as day follows night, we were punished.

One change that Curbs may have been expected to make for this game was to rotate the goalkeepers, as is the norm in modern-day football and by and large was back then as well. But this was a change he didn't make, as he stuck with Roy Carroll over Green, I presume as a vote of confidence in his new number one. What the manager really didn't need then was for the Northern Irishman to decide to do a bad superman impression in the 42nd minute, running out to try and punch a high ball launched to the edge of the area. He almost came fourth in a three-person challenge so far from the action was he, which led to the ball dropping to young striker Anthony McNamee, who lifted it over his shoulder and into the net. It was the 22-year-old's third professional goal in five years, and the last he would ever score for Watford. It was the last goal he ever scored above League One level. West Ham doing classic West Ham things.

The most classic West Ham thing of all happened three minutes into the second half, however, when Lucas Neill, he of an exemplary fitness and injury record which had seen him play 157 of Blackburn's last 172 Premier League games, was stretchered off on his West Ham debut with an ankle injury.

Zamora missed a hat-trick of excellent chances in the second half, including a sitter in the last minute that was again headed off the line by Stewart, and Boa Morte blazed over when well placed. As I've already said, hopefully the goals would come soon for the £5.5m attacking midfielder. The 1-0 loss knocked us out of the cup and provided Watford with win number three of their season, and their first away from home.

Curbishley was in his normal pragmatic mood after the game. 'They tried their hardest – I've got no complaints about that. Perhaps second half we could have got ourselves back in it. Perhaps we deserved a draw but we haven't got it, so we move on.'

It's incredible that he never made a fortune in after-dinner speaking.

Saturday, 27 January 2007:
West Ham 0
Watford 1 *McNamee (42)*

The one positive of being out of the cup, as January ticked into February, was that we had no other distractions and our position was clear. The next four games were pivotal if we were going to remain a Premier League club. Funnily enough, my dad ran into Lee Bowyer in a supermarket around this time and he said the same, so clearly the players knew it as well.

A home game with Liverpool, which could be classed as a 'freebie' of sorts, was followed by three games against teams at the wrong end of the league, an away game to 14th-placed and out-of-form Aston Villa, and then matches against the two sides below us in the bottom three, a home game against Watford and a trip to the Valley to play Charlton.

We had amassed 20 points from 24 games and had 14 games left to nigh on double that tally. With that in mind, the next four games would need to account for a decent percentage of the 20 further points required. The other side of this run would see ten games remaining, including against seven of the top ten sides as the league stood at the end of January. That meant trips to the Emirates, Old Trafford and Ewood Park among others.

February had to be the month the tide turned. It ended up being as bad a month as it was possible for a football club to have.

CHAPTER NINE

The Next Five Games

THE SEARCH for new additions prior to the window 'slamming shut' (Sky Sports News) the day after the Liverpool game continued apace after the Watford defeat. Upson oddly decided that the day after being beaten at home by the bottom team in the Premier League was the day to announce his interest in moving back to London from Birmingham, stating his belief in the media that the Blues should accept the offer that had been presented to them. 'I think Birmingham have had a pretty good offer for me and have decided to decline it. I can't control those decisions, so I have to get on with it. Is £8m or £10m silly money? Yes, I think it is given that I've only got 17 months left on my contract and I've declined to sign a new one. But Birmingham are desperate to get back into the Premier League and it's their decision – although West Ham is an attractive proposition for me.'

We also continued with our not-very-subtle plan to try and rob Charlton of all their players, with bids for

Hermann Hrediarsson and Darren Bent (again) being turned down, so it seemed leading into deadline day that the potential Upson move would be the focus.

Before that would be the small matter of a match with a bang in form Liverpool side. Rafael Benitez's men were coming into the contest on the back of four straight league wins, including a 2-0 win against Mourinho's Chelsea in their most recent league match. They were also in the process of adding to their squad by signing a young, highly rated Argentinian international defensive midfielder. You can guess who that was. I assume we had told them Hayden Mullins wasn't for sale, so they went for the second-choice option. Mascherano would make 11 appearances after signing for Liverpool on an initial 18-month deal, and finished the campaign playing for the Reds in a Champions League final, so his season ended somewhat better than it began, it is fair to say.

Curbishley again made only minor changes to the side. Neill's injury was not as serious as first feared – he was projected to be back in a fortnight – so while he dropped out for Davenport to return, we at least knew he would be back soon. Also, Marlon and Yossi were available, and replaced Zamora and Newton. Kepa made the bench, as did John Pantsil randomly, and Roy Carroll somehow kept his place in goal.

Oh, and Christian Dailly was still in the team. I had no memory of him still being at the club at this time before starting this book, and it turns out he played about 57 sodding games. What a year this was.

Liverpool's team selection seemed to indicate that they weren't in the mood to show us any mercy. A front three of Kuyt, Crouch and Bellamy were selected, which appeared to be quite a task for Davenport and Dailly to handle. And yet, in the first half they managed to achieve this successfully, despite the nervous wreck of a goalkeeper playing behind them. In the first 20 minutes, Roy came for a couple of crosses and got absolutely nowhere near them again, which led to a crowd understandably lacking in patience at this point, chanting 'there's only one Robert Green' at both the keeper and the management.

Not a particularly helpful chant for anybody involved, but I can understand the sentiment. If Carroll had been playing well since being brought back into the side, I could have seen why he had been retained. But essentially a clean sheet against a League One team had kept him between the posts for a month now, a month in which we had conceded six goals in three games, lost leads in both league outings and gone out of the FA Cup.

We were struggling to get the requisite quality in some areas of the pitch due to factors out of our control – e.g. the injuries at centre-back – so choosing to go with lesser quality in areas we could control was utterly baffling. Keep in mind, we were asking Calum Davenport and Christian Dailly, who were not only fourth- and fifth-choice centre-halves at West Ham but would have been at most teams in the same league, to mark three international-calibre strikers. Surely to God picking clearly your best goalkeeper to assist with this would have been a no-brainer? It seemed that it was, to everybody except the manager. Sadly, this negative chant would be far from the last or the nastiest one heard in the coming weeks.

The first 45 minutes came and went with us holding on at 0-0 despite a chronic lack of possession, and as the half progressed we even managed a couple of half-chances of our own, with Harewood and Benayoun having attempts from which Reina had to make competent saves.

At half-time and as the second half kicked off, there were reasons to feel positive. Despite Carroll's jittery display, we had looked by and large secure at the back and had created opportunities ourselves. We had shown that we could compete with Liverpool on the very biggest of stages a few months previously, but could we manage that over 90 minutes again and potentially get some unexpected points out of the contest, which could maybe even signal a momentum change at the bottom of the league in our favour?

Dirk Kuyt put Liverpool 1-0 up ten seconds into the second half. Sometimes this stuff just writes itself.

It was a fantastic goal in all fairness, a sweetly struck effort from 25 yards that arrowed into the corner, but in that moment you could feel the optimism leave the stadium as quickly as air from a burst balloon. Nine minutes later, Crouch doubled the lead for the Scousers and that was all she wrote.

In fairness, we did rally as the game went on. We made a double change up front with 17 minutes to go that saw Zamora and Kepa replace Harewood and Cole. The switches paid an immediate dividend as a cross from the former was turned into the net by the Spaniard for his first goal for the club, within 90 seconds of him coming off the bench. A new hero was born, sort of. You don't need me to tell you that he never scored for us again.

It did lead to possibly the shortest-lived player chant of all time, though, with 'what's that coming over the hill, it's Kepa Blanco, it's Kepa Blanco' to the tune of 'Monster' by the Automatic, which was a massive song at the time, bellowing out from the Bobby Moore Lower and beyond.

Liverpool held out after that with relative comfort and in truth had better chances in the last few minutes – Bellamy hit the post and Carroll in fairness made an excellent stop from Kuyt. But it ended in a familiar story, a defeat with a few positives sprinkled in, but a defeat nonetheless. The players would have walked off the pitch to find out that Sheffield United had done something that we couldn't manage, which was beat Fulham at home to go seven points clear of the bottom three, and the following night Charlton got a 1-1 draw at Bolton (something we hadn't done either) which put them level on points with us. Everybody else was picking up points periodically, while we were stuck.

After beating United in Curbs' first game, we had 17 points. Six weeks and seven games later, only three more points had been added. Time was running out, and the next three games were officially being played at Villa Park, Upton Park and the Valley, but for West Ham they may as well have been played at the last chance saloon.

Tuesday, 30 January 2007:

West Ham 1 *Blanco (77)*

Liverpool 2 *Kuyt (46), Crouch (53)*

BOTTOM 7: (31/01/2007)

	P	Pts	GD
Aston Villa	25	29	-4
Fulham	25	29	-12
Sheffield United	25	27	-12
Wigan	24	22	-16
WEST HAM	*25*	*20*	*-22*
Charlton	*25*	*20*	*-24*
Watford	*24*	*15*	*-22*

The following day, the on-off/will they, won't they transfer saga (why use one cliché when you can use three?) of Matthew Upson was resolved with Birmingham reluctantly accepting an offer in the region of £7.5m for their captain, and the signing being formally announced shortly before the window closed. Upson signed a four-and-a-half-year contract, which apparently included a clause that he could leave at the end of the season if we were relegated.

Two players departed that day as well, Mears went to Derby on loan and would end up joining them permanently at the end of the season, and Mascherano's protracted move to Liverpool was confirmed, with the player giving us a genuinely fond farewell in the media, while sharing the same confusion we all had as to why he was used so infrequently. 'I am sad that it didn't work for me at West Ham. I came with great hope and I don't know why they didn't pick me. Every day I was there, training hard, just in case. I didn't complain, but I accepted that I was not in the plans of Alan Pardew or Alan Curbishley.

'My time at West Ham wasn't what it was meant to be. I was excited to be joining the club. They haven't won much and I wanted to help to change that – and I feel bad that I couldn't. Today I went and said goodbye and the players wished me good luck. I have to take a positive from this; I have never been at a club where I was not wanted in the team, where I wasn't an important player. It is an experience I would not wish to repeat.' Maybe at some point during his spell playing with Messi, Villa, Xavi, Busquets, Iniesta, Suarez, Neymar and everyone else in those magnificent Barcelona sides, Javier Mascherano may have thought, 'God, this is so much easier than it was at West Ham.' You have to laugh otherwise you might cry.

Later that week, there were reports that the goalkeeper issue may have been more personal than it appeared on the surface, with rumours of a bust-up between Curbishley and Green after the Reading game making their way into the papers. These were swiftly denied by both parties, with Curbishley branding the reports 'totally untrue' in an interview with *The Sun* while explaining a little more on Green's continued omission from the starting line-up. 'I came here with no agenda or favouritism and I kept Roy in. He did well against Fulham and Newcastle but obviously was at fault for the Watford goal in the FA

Cup. Everyone's under scrutiny but particularly in goal. Now there is competition in that role. The fans have had a pop at Roy and everyone knows that – you can't play here and not hear it.'

Green also played down the reports while toeing the full party line that all footballers follow in interviews of the club being more important than the individual. 'Up until the Reading game, I thought I had done well and it is always disappointing to get dropped,' he said. 'But you pay the price for losing 6-0. It is ridiculous to get down about these things, though. You are no good to anybody if you get depressed and start moaning and groaning. I know the size of the task just to play for West Ham. You have one bad game here and you are out. The club is bigger than any individual and if Roy can come in and keep West Ham up, then that is a wonderful thing.'

Whether there was any truth in the story or not, it seemed unlikely that if we stayed up it would be down to Carroll in a big way, but maybe Green knew something we didn't. He worked with him in training every day, and also presumably wasn't watching the matches if he really did believe that Carroll could keep us up.

For the trip to Villa, just the three alterations were made to the 11 beaten by Liverpool. Upson came in for his debut, replacing Dailly, and the front two who showed promise in the last 15 minutes against the Reds started from the off, as Zamora and Kepa replaced Harewood and Cole. Carroll retained his place in goal (if this game had been a home fixture, I wonder if that would have been the case) and we kept the same four-man midfield of

Benayoun, the two Nigels and Boa Morte for the fourth game in a row.

We were on the back foot in the early stages as Petrov and Grant McCann fired wide, and our unrequited love Ashley Young forced a good stop from Carroll. But we were coming into the game a little more by the half-hour mark, when our luck with new signings turned from bad to downright ridiculous as Upson followed Neill's lead from the previous weekend and went off injured. A routine headed challenge with Agbonlahor resulted in Upson landing and pulling a calf muscle. He was immediately replaced by Dailly, meaning that neither of our two marquee defensive signings at a combined cost of six figures of wages per week were on the pitch, and Christian Dailly still was. (Just to be clear here, I actually liked Dailly over most of his time with us; it's just that looking back, his continued presence in the team in 2007 amuses me no end.)

Curbishley stood on the touchline with a wry smile on his face as Upson limped by, and I cannot say I blame him. He must have felt like a bloke who found a winning lottery ticket the week after it expired. A big job at a club with money to spend had come his way, and it was worse than the job he'd had before.

At that point Villa correctly sensed weakness, stepped up their game and battered us for the next 50 or so minutes. Somehow they only scored once, with big striker John Carew netting on his home debut just before half-time from Young's assist. Other teams got positive things from big signings on their debuts, so why couldn't we? They were even completing the games, for God's sake.

Martin O'Neill's side had won only one of their 13 previous league games and plummeted from the top six to the bottom half, but we couldn't get near them as the second half rolled on. Young shot inches wide, McCann got even closer but still sent his effort off target and Petrov forced Carroll into another very good save. But with a couple of minutes to go, they still hadn't got the second goal and put us to bed. Could we capitalise on this? It had been done to us often enough. Could we be the beneficiaries of a team who'd had most of the play but not scored the killer goal?

We won a corner in the 89th minute, which is generally a good start. The ball was half cleared as far as Etherington (on for the poor Boa Morte), who unleashed a volley that was brilliantly saved by Thomas Sorensen. The ball went for another corner, which was half cleared as far as Calum Davenport, whose volley was hit with technique belying his normal position at the other end of the pitch, and guess what, was brilliantly saved by Thomas Sorensen.

Hands were on heads in the away end behind the goal, and no doubt in every household containing a West Ham fan following the game. That save went for *another* corner. The ball was flighted into the six-yard box and flicked on to Etherington, who headed past Sorensen. It was headed by their left-back Bruma on the line, up on to the underside of the bar and out again. Not in. Not over the goddamn line. No goal. There was never a sodding goal this season. It was cleared and we lost 1-0.

We had managed to snatch defeat from the jaws of stalemate from the jaws of defeat. If that is even a thing. Spoiler, the agony felt from the minute or two of near misses was at best the fourth worst thing to happen to West Ham fans this month.

The defeat and the injury to Upson left our manager in disconsolate mood in the post-match interview. 'It just sums us up at the moment. We signed Lucas Neill and he didn't last 20 minutes and we have signed Matthew and he has only lasted a bit longer. I haven't even spoken to Matthew about it, so I can't speculate about how long he will be out. Everyone's just so disappointed, but we are just going to have to get on with it. We need some three-pointers now. We laid siege near the end, but Thomas Sorensen made some great saves.'

His mood wouldn't have been improved when he found out that Wigan had beaten Portsmouth 1-0 and moved five points clear of us now, with a game in hand into the bargain. We got lucky when Blackburn did us a favour, beating Sheffield United 2-1 with a Morten Gamst Pedersen goal in the 92nd minute. Any positives were welcomed at this point. They were in very short supply.

Saturday, 3 February 2007:

Aston Villa 1 *Carew (36)*

West Ham 0

BOTTOM 7: (03/02/2007)

	P	Pts	GD
Fulham	26	32	-11
Manchester City	25	30	-11
Sheffield United	26	27	-13
Wigan	25	25	-15
WEST HAM	*26*	*20*	*-23*
Charlton	*26*	*20*	*-25*
Watford	*25*	*15*	*-23*

As the league table showed, things were going past worrying, past concerning and into full-on critical. Upson would be ruled out for three to four weeks, meaning the game at home to Tottenham was realistic for his return and he should only miss two games, which on the face of it wasn't too bad. However, with those two games being so pivotal, if they went wrong it seemed that Upson's return would almost be an irrelevance.

Four points from the three games seemed like the bare minimum, six was badly needed. One game had been and gone with no points added, so there was zero margin for error. Watford, purely and simply, had to be a win. And it really should have been, for as bad as we had been all season, they were clearly worse by any measuring stick. Only two wins in 25 games, none away in the league (we know where their only away win in all competitions had been) and they had somehow managed to score fewer goals than us, despite our almost total aversion to the task from September to December. They travelled to Upton Park having scored 14 goals all campaign compared to our 18 and had only scored in two of their previous eight games. As must-win games go, there weren't many better teams in the history of the Premier League we could have asked to play.

Almost half the starting 11 were changed for reasons that were a mixture of a lack of form and various returns to fitness. Carroll, Boa Morte and Kepa were left out in favour of Green, Etherington and Harewood, and Neill and Ferdinand returned from injury to replace Spector and Upson. Pleasingly, Tevez was also fit enough to make the bench. Maybe the potential X factor he possessed could make a difference during the run-in, even though it had to be admitted it had made barely any difference at all up until this point (let's remember that fact for later, eh?).

Now, the first goal in any game of top-flight football is always important, we can all agree on that. In a six-pointer, it is doubly important. In a six-pointer as big as this one, when third from bottom is playing bottom, it is trebly important.

Against this Watford team it was even more so still, as one stat I left out earlier that was actually in their favour was that while they had barely won a game and could hardly score a goal, defensively they weren't that bad. They'd conceded 37 goals in 25 games, which for a team at the bottom is actually pretty good. We'd conceded four more than that, and in fact were one of four sides who had done so. Blackburn in ninth had shipped the same amount, and Tottenham in 11th only one fewer. Their manager Aidy Boothroyd, through a style of what might be called functional play, had built a side that played to their limited strengths, which was namely to work hard and make teams beat them, rather than over-attack and be picked off.

This wouldn't have been news to the management team and therefore the players. The first goal was everything in this game, so it was crucial not to hand Watford anything easy, anything on a plate. So quite why Anton Ferdinand in the 12th minute thought it was a good idea to tug back their striker Darius Henderson a couple of inches inside the corner of the penalty area, I will never, ever know. I didn't know then, I don't know now and if Anton ever for some reason turned up at my house with a detailed hour-long presentation (complete with slides and diagrams) as to why he did it, I *still* wouldn't bloody know. It sure as hell wasn't because of the massive threat Henderson posed as he hadn't scored a goal all season, despite appearing in 23 of their previous 25 games.

Well, he hadn't scored a goal at *that* moment anyway. About 90 seconds later he had, as he buried the resulting penalty past Green.

We were 1-0 down, then. In a game we had to win. Against a team who weren't that bad defensively and were sure to hang on for their lives. But those of us in the crowd kept the faith at this point. There were 78 minutes still to play, plenty of time, there were options on the bench and some leaders on the pitch who could get stuck in. They included Lucas Neill, who we'd heard was a leader and was back from injury quite quickly and could help out, right? Right? Thirty-two minutes in, Neill went in for a tackle, got up, waved his arms in frustration and just walked off. Injured. Again. He'd gone six years at Blackburn without an injury and had knocked out two for us in an hour of playing.

This was the moment the crowd turned in my opinion. I'd never heard such a 'oh just **** off' type of reaction before from a West Ham crowd. What I mean is in the sense that it wasn't at one player or a goal conceded or chance missed, more at the entire miserable ridiculous situation we were in. Miserable is the operative word to describe this whole afternoon. Zamora missed two good first-half chances, heading over both times, and the only other memory I have of the opening 45 is Watford's young keeper Ben Foster (he is now Watford's old keeper Ben Foster as I write) taking *hours* to take goal kicks. He wasn't even booked the entire game, which is incredible.

Tevez was brought on for Zamora at half-time. Could this be the day, the moment when he turned his promise into an end result? We continued to huff and puff. We would end the game with 62 per cent of the ball and 24 shots on goal. This wasn't a day when you could accuse the players of not being interested or downing tools. But shots such as a free kick from Tevez that went just over continued to go high or wide and the frustration in the crowd got close to boiling point.

And then, with half an hour to go, Reo-Coker for two wonderful minutes turned into the player of the season before, just as Yossi had against Fulham. Collecting the ball, he drove through midfield, past their backline and was clean through on goal. Fellow centre mid Gavin

Mahon had tracked him but wasn't quick enough, and his tackle scythed him down. In the area. Penalty given. Our first penalty all season, and a possible first step to salvation was right there in front of us. Nige knew it as well. With the punch of the air he gave to those behind the goal, this was the moment we so desperately needed.

We all thought it was going to be a moment not only for us, but also finally for Carlos. Surely he would take the penalty, score, celebrate wildly (we hadn't seen it yet but it felt like that might be his kind of thing) and buoyed by the crowd favourite scoring a goal that would lift not only his confidence but the mood of all around him in claret and blue, we would go on to earn the win we all craved so much.

Who knows what could have happened then? We might win at Charlton, beat Tottenham. We might even be able to refer to this season as a 'Great Escape' in years to come or something like that.

Then two very strange things happened. Firstly, it occurred to me that in all the celebration of the penalty awarded, I must have missed the red card shown to Mahon. After all, Reo-Coker was clean through, about to shoot in a one-on-one situation and was hacked down in what was a definite booking anywhere on the pitch. But in the area, as the last man, it was a clear professional foul, and thus not a yellow card. It was a sending off. In the moments leading up to the penalty that Tevez was definitely, 100 per cent going to take, I counted the yellow Watford shirts just to make sure. There were ten of them. Plus the goalkeeper. That makes 11. Trust me it does, no need to check. The referee, Alan Wiley, hadn't sent him off. How had he not sent him off? How did he decide it was only a yellow? It wasn't until I got home that night that I checked and realised that he hadn't even booked him.

Now I know nowadays in the Premier League that it may not have been a red card. There is the 'double punishment' rule that if a foul leading to a penalty doesn't merit a red in and of itself, it doesn't have to be a sending-off. But in March 2007, there was no such law. Any referee at any level would have known that it was a straight red card, and Watford would have been down to ten men. It was in the rules, and one of the more basic and straightforward ones at that. Any referee would have known that rule. (Another basic rule that all refs would know was the offside rule, which we had been the victims of a couple of games previously at Newcastle. It never rains.) I can only assume that in the commotion following the penalty award, referee Wiley just forgot to send him off. I cannot fathom any other excuse. Because there was no excuse, simple as that.

The second strange thing was that the taker of the penalty, 5ft 10in white Argentinian Carlos Tevez, looked a lot like 6ft 4in black Englishman Marlon Harewood. Now I had never got the two mixed up visually before, so this was most odd.

It turns out my eyes were not deceiving me. It had been decided, either before kick-off or on the pitch, that Harewood would have the responsibility of dragging us back into the game. This, even without hindsight being a factor, was a decision I could best describe as brave. Marlon had taken plenty of penalties before with a large degree of success, but none carried anywhere near as much pressure as this one did. Plus, there'd been a fair delay since the award of the penalty (probably due to a lot of waiting around for a sending-off that never happened), and as I have stated before, the Marvellous one was never at his best when he had time to think about things. This was a fair amount of time to think about something very important indeed.

He stepped up, we held our breath. Always a short run-up from Marlon, so not long to have to wait. He sent the keeper the wrong way. Thank Christ for that. In my seat, facing the side of the net to the keeper's right, I and all the fans around me started to cheer as we saw the ball fly towards the other corner, and quickly wondered why all those not sharing our view weren't doing the same. He had stuck it a yard and a half wide of the other post.

Salvation – gone. Motivation – gone. Confidence – gone. Happiness – gone. Premier League – all but gone. The air and hope left the crowd. Only anger remained.

The last half an hour was football's equivalent of sitting in an electric chair waiting for it to be turned on. You know all hope barring a miracle is gone, but you have to hang around anyway. The only proper chance we created was when Tévez managed to round the keeper but then partially scuffed his shot, which allowed it to be cleared off the line by centre-back Malky Mackay, who had played for us in the Championship two years previously and looked about 47 then. Seriously, he was a tough and very good player in his day but the man could barely run when he was in our colours. How he was part of a defence keeping a clean sheet in the Premier League in 2007 should be a case for Mulder and Scully.

By the end we'd reached the anger stage of grief, which led to chants around the ground of 'you're not fit to wear the shirt' among others. In truth, the performance wasn't lacking effort, more quality and confidence, which had been eroded by defeat after defeat, disappointment after disappointment. The final memory of the afternoon I have was Tevez diving full stretch, goalkeeper-like, to block a clearance with his arms, which managed to bring a murmur of laughter and sympathetic applause from the otherwise hostile locals.

While funny, it was our season summed up in a way: this apparently world-class forward with the world at his feet, who was going to help take us to the next level, had been reduced to diving around in desperation to stop Watford clearing the ball on the way to a turgid 1-0 defeat. It wasn't where we thought the situation would ever get to, but it was now where we were.

The final whistle saw boos and anger from the fans who had bothered to stay to the end. We didn't quite need snookers to stay up now, but we were five frames to nil down in a best-of-11 match. In his press conference after the game, Curbishley referenced the penalty and non-sending off, and the terrible run since his arrival, as well as the chants from the stands. 'We need a lift. Everyone needs a lift. When we missed the penalty, it had some effect on us. I was pleased to get the penalty but the referee has to make a decision. Mahon appeared to be the last man – and I've seen it on the video and he definitely was the last man. Wiley's got to make a decision. I've seen people sent off for it but somehow he decided it wasn't a sending-off offence. I'm more disappointed with not scoring. That would have changed the game.

'Since I've been here, we've won one game. It's been a dreadful run. No matter what I say, I'll be criticised, so I won't say too much. We need a lift. We'd like to think it's going to be against Charlton. It's a desperately disappointing day and a desperately disappointing result, but it's not over. One thing I am about is trying to keep a settled side but we've had too many changes through lack of form, injuries, lack of results. We've had some coming on as subs in previous games looking sharp but perhaps that's not been the case when they've started.

'The "you're not fit to wear the shirt" chant? It's not nice. To be fair to the fans, they've been constant in their support. They've got behind us in their droves and got behind us at the start but we haven't delivered enough to them to keep them going throughout the match. We've not given them anything to get behind.'

Saturday, 10 February 2007:
West Ham 0
Watford 1 *Henderson pen (12)*

We were now five points behind Wigan, who had two games in hand, both of which would be played before our next game at Charlton, which was two weeks away due to international fixtures. The following day, all Hammers fans hid behind the sofa as Jewell's side gave Arsenal an almighty fright, taking the lead in the first half and holding the advantage until the 81st minute, when an own goal and a Rosicky strike gave Arsenal a narrow 2-1 win. The second game ten days later saw the Latics travel to our most recent conquerors Watford, where the two sides played out a 1-1 draw that saw Henderson score again to double his tally for the season. Clearly there was no stopping him now.

So only one further point gained by Wigan across the two games but still a convincing gap to ourselves in 18th position; six points with 11 games to go and a far superior goal difference was an enviable position. Sheffield United and Manchester City in 15th and 16th sat even prettier, ten points clear with again a far superior goal difference. Losing 6-0 will do that.

BOTTOM 7: (21/02/2007)

	P	Pts	GD
Fulham	27	32	-12
Sheffield United	27	30	-12
Manchester City	26	30	-12
Wigan	27	26	-16
WEST HAM	*27*	*20*	*-24*
Charlton	*27*	*20*	*-27*
Watford	*27*	*19*	*-22*

Not only were the sides above a long way clear of us, but the two teams who had been consistently below us had closed the gap to the point that the very bottom of the league wasn't far away now either. The four points Watford collected from ourselves and Wigan meant they were now just one positive result from going clear of us, and Charlton were level on points going into our encounter at the Valley. Pardew's men had lost their previous two games admittedly, but these were against Chelsea (1-0) and Manchester United (2-0), so it wasn't as if we were playing a team out of form. They were largely on the up and had been since Pardew's appointment two months earlier. In comparison, we had not won a single league game in the time Pards had been in control at the Addicks.

The match between the two sides was as big a relegation battle as they came. The loser would be second from bottom at best and at least six points from safety with ten games to go, if not more. I don't think it needs to be spelled out any clearer than that. It was also a unique situation. Seldom does a manager have the tenure and popularity at one club that Curbishley quite rightly had at Charlton, and while it's not uncommon to see managers of this ilk return to their former employer, I cannot imagine the return has come in a game as important as this one for both managers' previous and current clubs.

And not only that, when has the manager in the opposite dugout been the man that the returning former manager replaced at his new club? But that was what was in store when Curbishley's West Ham met Pardew's Charlton. The game was played somewhat surprisingly at 3pm on a Saturday. Looking back, I'm staggered that with all the subplots at play it wasn't selected for live broadcast, but maybe Sky felt like they owed us one after screening the disaster at Bolton live.

The day before, Curbs briefly spoke with the club website about the match, stressing its obvious importance and expressing some optimism for the challenge ahead. 'We know how important the game is. This and the Watford game have been of massive significance; we've blown the first one and we can't blow the second. We're waiting for that boost to come and give us a bit of a lift. The other clubs [around us] have had that lift and you can see how much it's helped them. We're desperate for that and we'll get it on Saturday. This has been the best two weeks that we've had with the players – and hopefully it will show.'

Pards, for his part, played down the significance of the links between the managers, while respecting the enormity of the game. 'I have nothing to say because nobody at this club is going to try and rev up the game – it's revved up enough. I am not going to cause any waves and while I have respect for the West Ham United players, I am the Charlton manager and my priority is three points for Charlton.'

So, to the Valley then. My dad and Barry were in attendance. I chose not to go, in a decision that has aged magnificently. Dad was excited, though; this was a chance for the terrible memory of Reading away to be put to bed. I don't know what Barry felt about the game, but I can only assume he took his coat off two minutes before the match kicked off.

The almost standard five changes were made to the line-up for this one. Both full-backs were switched as Dailly (of course) and Konchesky came in for the stricken Neill and the dropped McCartney; Reo-Coker and Zamora missed out due to injury and were replaced by Mullins and Cole, and Tevez replaced Harewood to reunite the striking duo that had started positively against Fulham six weeks prior. Charlton in comparison had a largely settled side, which was boosted for this game with the return of top scorer Darren Bent and England international (and former transfer target) Luke Young.

I was following this game at my friends Neil and Owen's flat in Portsmouth, watching *Soccer Saturday* with a couple of beers prior to a night out in the town later that evening. We heard that Charlton were comfortably the better team and swarming all over us, and after 20 minutes or so Owen (my fellow Hammer from uni) and I decided we would go and get some early dinner to line the stomach for the night ahead from a baguette shop a couple of minutes' walk from their house. We barely spoke about the match while we were out; we could sense what was coming.

The game, the day, just had that feel to it. In truth, despite the rhetoric coming from the manager and players that we could still stay up, we knew it was over and this felt like the day it was going to be confirmed. As we walked back up the stairs to the flat, baguettes in tow, we mentioned how we had zero hope of walking back to see good news. We fully expected to walk back into the flat seeing we were a goal behind. What we saw on the

TV left us open-mouthed. We expected it not to be good news, but this? Our appetites vanished instantly.

Owen and I had been away from the TV for about 15 minutes. We were 3-0 down.

To be as brief as I can, 24 minutes in Darren Ambrose evaded our central midfield and back four as Bent crossed the ball in from the right-hand side, and volleyed with his left foot past Green. We literally had six players goal side of Ambrose prior to him making a run into the area. They either watched him make the run or lightly jogged after him. There was no other Charlton player in the 18-yard box; it wasn't that we were overloaded with players to mark. There was just no awareness and/or no desire to deal with the danger presented. Purely and simply, Ambrose wanted to score more than any of our players wanted to stop him.

Five minutes later, winger Jerome Thomas received the ball in behind Dailly and drove at Davenport towards our goal. Thomas pushed him back and back towards our area, shifted the ball on to his left foot and put it in the far corner of the net. My youngest son currently plays for an under-9s team and I have seen defenders of that age make it harder for an attacker than I saw here.

In the slightest defence of the centre-back, he could have been helped by our midfield a little more, but Quashie decided to just amble along behind Thomas rather than sprint to catch up and make things more difficult for him. I guess playing for a team about to be relegated was in his comfort zone and he wasn't prepared to try and rock that boat.

The third goal came when Konchesky tackled Zamora in mid pitch. Yes, you read that correctly. I'm not sure what was more surprising, the two of them flailing around, falling over each other and losing the ball or one of our players actually making a tackle. The ball was played to Bent, who was clean through on goal as Ferdinand had stepped up to play offside with his defensive 'partner' Davenport unaware of his decision. Well, I hope he was unaware seeing as he was stood six yards behind him. Bent scored and sealed the game for Pardew's men before half-time. Pathetic doesn't begin to cover it.

You might expect that the reaction from the fans would be fury and bile almost unmatched by a crowd, remembering that those who travel to away games are often the most passionate and hardcore of football fans. Also, these fans had not seen a single away win all season, and barely even a goal. And while there certainly was anger, with further chants of 'you're not fit to wear the shirt' and the like, the shambles of the situation brought more irony and gallows humour from the Hammers faithful. And trust me, no fans do gallows humour quite like West Ham's. We've had enough practice over the years.

So the second half, in which Thomas completed the scoring with a drilled shot past Green to make it 4-0, saw West Ham fans doing the conga around the stand and the concourse, while various songs were made up referencing the Championship and how 'we're s**t and we know we are'. But then, miraculously, West Ham made a comeback, scoring goal after goal, sending the fans into raptures. Well, that's what the away fans decided anyway. This was the day the song 'let's pretend we've scored a goal' was born.

The players on the pitch clearly weren't going to provide anything to cheer about, so the fans provided it themselves. The chant would begin, followed by a countdown of five, four, three, two, one ... and then mass cheering broke out. This happened four times, and amazingly we had equalised! Sort of. '4-0 up, you ****ed it up', the fans sung to the laughing Charlton supporters, who were probably wondering what had been put in their counterparts' drinks at half-time.

Simply put, for a lot of the people investing their hard-earned money to watch this utter rubbish, the stage of grief had now hit acceptance, and a good time was going to be had by all come what may. Personally, I can tell you the result didn't bother me anywhere near as much as the results against Bolton or Reading did. I still had hope after those games that things could be salvaged. I now had absolutely none. I went out that night, had a great time with my mates and barely thought about football for a few days.

Saturday, 24 February 2007:

Charlton 4 *Ambrose (24), Thomas (34, 80),*

Bent (41)

West Ham 0

Curbishley, however, was a broken man after the game. He admitted in an interview with *Match of the Day* that he 'hadn't enjoyed this for one minute' and spoke of 'yet another miserable weekend'.

If you were looking for a last-gasp rallying cry, there erm, wasn't one. 'Before I got here, West Ham had lost 13 out of 16 games and eight on the spin, and I've not been able to change that. One win from 11 is just not good enough and no matter what I throw up, it's just not good enough. It's going to be extremely tough now. We've had two opportunities in recent weeks against Watford and Charlton and haven't taken them. We're on the receiving end of it at the moment and we don't look as if we're going to get out of it. The question is, are we going down with a fight or a whimper? There are ten games left, lots of points at stake.'

You always know a team is utterly screwed when the manager starts pointing out how many games are left and the amount of points there are to play for when nobody has asked for that information. And there really can't have been many managers ever who have said in an interview in *February* that it doesn't look as if they will get out of a relegation battle. Can't say he was wrong, mind.

He also complained about the injuries and how he hadn't been able to keep the same team together, which I sympathise with in part. Yes, the injuries had been brutal in some areas, particularly in defence, where we had lost Gabbidon and Collins for months and Anton had been out on three separate occasions in the time Curbs had been manager. But at the same time, nobody made him go out and spend £3m on Tottenham's fifth-choice centre-half, who anybody with functioning eyeballs could see was nowhere near good enough to be near a team in our position. Upson had been injury prone throughout his career – bad luck, yes – but if you are buying players to help attain a short-term goal, these were not signings that should have been made, for the better part of £10m no less.

Curbishley had also fallen into the same trope as Pardew whereby he seemed to draw the two forwards out of a hat every week. Any game in which you came on and played well guaranteed a start in the next one; any bad game and you were out. Never any continuity or thought was given as to what could be an effective partnership. In his time as manager, Harewood, Zamora, Sheringham, Cole, Tevez and Kepa had all started up front. He had only been manager for 11 league games. He picked Harewood and Zamora for the first three games of his tenure. The list of combinations used thereafter is below:

(Changes in bold)

MANCHESTER CITY (H): Sheringham, Harewood

READING (A): **Zamora**, Harewood

FULHAM (H): **Cole, Tevez**

NEWCASTLE (A): Cole, **Harewood**

LIVERPOOL (H): Cole, Harewood

ASTON VILLA (A): **Zamora, Kepa**

WATFORD (H): Zamora, **Harewood**

CHARLTON (A): **Cole, Tevez**

Nine alterations in just eight games. Those who do not learn from history are doomed to repeat it.

The following day saw Wigan hammer another nail in the coffin as they beat Newcastle 1-0 at home. The gap was now nine points with ten games to play, effectively ten points such was the disparity in goal difference between the teams.

Essentially, we had ten games left to double the points we had so far acquired in the 28 previous matches. The ten games included home matches against Tottenham, Everton, Bolton and Chelsea, who were all in the top nine, and away trips to Arsenal and Manchester United. Overall, seven of the ten games were against teams in the top half of the league, and two of the remaining three were away games at Wigan and Sheffield United. Yep.

BOTTOM 7: (25/02/2007)

	P	Pts	GD
Fulham	28	32	-13
Manchester City	26	30	-12
Sheffield United	28	30	-16
Wigan	28	29	-15
Charlton	*28*	*23*	*-23*
WEST HAM	*28*	*20*	*-28*
Watford	*28*	*19*	*-25*

The good news kept coming in the days after Charlton, as it was announced that we had been charged with a breach of Premier League rules regarding the transfers of Carlos Tevez and Javier Mascherano on deadline day. Who saw that coming, eh?

We had been accused of breaching two regulations when signing the players, regs U6 and U18. U6 read, *'No person may either directly or indirectly be involved in or have any power to determine or influence the management or administration of more than one club.'*

U18 stated, *'No club shall enter into a contract which enables any other party to that contract to require the ability materially to influence its policies or the performance of its teams in league matches.'*

The Premier League's official statement when announcing the charges was as follows, 'It is the Board's complaint that there were agreements in relation to both these transfers that enabled third parties to acquire the ability materially to influence the club's policies and/or the performance of its teams in league matches and/or the competitions set out in Rule E10.

'The Board's view is this constitutes a breach of Rule U18, which states, "No club shall enter into a contract which enables any other party to that contract to acquire the ability materially to influence its policies or the performance of its teams in league matches or in any of the competitions set out in Rule E10."

'Furthermore, at the time of the transfer agreements for both Tevez and Mascherano, and until January 24, 2007, West Ham United failed to disclose the third-party agreements to the Premier League and/ or deliberately withheld these agreements from the Premier League.

'The Board's view is this constitutes a breach of Rule B13, which states: "In all matters and transactions relating to the league, each club shall behave towards each other club and the league with the utmost good faith."'

The issue arose when Mascherano was signing for Liverpool, and thus having his registration transferred from one club to another. Liverpool registered the player with the Premier League on the same terms he was on with ourselves before the governing body intervened, saying that a transfer including a provision that the player could be sold without the consent of the club they were playing for wasn't allowed. It then came out that this provision was in the contracts we signed with Tevez and Mascherano but we hadn't told the Premier League about it.

The governing body swiftly asked the club for further information. We then provided the required info and were then subsequently told by the Premier League that if this had been submitted when the transfers were completed originally, the duo would not have had their contracts ratified by the league and wouldn't have been allowed to play for West Ham.

Ah. That's not ideal.

Mascherano signed for Liverpool with the suspicious provisions removed, and Tevez somewhat oddly was announced as being allowed to play for us until the formal hearing was held, which would be some time in late April.

Now I will air my opinions on the results of that hearing (and all that followed it) later. Right now, I will just look at the initial charges and process that was announced. Regarding the charges, were we guilty? Of course we bloody were. As I've said, we basically admitted it, several times? As I have previously covered, Pardew and Magnusson were both on record in the media in admitting we didn't know how long they would be with us. That isn't something you say when you are in control of the players' transfer rights. We admitted this multiple times and somehow nobody noticed until Liverpool naively assumed they could do the same thing and not hide bits of the agreement.

Now, clearly we weren't guilty if the charge was relating to the transfers involving a clause that they had to play at all times. Because they hadn't. Tevez had been in and out of the side when fit, and Mascherano hardly ever played at all after the first fortnight, making a grand total of five starts and two further substitute appearances in his spell at Upton Park. So, we were as clean as a whistle on that front. But we had no say as to whether the players were sold on to another club, nor would we have profited on it past a sum of £2m, as was found out later, and that broke the Premier League rules at the time. In truth, we didn't have a leg to stand on as far as I could see, and we would have to accept a punishment when it was handed down.

So yes, we had done wrong, broken the rules and would have to face the consequences. But why was it decided that these consequences wouldn't be passed down until April, and why was Tevez allowed to keep playing for us in the meantime?

Keep in mind for later, neither of those decisions had anything to do with West Ham United. The charges were announced on 2 March and the club had 14 days to respond. If the hearing had been held by the end of March, which surely could have been feasible, or if Tevez was barred from playing for us until the hearing, however far in the future it would be held, none of the later issues would have arisen. Again, neither of those decisions were anything to do with us.

In my opinion, the reason the hearing was slated for late April was because it was assumed we would be mathematically relegated by then, which meant all possible sanctions could be on the table. If we could still stay up, the punishment could have been interpreted as 'relegation' if we were deducted points (widely assumed to be the expected outcome), which would have likely led to a lengthy legal battle.

But if we were already down, there would have been next to no arguments at an immediate deduction, which could then have served as a precedent to deter clubs from considering doing this in future.

A safe bet by the Premier League authorities, then. No way were we not going to be mathematically relegated by late April, and why did it matter if Tevez played for us or not, I dare say they may have thought? He hadn't scored a goal all season and allowing him to continue doing his job would stave off any potential 'restraint of trade'-style lawsuits from any of his people.

In Curbishley's pre-match press conference on the Friday, two days before the home match against

Tottenham, he confirmed that Tevez would indeed start up front in the coming game.

The Argentinian was one of six players who had started at the Valley to keep his place for the London derby, as the seemingly obligatory five changes were made to the team. The fit-again trio of Neill, Upson and Bowyer returned in place of Dailly, Davenport and Benayoun, Harewood replaced Cole to partner Carlos up front, and with Mullins joining Reo-Coker on the injury list, Mark Noble was brought into the side for his first sighting since he got the man of the match award against Brighton, making not only his first Premier League appearance of the season but first for 16 months. The full squad was as follows:

Starting XI: *Green, Neill, Ferdinand, Upson, Konchesky, Bowyer, Noble, Quashie, Etherington, Tevez, Harewood*

Subs: *Walker, Spector, Davenport, Blanco, Zamora*

The day before saw a full programme of Premier League fixtures that rained further pain down on to us. Charlton battled back from 2-0 down at Vicarage Road to draw with Watford, Sheffield United drew 1-1 at home to Everton and Wigan won 1-0 at the not yet Etihad against Manchester City.

These results meant as we kicked off against Spurs we were bottom, ten points behind 17th-placed City, with ten matches and 30 points left to play for. At this point, we were now 11 points behind Sheffield United and 12 adrift of Wigan, both of whom had comfortably superior goal differences into the bargain. Hell, Charlton had even moved four points clear and were now in 18th. This match was the footballing equivalent of a desperate gambler having £1 left in his pocket and needing to win the £200 jackpot with it.

Maybe it was knowing the futility of the situation, in a way being able to play without pressure or expectation for the first time in months, maybe it was picking the right team and combinations eventually, maybe it was the leadership of Neill returning to the team (he started as captain), maybe it was the alignment of the solar system, I have no idea. But whatever it was, for the first 45 minutes of the game we were outstanding.

Noble snapped into tackles immediately, earning a yellow card in only the sixth minute in what was a minor preview of things to come over the next decade and a bit. Tevez buzzed around the pitch with class, workrate and purpose. Neill provided a calmness at the back that we hadn't seen all season. When Green was called upon by Berbatov on two occasions, he saved with quality and confidence. What was going on?

We lost Upson in the 12th minute to injury; he wouldn't be seen again all season. His part in this story was over, two appearances and 42 minutes on the pitch for a £6.5m signing designed to help keep us up. But in the first half his absence barely registered; we didn't miss a beat. Four minutes after he left the stage, Noble made that stage all his own. A cross from Konchesky fizzed in towards Tevez, the Argentine used his chest to cushion the ball back to Noble, and the young midfielder's half-volleyed drive went through Dawson's legs and past Robinson in the Tottenham goal.

We were 1-0 up and it was thoroughly deserved. Noble ran towards the East Stand, arm in the air and legs pumping. Whatever happened from this point to the end of the season, here finally was a positive, one of our own, years before a chant made that phrase cool to say, who we could build the team around and have as a key player for years to come. How right we were.

We held on through the next 25 minutes and looked just as likely to get the next goal as our more fancied rivals. Then, five minutes before half-time, Tevez wriggled past one challenge and was then brought down by Dawson around 20 yards out. Six Spurs players lined up in the wall, with three of our players for company. Tevez stood over the ball, alone. He'd had three set plays in similar positions at the Centenary Stand end of the ground, against Watford which went just over, against Newcastle, which hit the bar, and against Man City, which missed by inches. He stepped up, curled the ball over the wall, over Robinson, who had taken a step too far off his line, against the underside of the bar and into the goddamn mother loving net.

'He's scored! He's scored!' was all I could scream. It was the only thing I could think of to say, it was the only thing that mattered in that moment. To me, to every West Ham fan. We had grown to love this boy, we marvelled at his hard work for a club he would have barely heard of seven months earlier. We loved him and we knew he loved us. And we just wanted his luck to change, we wanted him to succeed, firstly for us but then also for himself. Whether it made any difference to the end result of the season wasn't important as the ball hit the net. It just mattered that finally, at long last, Carlos Tevez had scored for West Ham United.

And it was all that mattered to Tevez himself as well. In one of the most iconic goal celebrations of all time, he ran to the crowd in the West Stand Lower, shirt already off, grinning from ear to ear. At the pace he was running, he was going to do well to stop before he got to the hoardings. Only stopping was never his intention. He leapt the hoardings to celebrate with the fans. *His* fans. We had stuck with him, and he had repaid that faith and stuck with us. And he wanted us all to celebrate together. Within seconds, he was engulfed by over a hundred supporters. No malice, no danger to anybody involved, only happiness and gratitude. Finally, the season had a moment to savour. One that would make a West Ham fan smile for years to come. Case in point, writing about it is making this West Ham fan smile 13 years later.

Tevez was booked for the crime of removing his shirt. And jumping into the crowd. And holding the game up for too long. And just about any other offence that can be committed during a goal celebration. We calmed down and got ourselves in at half-time 2-0 up. It wasn't quite the first step on the road to survival, but it was a reasonable start to crawling. The big question now was could we keep the level of performance up? And could we get the result? Performances counted for nothing in the situation we were in; there was no more room for 'taking the positives'. All that mattered now was points.

Curbishley would have no doubt been delighted with the opening 45 minutes, and I am sure would have been at pains to ram down the throats of his players the importance of the first quarter-of-an-hour of the second half. 2-0 leads, as we all know, can often be perilous. Even more so when you're bottom of the league, bereft of confidence and haven't won a game of football for three months. It was vital we defended well, played sensibly and did nothing rash.

Lee Bowyer's decision to slide in on, and completely wipe out, Aaron Lennon (him again) as the winger drove into the area was poor defending, not sensible and extremely rash. Not what we were looking for. Defoe converted the ensuing penalty to make it 2-1 six minutes into the second half.

We could all see what was coming now. We started to defend deeper. Spurs, who Berbatov apart had looked toothless up until Bowyer's lunge, were now on the front foot. On 63 minutes, a well-worked move from Berbatov, Lennon and Tainio led to the diminutive winger flicking the ball back for the Finnish midfielder, who hammered it into the net. 2-2. We had thrown away the lead within 18 second-half minutes – the way teams in the position we were in so often do. It wasn't a shock that we had done it, but my God was it still disappointing.

The game lost its shape somewhat after Tottenham's quick-fire double. In normal circumstances we may well have taken the draw, licked our wounds at throwing away a lead but tried to see that overall a draw against a side much higher in the league than us was a positive result. But in the mess we had found ourselves, a draw having been 2-0 in front just wouldn't do. First Kepa was sent on for the injured Quashie, then three minutes later Zamora was on for Etherington. We had four forwards on the pitch for the last seven minutes in our desperation to try and find a winner, with a midfield comprised of just Bowyer and Noble. All this to just have a toehold again in our climb to safety.

And then, with five minutes of normal time to go, it happened. A free kick from Tevez (who else) on our right-hand side was met by Zamora, who headed the ball past Robinson's outstretched left hand and into the far corner of the net, to put us back in front at 3-2.

We'd done it, thank God we'd done it. It might all count for nothing in the end, but at least this day, against *them*, wasn't going to be the day the last rites of our season were read. We only had a couple of minutes to hang on this time as well. There was barely enough time for the obligatory panic to set in. Spurs brought Adel Taarabt (a footballer who the word 'mercurial' could have been invented for) on, we had made all our allotted changes, so seeing as nearly half the ten outfield players were central strikers, settled on a formation of 'everybody back'.

Into the last minute of normal time, Spurs attacked and got to within 20 yards of our goal. A shout for handball against Ferdinand seemed to panic the defender, who in his haste to get the ball put an arm somewhere near the vicinity of Taarabt, who went down and was 'fouled'. Seriously, if you look up the word 'weak' in the dictionary, you would see a picture of this free kick being awarded. The referee for the game was Mike Dean, by the way.

The one slight result we had was the offence was no more than half a yard outside the area. It was, as many summarisers say, 'almost too close', in that to get the ball over the wall and down again from such a short distance was extremely difficult. For that reason, I was worried but not to the point of full-on panic.

I've also long had a theory that if you are hanging on to a lead with not long left to play, giving away a free kick where the attacking team will go for goal isn't actually as bad as it seems at the time. The method to my madness is that the time from when the offence is given to when the ball is struck is normally at least a minute, if not nearer two, and this time is never added back on to the game. It's not time wasting, is it? You are setting up a wall, defence etc, and often the attacking team take just as much time to be ready. So, if the ball doesn't go in, which for all the danger and excitement free kicks provide the majority of them do not, a free kick can amount to a missed chance the same as in open play, but one that may take a couple of minutes out of the end of a game.

Anyway, the free kick took the customary amount of time to be ready to be taken, and while nervous I still felt OK. As I have said, it would take a wonderful strike to get the ball up over the wall and down again from such a short distance, and even if it was achieved, we were going to drop Konchesky back on to the line, so please

God he could head the ball clear. It would need a free kick of magnificent technical ability to break our hearts. Thus, it would need to be a player of said magnificent technical ability to do so.

Spurs had Dimitar Berbatov.

Curled, up, over the wall, over Konchesky on the line, under the crossbar. 3-3. On a ratio of sickening to the quality of the goal, it was up there with Gerrard in Cardiff. Heads in hands everywhere. One point, after all that. All the hard work we had put into this game, and it was going to end with the same result, literally, as we got at home to ****ing Fulham. Still nine points behind with nine games to go. And we'd given so much, played so well. Hard to see how we could come back from this.

There were five added minutes. We poured forward again. We may as well have; we had to win and with the personnel on the pitch it was the only way we could play. A scramble in the Tottenham box fell to Tevez. It was the 93rd minute. He unleashed a powerful right-foot shot, arrowing towards the far corner. Please. Please go in. We deserve this. It went wide. Inches wide, and I mean inches.

The angle behind the goal showed the ball was in for 70 per cent of its journey, before for some stupid reason veering inches wide. Martin Tyler on TV even shouted '*Tevez*' in his 'super special, winning goal that is going to be shown for years' voice. Think '*Agueroooo*' but two levels down. Yeah, that one. But it went wide.

It was the 95th minute. The last added minute. We won a corner. The last chance. 'Please let this corner result in a goal', we all thought. Tevez took it, it was cleared to the edge of the area, but Zamora still had it. The ball had to go straight into the box, where we had at least seven players waiting. But he hesitated for a second. And a Spurs player nipped in and stole the ball. And all of a sudden there were hundreds of them running forward, and we'd only left Konchesky back. Oh God, oh no, oh God. Marlon was busting a gut to get back to help, the ball was with Defoe, with Konch trying to shield him, trying to force him wider.

He shot. Green saved. Thank Christ.

Oh no, he hadn't held it.

Stalteri. 4-3. That's all folks.

Sunday, 4 March 2007:

West Ham 3 *Noble (16), Tevez (41), Zamora (85)*
Tottenham 4 *Defoe pen (51), Tainio (63), Berbatov (89),*
Stalteri (90)

What can you say? Just one of the worst moments I've ever had as a football fan. It felt like I'd been punched in the gut. I know I'm not alone, any West Ham fan, hell, any football fan who cares about their club, would understand how it felt, would empathise. They quite possibly had gone through something similar themselves.

Even on the TV commentary, Tyler and Andy Gray, neither West Ham fans or with any connection to the club, both said 'oh no' as the goal went in. Because anybody could see how much we had put in, how much it meant on the day to players and fans alike, how unbelievably *unfair* it was. Noble left the pitch in tears, Bowyer, Anton, Zamora, Konchesky all nearly joining him. They knew what was to come now. However bad it had got through this season, it was never meant to lead to *this*.

At 6pm on Sunday, 4 March, the league table looked like this:

BOTTOM 7: (04/03/2007)

	P	Pts	GD
Fulham	29	33	-13
Wigan	29	32	-14
Sheffield United	29	31	-16
Manchester City	28	30	-14
Charlton	*29*	*24*	*-23*
Watford	*29*	*20*	*-25*
WEST HAM	*29*	*20*	*-29*

No summing up necessary.

And yet, for the first time in a long time there seemed the slightest bit of hope. Maybe not for this season, but maybe there was an outline of a team that we could build around for the future. I spoke to my dad on the phone for a couple of hours that night, speaking of my hope that maybe Tevez loved us enough to stick around for another year, possibly even until January. Five months of him in the Championship would be too much for anybody else to handle. Ashton too, he wouldn't be able to leave. So Tevez and Ashton up front, Noble in midfield, Green and Neill leading the defence. The stay in the league below would surely be one season and then back up to try and kick back on. I almost felt optimistic, of all things.

Looking back now, the reason for the optimism was clear; that day against Tottenham despite the heartbreak, the West Ham of the previous season, of any successful season I'd witnessed, had returned. We attacked fearlessly, played well, played as a team and Spurs needed outrageous luck to beat us. In truth, they didn't even beat us. We beat ourselves.

So, looking back, maybe there was just a little bit more hope for the last nine games than I realised. The gambler hadn't won the jackpot with his last £1, but he had found another fiver just as he was about to leave the pub.

CHAPTER TEN

March

EVERYONE HAD a gap of 13 days to spend in Heartbreak Hotel on the back of the Tottenham game before we played again. The next match would be back on the road – a trip to Ewood Park to play Blackburn Rovers. Mark Hughes' men went into the game with European aspirations. They sat tenth but were only three points behind Everton in sixth, as part of a clutch of clubs tightly bunched in the upper-mid realm of the table. Two of these clubs were Portsmouth and Reading, with Bolton just above the group in fifth. How times change.

We were the late game that Saturday, 17 March, a 5.30pm kick-off on St Patrick's Night. I'm sure our travelling fans weren't complaining at an extra two-and-a-half hours of the afternoon to celebrate the day in the well-known party streets of, erm, Blackburn.

In acknowledgement of the improved performance against Tottenham, Curbishley only made three changes to the starting line-up rather than the normal five, and two of those were injury related. Upson dropped out but pleasingly was replaced by James Collins, returning from injury after a near-three-month absence, and Reo-Coker had regained full fitness, which meant he replaced the stricken Quashie. The only non-enforced change was McCartney coming back in instead of Konchesky at left-back, which meant the team looked like this:

Starting XI: *Green, Neill, Collins, Ferdinand, McCartney, Bowyer, Reo-Coker, Noble, Etherington, Harewood, Tevez*

Subs: *Walker, Spector, Mullins, Boa Morte, Zamora*

Before I describe the game, an admission: this was the first time in my life that a West Ham game was live on TV and I chose not to watch it. I was still very much in an 'I hate football' phase after the Spurs game, and this match coincided with a Cricket World Cup match in which the massive underdogs of Ireland were chasing a target of 128 to upset Pakistan. I had watched the Irish innings for over an hour prior to our match kicking off and I decided to stick with it. I saw it as a chance to watch a team I wanted to win a sporting contest actually win one. That hadn't happened to me for three months (England's cricket team had been obliterated 5-0 in Australia to lose the Ashes over the time of this season as well). I hang my head in shame, of course.

I didn't miss much over the first 45 minutes, just us hanging on grimly while Morten Gamst Pedersen peppered our goal with attempts, one on the half-hour mark whistling inches wide of the left-hand post with Green well beaten. There was also a near-miss for one of the oddest own goals of all time as Green, who had come out of his area to try and dispossess the on-rushing Jason Roberts, met the forward's cross into the box with his left foot as he was running back towards goal, firing a yard over his own crossbar. If you don't remember it, trust me, a yard lower and it would be regularly shown on social media to this very day.

Our only attacking outlet was Tevez, unsurprisingly. He set up Harewood, who fired a half-chance over the bar and also forced an excellent block from Khizhanishvili, the defender having to throw himself at an effort that looked goalbound. We managed to get into the break scoreless, which again in a vacuum would have been a perfectly acceptable result come full time, a point away at a ground a long way from home against a team in the top half of the table. But as with the Tottenham game, it obviously wasn't enough because of the position we were in.

That position had actually got worse prior to our kick-off, as the 3pm games saw Manchester City win 2-0 at Middlesbrough, which moved them up from 17th to 15th, and dropped Sheffield United into the position one place above the bottom three, with the ever so slight lead of 11 points on us (*11* points. Let's all remember that for later on. Eleven points, with nine games to go). The other result that went against us was Wigan drawing 0-0 at home to Fulham, which took them 13 clear of us prior to the Blackburn encounter.

So clearly, a point wasn't enough here. Three was barely enough, but as it was the most we could get, that was what we had to aim for. So, when man-mountain centre-half Christopher Samba put Blackburn ahead with a thumping header from a Pedersen corner three minutes into the second half, things were looking grim. Even grimmer than they were already, which as we know was pretty bloody grim.

We made a change up front before the hour mark as Zamora replaced the ineffectual Harewood, which at the time didn't look too important, just another shuffling of deckchairs on the *Titanic*. But as we know, it ended up being one of the most pivotal decisions we made all season. With 20 minutes to go, Zamora and Tevez linked up, not for the first time that season but very definitely not the last, the ball got to Tevez wide on the right-hand side of the area, he teased and tormented Brett Emerton, and as he dragged the ball back his back leg was swept away by the Australian. Penalty.

Emerton was predictably 'furious' after the award but it was a clear-cut penalty, however much of an 'injustice' their manager Mark Hughes thought it was. In truth, Emerton was probably embarrassed at being unable to get near the Argentine or the ball for about 15 seconds of play.

Pleasingly, the right decision was made regarding the taker of this penalty. Tevez, bottom right corner, keeper sent the wrong way, easy as you like, 1-1. Carlitos stayed out of the crowd this time but still ran towards them, celebrating with fist pumps while screaming something in Spanish. I like to think it was 'God, I bloody love this club and whatever happens I will do the crossed Hammers sign to you lot every time I ever play against West Ham ever again'. That's what I like to think, anyway.

While Tevez was celebrating and professing his everlasting love to the club, the rest of the players led by Neill ran back to our half to kick off again. The work for the day was not done. We got the ball almost straight from kick-off and went back to attacking. A Bowyer cross was met by Collins, whose header was turned over the bar by Friedel, a decent save but one a goalkeeper worth his salt would always expect to make.

From the resulting corner, chaos ensued. A scramble just outside the six-yard box ended with a shot hitting Zamora, completely unmarked. His improvised flick was blocked by Friedel, who while saving also diverted it wide of an incoming Tevez, who was looking to tap the rebound home. The ball, however, did come back to Bobby, whose curling effort this time beat the big American in goal and hit the jumping Tevez on the line. Brilliant.

He had tried to get his feet out of the way, jumping with one of them actually going over the line, but the ball very clearly did not. For God's sake. The linesman appeared to have seen it as well as he was waving frantically, presumably to give offside.

Or, for reasons known only to Mr Linesman, he was waving to give a goal.

Yes, a goal. Despite the ball not crossing the line and clearly hitting a player in an offside position, a goal was given. The best reason I can give for the decision was Tevez wearing white boots, and as he jumped the linesman may have seen a flash of white go behind the line. I'm aware that's a reach, but I've got nothing else. This was the third such example in a game involving West Ham this season of officials appearing not to know the basic rules of the game, but this time it had benefitted us rather than hurt us.

Still 15 minutes to play, though, and let's face it, we knew panic would ensue. Blackburn would probably miss a couple of good chances before equalising, and then probably win it in the 103rd minute with a cross deflecting off seven of our players, two of our fans, Curbishley and Herbie the Hammer, before hitting Green in the head, knocking him unconscious and dribbling into the net. Fair to say reliving this season is getting to me at this point, dear reader.

But then something odd happened. The 15 minutes drifted by, injury time passed, and we erm, won. By two goals to one. Professionally, comfortably, we saw the game out. And I'll repeat, *won* the game, *away* from home. We hadn't won an away game all season, and we were the last of the 92 Football League clubs to do so. But we had done it now, with a minimum of fuss after the craziness of the 'ghost goal', as it was fashionable to call these things in this era.

Curbs was unsurprisingly on good form post-match, particularly regarding his opinion of said winning goal. 'I don't think it's over the line – but I'll take it! I've seen the incident and I don't care. It hasn't gone over the line from what I can tell, but we've not had the best of luck. I'm delighted because that's the first time we've managed to hold on for a long while, but in the end we made our own luck. It's a great three points, and it ain't all over yet.'

Bobby Zamora said similar in his interview with the TV cameras after the game when told his goal shouldn't have stood. 'Too bad! It's three points now, that's all that matters, and any other striker would say the same. In our position, we will take it and we definitely feel we can still stay up. There are still points to be had and we are going to give it everything we've got until the end.'

So, fair to say the long overdue win on the road had given the players hope, publicly at least. Me, not so much. I was delighted that we'd won the game, for the fans who'd been going to away matches all season and had put up with so much, but I couldn't see it affecting the end result particularly. There was still so much that would need to be done for there to be even the slightest chance, and although the next game at home to Middlesbrough looked winnable, there was the small matter of a trip to the Emirates the week after that we'd need a result in as well, which I just couldn't see happening. Even if that miracle happened, games with Chelsea, Bolton, Everton and a last-day trip to Old Trafford still loomed in the background.

We clearly looked a different proposition suddenly with an in-form Tevez, Neill at the back and players returning from injuries, but I still saw it all as too little, too late. We were off the bottom now, but still eight points behind with eight games to go. Charlton in 18th kept their four-point lead over us by beating Newcastle

2-0, and they still looked a far more likely side to claw themselves to safety than we did.

Saturday, 17 March 2007:

Blackburn 1 *Samba (47)*

West Ham 2 *Tevez pen (71), Zamora (75)*

BOTTOM 7: (18/03/2007)

	P	Pts	GD
Fulham	30	34	-13
Manchester City	29	33	-12
Wigan	30	33	-14
Sheffield United	30	31	-19
Charlton	*30*	*27*	*-21*
WEST HAM	*30*	*23*	*-28*
Watford	*30*	*20*	*-27*

We had another two-week break before the next game, with Gareth Southgate's Boro side making the long trip to the Boleyn Ground. The starting 11 pleasingly showed just one change from the win at Ewood Park, always a sign that things are improving, with Zamora's reward for the winner in that game being a starting berth in place of Harewood.

This game is a very odd one to write about, as it is the first time I have had an opportunity to describe a match like this in this entire book. It was a comfortable, routine win for West Ham.

No last-minute winners with managers clashing on the touchline, no randomly beating Manchester United, no winning goals that didn't go anywhere near over the line, none of that. We just played well, came up against a team that didn't play well at all, and comfortably took the points.

We started the game with something that we hadn't managed all season long; a goal in the opening ten minutes. The afternoon was only two minutes old, in fact, when a crunching tackle from Noble on Rochemback led to the ball falling to Tevez; the Argentine drove to the byline and pulled it back for Zamora to lash us into the lead. An early goal for any team is a massive boost, but for a team in a relegation scrap they are nigh on gold dust, and this was no exception. We held on to the lead with comfort as the game progressed, and as injury time at the end of the first half began, we doubled the advantage.

A cross-shot from Zamora was palmed away by Schwarzer in the Middlesbrough goal but only as far as McCartney, whose cross hit their defender Taylor and fell perfectly for the irrepressible Tevez, who tucked the ball home for his third goal in three games, the same scoring run as his strike partner.

Two up at half-time, then, and like Blackburn two weeks previously, now the worry came on strong that we would mess it up; the scars of Tottenham, Fulham and Newcastle before that still at the forefront of people's minds. But just like Blackburn two weeks previously, the collapse didn't come. We managed the game effectively throughout the second 45, limiting the Teessiders to a header apiece from the, erm, beefy strike partnership of Yakubu and Viduka, and just the one shot on target during the whole game. Indeed the best chance of the half fell to us and Boa Morte in particular, who when clean through shot straight at Schwarzer. It was a slight worry that the attacking midfielder we had bought to score goals still hadn't scored any, but we were still sure they would come in time – I think.

We won 2-0, a second consecutive victory and hope among Hammers fans was beginning to grow. In addition to the positives I listed after the Blackburn game, Noble had been outstanding in the middle of the park, producing a man of the match-level display, Collins and McCartney also had excellent games at the back, and for the first time all season we looked a good side all over the pitch, with positives throughout the team.

Saturday, 31 March 2007:
West Ham 2 *Zamora (2), Tevez (45)*
Middlesbrough 0

A personal memory of this game for me is that while it was taking place, I was aware of absolutely none of it. The game took place while I was on an aeroplane with my brother Michael travelling to America, the two of us fulfilling an ambition we'd had since we were little kids to go and watch Wrestlemania. I will spare you a complete rundown of the card, as I assume if you're interested in the great sport (yes, sport) of professional wrestling you probably already know what most of the matches were. But I will share a couple of stories regarding the trip and promise to do my best to keep them as non-geeky as possible, never fear.

Firstly, even though the show was in Detroit, I found out the good news of our second win in succession in a hotel room in Philadelphia. We hadn't got ridiculously lost, we'd just missed our connecting flight from Philly to Detroit due to us taking off two hours late from London. While normally this wouldn't be too much of an issue, the fact that this was on Saturday and the show was the following day made it a bit of a problem.

There were only three planes travelling to Detroit on Sunday morning that we could get and still make the show in time, so we had a nervous wait ahead of us. We arrived back at the airport first thing on Sunday morning from the hotel that had been provided for us by the airline and waited. The first plane was full so tough luck, but the second looked pretty good. Five minutes before last call and there were still at least 20 people with tickets who hadn't turned up for the flight, so this seemed a formality. A couple of minutes later, we were beckoned to the front and were getting ready to receive our tickets when, I kid you not, the Detroit under-15 girls' swimming team ran around the corner and straight past us in the queue. They had every remaining seat booked for themselves. It was like my life had become a bad American sitcom.

Thankfully, we did manage to get on the next flight and made it to the arena, Ford Field in Central Detroit, with an hour to spare. As I said, I will spare you the blow-by-blow details of the show, but I will share that it was the only time in my life that I have ever seen an American president, as one of the performers that night would go on to be the man in the White House.

Now I won't lie, had I been told that night that this would be the case and was asked to guess who said performer would be, Donald Trump wouldn't have made my top five. Or top ten for that matter. But he did, and he was indeed involved in Wrestlemania 23, as he managed Bobby Lashley to a victory over 'The Samoan Savage' Umaga, which meant that Trump got to shave Vince McMahon's head in this special 'Battle of the Billionaires' match. He was even the recipient of a 'Stone Cold Stunner' from guest ref 'Stone Cold' Steve Austin after the match. His hair stayed on throughout. Personally, I think President Austin, or President Undertaker seemed much more realistic at the time. Part of me still does.

(On that note, and wildly off topic, trust me on this prediction, The Rock (Dwayne Johnson) will be president of the United States of America one day. When it happens, remember that you read it here first. Tell people that you read the prediction in a book about West Ham's 2006/07 season. And amuse yourself with their confusion.)

Meanwhile, while I was knocking around in hotels and airports in Philadelphia trying to get to Detroit, back in east London Curbs was crowing about the performance and the result and growing in belief about our chances of survival, while being aware of the mountain there was still to climb. 'We're still alive, two results on the spin has been great for us. I think the results today have put a little bit more pressure on the teams above us, so we've got to keep going and see what happens in the end.

'But we've got to win some games. We've been saying that for the last couple of weeks, and we've won a couple. The way we played in the first half was terrific, we looked very confident. Can we take that on into our next game? We've still got to win the majority of our games.'

Regarding the other results that weekend, we had a good news/bad news scenario from the Valley, which saw Charlton win a game in the last five minutes through a Darren Bent penalty (bad), but the recipients of said late goal were Wigan (good). Sheffield United also lost again to Bolton thanks to a Kevin Davies goal ten minutes from time, and no other side in the bottom seven were victorious.

This meant that for the first time in months, a genuine battle for survival looked to be developing. At this stage, it still looked as if it would be one from Charlton, Sheffield United and Wigan to complete the bottom three, but with the gap to 17th now five points with seven games remaining, we were possibly just one more win from forcing ourselves into that conversation, albeit on the periphery. All we had to do was win our next game. Away from home, which we had just managed to do for the first time in ten months. Against Arsenal, at the Emirates Stadium. They hadn't lost a game there yet. They hadn't lost a home game to *anybody* for 14 months. Cool.

BOTTOM 7: (02/04/2007)

	P	Pts	GD
Aston Villa	31	35	-6
Fulham	31	35	-13
Wigan	31	33	-15
Sheffield United	31	31	-20
Charlton	*31*	*30*	*-20*
WEST HAM	*31*	*26*	*-26*
Watford	*31*	*20*	*-28*

Aston Villa. Dinamo Zagreb. Middlesbrough. Sheffield United. Porto. Watford. Everton. CSKA Moscow. Liverpool. Newcastle. Hamburg. Tottenham. Portsmouth. Blackburn. Charlton. Manchester United. Bolton. Wigan. Blackburn again. Reading. PSV Eindhoven.

These were the teams who had visited the Emirates Stadium to play Arsenal in the seven months since it had been opened. None of those teams had left with a victory. As we turned up as the 21st different opponents for the Gunners in their new home, we did so knowing that their record thus far was 21 matches played (Blackburn twice, don't forget), 12 wins and nine draws.

In addition, you can add the names of Bolton, Charlton, Liverpool, Aston Villa, West Brom, Tottenham and Wigan as teams who had played at the old Highbury since Arsenal had last been beaten at a ground they called home. That is 28 matches in total. That is impressive by any standard, at any time.

But all West Ham fans remember who the opposition was when they *did* last lose at home. As I mentioned earlier, it was Alan Pardew's claret and blue army, with an action-packed smash and grab of a 3-2 win 431 days prior. Could lightning strike twice in sort of but not quite the same place with a different Alan?

The day before we ventured to north London, we saw Alan Pardew's red and white army grind out a goalless draw at Man City, which took Charlton up above Sheffield United on goal difference and out of the relegation zone, five points clear of us in 19th. While the previous two results had meant that if we were added to the list of unsuccessful visiting sides to the Emirates it wouldn't be curtains for our hopes, with only six games to come after this we would be running out of time to make up that five-point gap.

In his pre-match press conference, Curbishley was oddly dripping with confidence – clearly the back-to-back wins had reminded him of why he wanted to be a football manager in the first place. He admitted that he 'fancied' the game, stating, 'I know Arsenal are a top side, but it's another game that we've got an opportunity to win – and that's what we're going to try and do. We have to win the majority of our games; we have to go for it. If we can get anything against Arsenal, it will take us into another big game against Sheffield United. We know we've got to win as many games as we can, so why can't we go and get a win at the Emirates?' Somebody put the man in a cold shower, he's got far too carried away.

Curbs briefly stopped checking how many points we were off a Champions League place to name an unchanged starting 11 from the Middlesbrough game. Completely the right decision as this was our best 11 by a mile at this stage. We finally seemed to have the spine of a team in place. Ferdinand and Collins looked an effective pair, particularly with Neill marshalling them from right-back, Noble and Reo-Coker in midfield formed a duo that combined hard work with tough tackling and endeavour (how had it taken until March for Noble to be considered?), and Tevez and Zamora up front were playing with confidence, cohesiveness and most importantly, goalscoring threat. So, we were all excited for Arsenal to rip all this to pieces.

You may remember when I briefly described the victory at Highbury earlier in this book, I mentioned that Arsenal absolutely pasted us in the early stages of that match. Well, the first ten minutes of this one made any West Ham supporter watching yearn for the glory days of only being battered that badly.

The Gunners' most recent outing had been a 4-1 spanking at Anfield, one of two consecutive defeats up on Merseyside after a loss to Everton prior to that, and they had clearly decided we were to be the recipients of the dreaded 'backlash' that bigger teams so often dish out to smaller rivals after a setback or two. And not only had they decided that the backlash was coming, it was to be dished out as quickly as possible.

Two minutes in, Fabregas clean through, just past the post. Shortly after, Adebayor headed wide when he should have done better. Six minutes in, Ljungberg was put clean through only for Green to speed from his line and make a very good save. Our keeper then made a smart stop from another Fabregas effort after intelligent play from Rosicky before Adebayor blazed over from inside the box after Ljungberg cut the ball back to him.

This all happened in the first ten minutes. Ten minutes, seven shots, four on target. But somehow no goals. We got through an onslaught to end all onslaughts unscathed.

The relentlessness of the attacks abated slightly, but still the chances came; Green made another fine save from a Rosicky snap shot, Ljungberg slid in to try and turn a cross home but missed the ball by inches, a cute chip from Fabregas was well saved, Adebayor tried one pass too many when in a one-on-one situation with the overworked keeper, but somehow we kept the scoreboard blank through a mix of profligate finishing, brave blocks from our defenders, Collins in particular, and nigh on perfection in goal from Green.

As the first half went into stoppage time, we were obviously desperate to finish the half without conceding, so when Lucas Neill found himself with the rare luxury of a moment on the ball midway inside our half, rather than doing anything too flashy he played what would best be described as a 'percentage' ball up to Zamora, who had been ploughing a lone furrow up front, with Tevez coming back into midfield to try and help stem the tide.

The long pass was likely only played with the aim to buy the defence some time before the half-time whistle, but somehow evaded the back-pedalling Toure and found our lonesome front man, who looked up and saw Lehmann too far off his line, so lifted it over him and into the net. Simple as that. With one of the two shots we'd had in the entire half, we had somehow gone 1-0 up.

Watching the score updates at home on *Soccer Saturday*, hearing the shout of 'goal' from one of the pundits, I swore loudly at nobody in particular. What good it did I have no idea as I was sitting by myself, but I was furious that all the hanging on had been for nothing. Your team never scores in those situations, do they? They concede. So when the news came through that we were actually 1-0 *up*, not 1-0 down, it was lucky I was sitting down as I would have fallen over otherwise.

I was on duty to keep my dad updated with goals that day as he was away on holiday, so I rang him intending to give him a detailed breakdown of the goal. But when he answered, I just shouted '*Zamora*' at the top of my lungs instead. I think he understood what I was talking about. It couldn't be denied now, there was hope. Real genuine hope, for the first time in God knows how long. Probably since the Harewood penalty against Watford, although it felt like much longer than that.

We just needed to coast through another 45 minutes, much like we had the first 45. Sort of.

Early in the second half came Robert Green's best save of the afternoon, and good Lord there were enough contenders. A shot from Gilberto from just outside the area was dipping into the keeper's right-hand corner. Ninety-nine times out of 100 the net would have bulged, but not on this day, against this man. Somehow, some way, he got down to the effort, got enough of a right hand behind the ball and turned it away for a corner. Gilberto was stood open-mouthed at not being able to celebrate an equaliser, and I'm sure he wasn't the only one in the stadium. Not long after that, our walking miracle of a keeper could celebrate another great stop, as he thrust out his left arm to block Adebayor's header from point-blank range after a Hleb free kick.

As time ticked down, Green was finally beaten by an Arsenal effort as a fantastic 20-plus yard hit from Fabregas whistled past the stopper, only to smash against the crossbar before being hacked clear. Then Gilberto hit the post with a left-footed shot, which we scrambled away. Aliadiere was put through on goal but couldn't beat the keeper, who smothered the effort.

Finally, a free kick from Fabregas was firmly met in the six-yard box by the head of Gilberto, who inexplicably nodded wide of the post. This sentence is used a lot in football but it was honest to God harder to head the ball wide than into the net from where he was, stood in the centre of the goal six yards out.

That chance seemed to knock the stuffing out of Arsenal's players, fans, and management as Wenger sat with that bemused look he would often wear when his charges have the majority or all of the play but fail to find an end product. Miraculously, we held out for the most unlikely, the most unfancied, the most unexplainable of 1-0 victories. We even had a great chance to make it 2-0 at the death as Boa Morte clipped a right-footed shot over Lehmann and wide with the goal at his mercy, but we were getting used to him missing chances like that at this point. Also, best we don't get greedy.

Arsenal finished the game having had 35, yes *thirty-five*, shots on goal across the 90 minutes, 11 of which were on target, in addition to 14 corners to our solitary set play. But we did it. We held on and became the first team to beat Arsenal at their new stadium, having been the last away team to be victorious at their old stadium. The rarest of doubles right there, and one that Gooners fans are still reminded of every time we play them to this day.

When Robert Green retired in 2019, in media interviews he referenced this game as his greatest ever performance, and I am sure that anybody who saw it or remembers it would agree.

The good news kept coming as well, as both Sheffield United and Wigan were beaten again; the Blades lost 2-1 at home to Newcastle thanks to a Steven Taylor header ten minutes from time, and the Latics surrendered a 1-0 lead at home to Bolton, going down 3-1. The gap was now only two points after their losses and our third win in a row, and second away win in succession (after nearly a year without one), and incredibly a win at Bramall Lane seven days later would take us above Neil Warnock's side and maybe even out of the bottom three.

Curbishley was delighted after the game and understandably full of praise for his goalkeeper. 'We've come here very confident on the back of two results but the way they [Arsenal] came out at the start of the first half was fantastic, so great credit to them. But Greeny stood firm. People will say that they missed some chances; I'd tend to say Greeny saved them, with some good defending. He kept us in the game, and we always had a chance then. When you play anyone in the top four, you need your goalkeeper to get ten out of ten, perhaps 11 or 12 out of ten, and Greeny has done that today.' Not often that a rating of 12 out of ten is accurate, but I think it was the case here.

Green himself was typically modest about his display when interviewed about it for the club website later that week. 'There was a lot of work for me but the game went so quickly [that] I don't recall much from it. But that is what I am there for and I was pleased to make the saves. Last week we played Middlesbrough and I don't think I had a save to make, but I had my fair share this week. It was just one of them days where we had a defensive unit that threw bodies in the way.

'We scored at the right time, which gave us that bit more belief. It was a great day for everyone involved at the club.'

Saturday, 7 April 2006:
Arsenal 0
West Ham 1 *Zamora (45)*

Two days later, Easter Monday saw three of our rivals in action again. Wigan earned a creditable 1-1 draw at Villa Park and Charlton played out a scoreless draw with Reading, while Fulham, who seemed to be imploding, were beaten 3-1 at home by Manchester City. This was enough to earn their manager Chris Coleman his P45 and presumably a good luck card from his friend Boa Morte; he was replaced by Northern Ireland manager and David Healy's biggest fan Lawrie Sanchez on an initial caretaker basis.

BOTTOM 6: (09/04/2007)

	P	Pts	GD
Fulham	33	35	-18
Wigan	33	34	-17
Charlton	33	32	-20
Sheffield United	*32*	*31*	*-21*
WEST HAM	*32*	*29*	*-25*
Watford	*33*	*23*	*-29*

CHAPTER ELEVEN

April

A WEEK later, we were back on the road and travelling north to Sheffield for what was now a critical game in the battle for survival against Neil Warnock's Sheffield United. It was 18th v 19th, an archetypal dogfight of a game. The Blades had taken only one point from their last five games, establishing what at one stage was an 11-point lead over us that had now been whittled down to just two. In truth, because of the lost lead this was probably more of a must-win game for them than it was us, but for us it was an absolute must-not-lose. Knowing the games we still had to come, a draw and a two-point disadvantage could possibly still be overturned. Five points would be almost back to needing snookers again.

We knew that we would face a metaphorical bear pit at Bramall Lane. This was a huge game for the home side and they knew it, and one thing for certain with Warnock was that he never had a problem using the right words and phrases to get a crowd baying for blood when it was needed most. This was proven correct as the game was played in front of a thunderous crowd. They didn't boo Tevez much, though, beyond the general 'frantic booing when you know the other team's best forward player has the ball' abuse that happens when people such as Ronaldo, Rooney etc get the ball. Odd that they didn't see him as a cheat or what have you at this point.

We named an unchanged team for the third straight match and began the game looking for a fourth win on the bounce. My dad and I had found a pub in east London that was showing the game and sat down to watch with real optimism that the run could continue and we could find ourselves on the brink of getting out of the drop zone by 5pm. What we ended up watching was essentially a 'greatest hits' compilation of things we had done wrong throughout the season, in one not-so-glorious 90-minute period.

The first 40 minutes or so passed by with the typical scrappy play that these games so often produce at the business end of the season, with once chance apiece for the two teams; Tevez curling over the bar from just outside the box and Kazim-Richards missing a great chance for the hosts, volleying wide from Gillespie's cross.

Then shortly before half-time, the oh-so-crucial first goal arrived. Ferdinand conceded a free kick just outside the area, for which he very conceivably could have been sent off, bringing down Nade 20 yards from goal having been booked for dissent no more than two minutes prior. Due punishment did arrive, though, as Michael Tonge absolutely blasted the ball into the top corner. Green had no chance, but I dare say if he'd got a hand to it his arm would have ended up in the net with the ball, such was the ferocity of the strike.

So, having gone 1-0 down as we had done so often this season, we started the second half creating chances, and not taking them. As I said earlier, this game was a real flashback to the multitude of bad days that we had seen prior to the spring revival. Tevez led a swift counter attack that ended with Lucas Neill of all people being free in the area 15 yards from goal, but his left-footed shot was magnificently saved by Paddy Kenny in the United goal. Kenny was no doubt eager to exact revenge for the misery he had endured in the reverse fixture the previous November. Shortly after that chance came an even better one for Tevez, but the Argentinian wizard returned to the misfiring striker in front of goal that we had seen earlier in the campaign, as he shot over from eight yards out with the goal at his mercy.

And again, as had happened earlier in the season, we were punished for our missed chances. It happened from a corner unsurprisingly as Jagielka leapt unchallenged to head past Green and all but seal the points for the Blades. With 12 minutes to go, Jon Stead turned Ferdinand inside out and curled the ball past Green to make it 3-0, and just like that it felt like the previous month's good work all counted for nothing.

We fell back to five points behind Sheffield United with only five games to play. Realistically, whatever we did now two wins seemed as if they would be enough for Warnock and his side to celebrate staying up in their first season back in the big time. They had the fixtures to do it as well, with trips to Aston Villa and Charlton along with home games against Watford and Wigan. All they had to do was not be as awful as we had been in the corresponding fixtures and their job was done.

Our remaining five games looked very different indeed. We had to play four of the current top six, including Manchester United on the last day and Chelsea four days later.

I know whose situation I would rather have been in.

Curbishley wasn't quite in despair in his press conference after the game, but clearly knew what a blow we had suffered. 'It was a big game with a lot at stake and Sheffield United got the points. I think the scoreline was a bit flattering.

'The first goal was always going to be important and they got it. But we came out in the second half and had three good opportunities to equalise, which would have changed the shape of the game – but we didn't take them and paid the price.'

Warnock was predictably delighted and full of fire post-match, taking the media to task for daring to suggest that two teams with significantly better form than his charges may have ended up catching them. 'We knew it was an important game. I don't think there was anything significant in the result other than we showed we are still very much in it after people had written us off over the last few weeks.

'I think the media have presumed both West Ham and Charlton would finish above us. But we have brought other teams into it now, which we wanted to do, and I don't think anybody can say who is safe and who is not. But we have given ourselves a fighting chance. We won as a team and we thoroughly deserved it. I thought we looked a Premiership side out there today.'

Odd that he didn't mention how unfair it was that Tevez played, and he shouldn't have been allowed, and they were cheated blah blah blah. He must have been saving that for later. Surely it was a world ending-level problem for him at this point and not just at the end of the season? How strange.

Saturday, 14 April 2007:

Sheffield United 3 *Tonge (39), Jagielka (68), Stead (78)*

West Ham 0

BOTTOM 6: (15/04/2007)

	P	Pts	GD
Fulham	34	35	-17
Wigan	34	35	-19
Sheffield United	33	34	-18
Charlton	*34*	*32*	*-21*
WEST HAM	*33*	*29*	*-28*
Watford	*33*	*23*	*-29*

The league table above includes two slices of luck that we were handed in the televised *Super Sunday* games as first Wigan managed to blow a one-goal lead not once, not twice, but three times at home to Spurs, with two Robbie Keane goals contributing to a 3-3 draw, and then

Charlton having their hearts broken at Goodison Park in a ridiculous last ten minutes.

Having gone 1-0 down to a Joleon Lescott goal in the 81st minute, it seemed as if they'd saved a priceless point when Darren Bent equalised in stoppage time. Celebrations were wild on and off the pitch, Pards was going crazy on the touchline (no reggae dance yet, though, that was a few years away) and it was clear how big this goal was to everyone involved with the club. An unexpected point at a top-half team's ground, achieved in the most dramatic and uplifting of ways.

So when Everton went straight up the other end and scored through James McFadden in the 93rd minute, the despair snatched from the jaws of salvation was up there with our loss to Spurs the previous month. Pardew looked utterly devastated at the end of the game and it was hard to see how the manager and his players could recover from the cruellest of defeats. It was a challenge that they would fail to accomplish; Charlton would not win another game that season.

We only had four days to recover from the disappointment in Sheffield before Jose Mourinho brought the reigning champions across London, looking to hammer another nail into our relegation coffin while also keeping their hopes of a third consecutive league title alive. The Blues were six points behind Manchester United at the time after the Reds had done us a favour by beating Sheffield United 2-0 the night before, and needed to win this game to close the gap back to three points with four games to go. We needed the points just as much, for reasons that we are all aware of at this point.

There did seem a window of opportunity, however. Mourinho's men were only three days removed from a bruising extra-time victory against Blackburn in an FA Cup semi-final, and the starting 11 chosen by 'The Special One' reflected that, with five alterations from the battle with Mark Hughes' men. The team chosen in response by Curbishley showed three injury-enforced changes from the defeat at Bramall Lane, as Ferdinand, Etherington and Bowyer all missed out, which saw Benayoun and Boa Morte come in on the flanks and Spector picked to play right-back, with Neill moving to centre-back to partner Collins. Davenport was only on the bench, which as a specialist centre-half must have been quite the confidence boost for him, as well as a glowing recommendation of his performances while he was in the side.

Whether Chelsea were tired or not, this was clearly a mammoth task to get anything against one of the strongest Chelsea sides, if not *the* strongest Chelsea side of the past 20 years. Cech, Terry, Lampard, Drogba, Makelele, Ballack etc; squads didn't come much stronger than that, before or since. Or more dislikeable, come to think of it. To get a result, we would need a raucous crowd, which we got, a committed and spirited performance, which we got, and Chelsea to have an off night, which we didn't.

What we got wasn't a poor Chelsea performance and a much-needed victory, but a very good Chelsea performance and a routine defeat. Previous transfer target Shaun Wright-Phillips rubbed our noses in it with two first-half goals, the first from a wonderful turn and feint that beat Spector and Collins in one move before he curled the ball into the far corner, and the second an excellent volleyed finish that came 30 seconds after a long-range effort from Tevez had levelled the game for us. The brief equalising goal to be fair was more due to an error from Cech, who failed to palm away a bread-and-butter shot for a goalkeeper of his quality, rather than any brilliance from the Argentine on this occasion.

Second-half goals from Kalou and Drogba ended the game as a contest after 62 minutes, and the game meandered to a 4-1 defeat, one which kept the gap to safety at five points, with now only four games to go.

Wednesday, 18 April 2007:

West Ham 1 *Tevez (35)*

Chelsea 4 *Wright-Phillips (31, 36), Kalou (52), Drogba (62)*

BOTTOM 6: (18/04/2007)

	P	Pts	GD
Wigan	34	35	-17
Fulham	34	35	-19
Sheffield United	34	34	-20
Charlton	34	32	-21
WEST HAM	34	29	-31
Watford	34	23	-31

After the second loss in four days, Curbs was disappointed but still believed the escape could happen. 'We will keep going. This could go right to the end, but for it to do that we need to do what we did recently and put three wins together. In the first half, we were excellent and I think the fans appreciated that. We had our chances, equalised and then could have equalised again, but you have to take your chances against Chelsea because they are a top side.

'It is not because of this game that we are where we are. We have lost big games against the teams around us.

'We don't need a miracle. We need to win football matches.'

At this point, the manager may have been the last person who still didn't think we needed a miracle. The run of three straight wins had kept us in with a mathematical chance, but a look at the table opposite shows how monumentally difficult the task now was.

We had four games remaining. Because of our awful goal difference, we needed a minimum of six points to overhaul Sheffield United. A minimum.

We needed a minimum of seven points to catch Wigan or Fulham, and for that to happen they had to lose all their four games. Five points for either side and we couldn't finish above them. Also, Sheffield United still had Charlton and Wigan to play, the latter at home on the final day, so we knew that at least two of the teams would have to pick up points.

Even if we managed nine points from the four games and went above two of Sheffield United, Fulham or

Wigan, two wins from Charlton would keep them above us and we would go down anyway.

Basically, to have any chance at all we needed at least nine points from four games.

Those four games were at home to Everton and Bolton, who on the night we lost to Chelsea were fifth and sixth respectively and battling for the European qualification places. The away games were at Wigan, where we also knew that a loss there would make it virtually impossible to catch them, and on the final day of the season, at Old Trafford against Manchester United, who might well need a result themselves to win the league.

To sum up, at the very least nine points were required from four games, three of which were against the top six, having won eight games and taken 29 points from 34 games all season up to this point.

Curbishley was partly right, we needed to win football matches. But he was also partly wrong. We very definitely needed a miracle.

CHAPTER TWELVE

The Last Four Games

THE FIRST stop on the long and unlikely road to safety was a home match against Everton. David Moyes' men were significantly closer to full strength than in the corresponding fixture in December, when they had beaten us with essentially half a team.

To that point, there was quite a level of irony that these fixtures against Everton, Wigan and Bolton, in which we now needed nine points to have any chance of survival, were the final run of games for Pardew five months previously, where a haul of zero points and zero goals in the reverse fixtures cost him his job.

As I mentioned, the Blues arrived for the game on an eight-match unbeaten run and sitting a very creditable fifth in the league, level on points with Bolton in sixth and six points clear of Reading in seventh. The sizeable gap to the Royals in seventh meant they were aware that six to nine points from their four final games would virtually guarantee European football, and it wasn't unrealistic for them to assume that three of these points were there for the taking in a game against the 19th-ranked team in the league at this stage.

As I said, Everton were far nearer full strength for this encounter, with only Tim Cahill missing of their main names. Mikel Arteta, Andy Johnson, Joleon Lescott and Leon Osman all started, whereas only Johnson and Osman of that quartet played in December.

We lined up with two changes from the Chelsea game, as Ferdinand and Etherington were both fit and replaced Spector and Boa Morte. We also oddly didn't name a goalkeeper among the five substitutes, as Curbishley wanted the maximum number of outfield options on the bench just in case. The full 16 for the game was as follows:

Starting XI: *Green, Neill, Collins, Ferdinand, McCartney, Benayoun, Reo-Coker, Noble, Etherington, Zamora, Tevez*
Subs: *Spector, Davenport, Mullins, Boa Morte, Cole*

The opening minutes of the game were quiet and devoid of any incident, which was quite surprising given our desperation for victory. This need was given a massive boost, though, in the seventh minute when an innocuous-looking collision between Reo-Coker and Johnson left the England striker unable to continue. Everton had no recognised forwards on the bench so winger James McFadden, fresh from breaking Charlton's hearts, was brought on in his place and a change in formation to a five-man midfield was necessitated.

Within five minutes of the restart while the reorganisation in approach was still being worked out by Moyes' men, we went and scored a bloody goal.

And what a goal it was.

Neill, Benayoun and Zamora were partaking in some fairly aimless keep-ball on the right-hand side, the ball was worked to the Israeli, who moved inside, still appearing to have no real plan of what we were going to do with this specific attack. He did a natty little backheel to Zamora and began jogging to the centre of the pitch, I assume expecting a return pass and hopefully a few more options to pass to than he'd had thus far. Bobby Z, clearly bored by this aimless play, collected the ball, took one touch with his right and absolutely smashed the thing into the top-right corner.

It was a stunning strike and looked so effortless it made you wonder why he didn't just do it every time he got the ball. It was such a good goal he even celebrated it with other players rather than run off pushing them out of the way looking furious, always the mark of an excellent Zamora goal. It was the forward's fifth goal in six games, bookending the season with two marvellous runs of form after his hot streak at the beginning of the campaign as well. These scoring runs, added to a goal of that quality, made the drought in the middle of the season look even more baffling, but thank God this run arrived when it did. We were sunk without it.

Shortly after that goal, Lucas Neill very nearly did a passable impression of the wonder strike, a left-footed curling effort from the right-back whistling just wide of the very same upright. At the other end James Beattie, without a goal in open play all season, missed two half-chances to end that drought against us, which no doubt every person in the crowd aware of the stat was thoroughly expecting to happen.

One of those half-chances caused a moment that led to every Hammers fan, and I dare say a few of the players, having their hearts in their mouths. Not because of a near miss, but because one of said chances led to Green coming out of goal and claiming the ball just ahead of Beattie, who in the resulting challenge accidentally dislocated the goalkeeper's finger. Remember, we had no back-up keeper on the bench.

As the physio came on to attend to Green, groans echoed around the ground. This was going to be the comedic punchline to end this most farcical of seasons. I have no idea who would have replaced the keeper in goal. After the match, Curbishley said that one of his staff had suggested 'Ludo', a reference to our then-goalkeeping coach and former playing legend Ludek Miklosko (from somewhere near Moscow from what I understand).

Thankfully Green managed to pop his finger back into its socket and play on through the pain, so we never got to see Calum Davenport, Lucas Neill or whoever it would have been play in goal for an hour in a Premier League match.

And that, somewhat surprisingly, is pretty much all there is to write about for this game. Everton looked toothless without Johnson; indeed they failed to fashion a single shot on target through the 90 minutes. Two efforts wide from Arteta in the second half, one with nine minutes to go in particular that he really should have done better with, were the only chances they created worthy of the name. For once in this season (and quite honestly this could apply to so many other seasons in my time supporting this club), we didn't decide to give a team offering nothing going forward an easy chance on goal through a balls-up of our own making.

Referee Mark Clattenburg tried to mess with us by adding six minutes on for no real reason, but we even saw those out with an odd degree of comfort for a 1-0 win that, were it not so precious, would be forgotten by all involved with it about a week later.

Saturday, 21 April 2007:
West Ham 1 *Zamora (13)*
Everton 0

Step one was complete. The results around the country were favourable to us as well, as our two main rivals Charlton and Sheffield United drew 1-1 at the Valley, Wigan were beaten 2-0 at Anfield and Fulham were held to a draw at home to Blackburn; they hadn't won in nine games and had tasted victory only once in their last 17 matches. Lastly, Watford were mathematically relegated after a 1-1 draw at home to Manchester City; they only won one further match after their win at Upton Park, continuing to prove how utterly terrible we had been for so much of the previous nine months.

BOTTOM 6: (21/04/2007)

	P	Pts	GD
Fulham	35	36	-19
Wigan	35	35	-19
Sheffield United	35	35	-20
Charlton	*35*	*33*	*-21*
WEST HAM	*35*	*32*	*-30*
Watford	*35*	*24*	*-31*

Curbishley displayed the necessary optimism in his post-game press conference after the victory but was aware of how much work still needed to be done. 'Once again we have beaten a top-six side, but now we have got to go to Wigan next week and get a result against one of the teams around us. We've given ourselves a chance, but at quarter-to-five next week it can all change round. That's what I said in the dressing room.'

So, the gap was now down to three points but again with the disparity in goal difference, we still needed four more points than Wigan or Sheffield United and had only three games to do it. The game at Wigan was now monumental; a victory and we would go level on points with them, all to play for with two, albeit still very difficult, games to go. A loss, however, coupled with Sheffield United beating Watford on the same day and with the goal difference, would mean we would be all but mathematically relegated.

Prior to the battle at the JJB Stadium, West Ham would be facing another very difficult battle: one in front of a Premier League tribunal. The hearing for alleged improprieties regarding the Tevez and Mascherano signings was, finally, going to take place.

On 27 April, three months since the issue had come to light and only 16 days before the end of the Premier League season, as well as the day before a critical game not only for ourselves but also for Wigan Athletic, the Premier League had finally got around to deciding what punishment, if any, would be handed down upon us.

The case was heard by a three-man panel, made up of Simon Bourne-Arton QC, Lord Herman Ouseley, at the time the chairman of 'Kick it Out', and David Dent, an ex-Football League secretary.

At around 4pm on Friday, 27 April, less than 24 hours before the kick-off at Wigan for what was going to be our 36th fixture of the season, it was announced that West Ham United had pleaded guilty to breaching Premier League rules regarding the signings of Carlos Tevez and Javier Mascherano and had been fined £5.5m.

But there would be no points deduction imposed on the club for either this season or the following one, as had been widely speculated upon, mainly because we had pleaded guilty, the Premier League panel said.

It was stated that when we signed the Argentinian internationals from Brazilian club Corinthians last summer, the players were actually contracted to four offshore companies rather than solely to Joorabchian's MSI, as had been reported and/or speculated on at the time, and had essentially allowed the companies to retain the transfer rights of the two players – a fact that, according to the commission, Hammers bosses deliberately concealed from league authorities.

'[West Ham] knew that the only means by which they could acquire [the players] would be by entering into the third-party contracts,' said the commission. 'Equally, they were aware that the FAPL, at the very least, may not – and in all probability would not – have approved of such contracts.'

We had broken the rules by allowing a clause that the two players could be transferred away from West Ham without the club's consent; reportedly for as little as £2m paid to us in the January transfer window, or £500,000 in any window after that. This was something we had alluded to regularly in press conferences, as I have mentioned previously, but it was the first time it had been formally disclosed. Again, the Premier League wouldn't have approved of a contract with this provision in it.

The club released a formal statement on the matter shortly after the verdict. 'West Ham United Football Club was given an opportunity to present its case and received a fair hearing. The club's submission that the contracts gave no actual influence to any third party was accepted by the commission.

'The club has not been found guilty of fielding an unregistered player and speculation about a likely points deduction has proved to be unfounded. The club regrets the fact that they fell foul of the FA Premier League regulations, but the new owners of the club now want to focus on matters on the pitch and remaining in the Premiership. The threat of a points deduction has now been removed and the club's fate remains in its own hands.

'The club believes that promotion and relegation issues should be decided on the pitch and we are pleased that the commission agree with that view.'

It was fair to say that our relegation rivals didn't necessarily agree with our viewpoint that the relegation issue should have been decided on the pitch. The following day's opponents Wigan, led by their rent-a-quote chairman Dave Whelan, were shouting from the rooftops that the decision was unjust. 'The Premier League have now established that no one can ever be docked points unless a club goes into receivership and then it's an automatic ten-point deduction.

'The rules are the rules and if this breach doesn't merit the docking of points, then let's make it clear – nothing does. That's fine by me. Let everyone be treated the same, I say. A precedent has been set.'

Useful to note that at this point, prior to us playing his team at the JJB Stadium, Whelan wasn't asking for the case to be looked at again, just that clearly nobody will be docked points again for anything other than going into administration. At the time of writing over 13 years later, he is correct; only one team has been deducted points in the Premier League since, which was Portsmouth, who went into administration. So good news Dave, you got what you wanted then, on that day anyway.

One person involved with our rivals was on our side in the media the following day, though, a manager no less, who didn't think a points deduction would have been fair.

'All things considered, it is best if football decides. On the pitch is where it matters.'

How nice of that manager to be on our side. Clearly a fair and honourable man. I grant you it was Alan Pardew, who was our manager when we signed the two players, but still, you take all the support you can get in these situations.

As well as the non-points deduction, the other headline from the tribunal result was that the registration of Tevez to West Ham could be terminated by the Premier League if it wished to do so, and that even if they decided against that, 'Tevez will not be allowed to play again for the club until it proves that a new, legitimate arrangement has been made that prohibits any influence by third parties.' Again, keep in mind we had our biggest game of the season the very next day.

It was widely assumed for the next few hours that Tevez's time with the club would be up. The Premier League had been given the power to cancel his registration and it seemed logical that they would exercise that option, which would seemingly bring this saga to a close. But then, late on the night of Friday, 27 April, the following statement appeared on the West Ham website:

'Following discussions with the FA Premier League, West Ham United can confirm Carlos Tevez is available for selection for the rest of the season, including Saturday's game against Wigan Athletic. The actual registration of Carlos Tevez has not been called into question and he remains a West Ham United player approved by the Premier League.'

Right.

Here, for me personally, is the second part of this whole saga that still baffles me to this day. The first part, as I've said previously in this book, is how it took so long for anybody to notice something fishy was going on, particularly when club personnel kept doing interviews alluding to something fishy going on.

The second part is how in the blue hell did the Premier League let Tevez finish the season playing for us? Keep in mind here, I am not blaming West Ham United for this. Damn right we should have tried everything to keep Tevez available; he had been a major part, not the sole part (we'll get to that in a bit, don't you worry), but a major part in the revival over the previous seven games, and without a doubt our chances of getting the six points minimum required to stay in the Premier League in the final three games were far greater with him on the pitch. We would have been morons not to try.

But we should have been told no.

Now I understand that technically, Tevez wasn't 'an ineligible player'. We hadn't picked 'an ineligible player', as so many people who just listen to football phone-ins and shout at their radios thought and would repeat over the coming days, weeks, months and even years. His registration had been ratified by the Premier League and he had been eligible to play every game that he had played for West Ham.

But we had just been given a fine over 18 times higher than the biggest fine ever handed out by the Premier League before, as we'd left bits out of the agreement that would have made him ineligible. (£300k to Chelsea for tapping up Ashley Cole, if you're wondering.)

It was a messy situation. If Tevez played the rest of the season, scored a couple of goals and helped us stay up, the Premier League was opening itself up to a myriad of questions and potential appeals.

Yes, if they had stopped what was technically an eligible player appearing for us, we could have kicked up a stink, threatened an appeal etc, but having just admitted guilt of a transgression involving the player, the chance of any appeal court siding in our favour over an issue involving the same player was minimal.

The sensible thing for the Premier League to do was announce that Tevez couldn't play for the club again unless his entire registration was signed over to West Ham United, in the way that Liverpool were going to officially sign Javier Mascherano at the season's end.

But they didn't do that.

They just asked us to take the dodgy bit out and we could keep playing him. So, we e-mailed them and told them that we had, and they said that we could keep playing him.

I hope to God that the next e-mail wasn't from a Nigerian prince locked in a cave, as the Premier League could have been massively out of pocket come the following Monday.

Jokes aside, I'm not saying we lied about removing the provisions from the arrangement (although much later on it was inferred that we had, but we'll look at that later). It's just, having lied about it once, you would think that they'd want more than just an e-mail confirming that we had, but nope, happy to take us at our word. The nice people.

The Premier League would later release a statement saying they were 'satisfied the club acted in a manner that is consistent with them having terminated the offensive third-party agreement', and the club certainly agreed with that sentiment. So Tevez could still be on the coach to Wigan, or more likely could remain in Wigan as I assume he was already there. I'll say this again: this all happened the day before we had our biggest game of the season, and was 16 days before the season finished.

And that is the main issue with this whole case really. The timing of it, and how long it took for any verdict to be decided. That's the real reason we weren't deducted points, and why Tevez could continue playing for us.

As I said earlier, in my opinion the reason the hearing was scheduled for late April was because the Premier League wanted to make an example of us and deduct points. The 'third party ownership' issue was creeping closer and closer on to these shores; it was something we didn't seem to understand as football people in England and didn't want to become a thing in our game. This was the first major example of it in English football and West Ham hadn't done it in accordance with the rules set out, so the Premier League in my opinion saw this as an ideal chance to hammer (pardon the pun) us with a hefty points deduction and make sure it didn't happen again.

Because as we all know, back in February when the charges were brought, we were going to be gone and relegated by late April, probably mathematically but at worst on the verge of, so a ten-point deduction (which had been widely rumoured) wouldn't have made a difference, no appeal, no complaining etc, and we could all go on our merry way.

Even in March this still looked likely, so no need to worry. But then we started winning. And kept winning. So, by the time we got to the hearing, the punishment for the rule breach wasn't then a points deduction. It was relegation. And that was an issue for the Premier League, as we would definitely appeal then, and they faced an issue when their final *Super Sunday* of the season would have to be played with an asterisk. Nobody would know whether West Ham had gone down or not, or whether Wigan or Sheffield United had stayed up or not, as that would have been decided in the courts over the summer. But what if there was an appeal after the appeal, or the case took too long, and August rolled round and nobody knew what league to put West Ham in?

In my opinion, what looked a safe bet was now the riskiest one of all. So they just decided not to place the bet full stop.

This was near as dammit admitted by the committee in their reasons for not deducting points, which were that we had pleaded guilty, but also, and this is a direct quote from the report of the verdict, 'A points deduction so late in the season might have consigned the club to relegation', and also, again a direct quote, 'The players and fans of West Ham are in no way to blame for the situation and therefore should not suffer.'

As we will get to, the clubs we were competing with for a Premier League place for the following season had a right to be aggrieved if we stayed up at their expense. They just directed their anger at the wrong people.

After all that kerfuffle, it was time for actual football to be played again. We made just the one change to the team for the six-pointer/basement battle, with Etherington missing out through injury and Boa Morte returning in his place.

The club, Eggert in particular, led the way on this so all credit to him. He made the very smart decision to pay for free coach travel for all Hammers fans journeying from Upton Park. For a match like this, without a doubt the claret and blue faithful would have travelled in large numbers anyway, but this move helped facilitate nearly 7,000 fans descending upon the JJB Stadium, which made up nearly a third of the 24,000 people in attendance overall.

Plenty of those fans would have read an interview with Carlos in *The Sun* that morning, in which he railed against people who had blamed the signings of himself and Mascherano for the struggles we'd had over the season. 'The people who have blamed me and Mascherano for everything do not understand football. These problems have never been caused by us either because of the transfer or the problems on the pitch. Javier and I are not to blame. Anyone who says that is wrong.

'I care for this club and have only ever done everything I can as a player and as a person to help West Ham this season.' God love him.

The first half-hour of the game was somewhat tepid, with us generally on top but failing to create any clear-cut chances. One big boost for us was the Latics captain and leading centre-half Arjan de Zeeuw going off injured in the 24th minute, to be replaced by former Hammers defender David Unsworth. While not a household name, de Zeeuw was the archetypal experienced pivotal defender for a lower or mid-range Premier League side, capable of galvanising a team or leading from the front, particularly in a game such as this.

Five minutes later, we took full advantage of the weakening in the Wigan backline. A long ball played forward by Neill landed between the defence and goalkeeper John Filan, the keeper saw this and hared from his goal towards the ball. He didn't get there first, though; the onrushing Luis Boa Morte did. The Portuguese lobbed the ball up and over the keeper, the ball taking flight and landing in the net.

Boa Morte finally had his first goal for the club, and what a time to do it!

Surely now we would see goal after goal from the attacking midfielder over the rest of his time with the club (spoiler: we wouldn't). But the future goals weren't important right now. This one was. 1-0 in front in a game we had to win.

Heskey headed not too far wide but other than that we were largely untroubled and got in at half-time with the lead intact. An enormous second half laid ahead of us. After looking down in all but name only, we were so close to being level on points with a team who had been

12 points ahead of us just six-and-a-half games ago. But as all West Ham fans know, these moments of hope are always followed by spells of abject terror at the idea of a positive situation going wrong, and then very often despair at the situation actually going wrong and all hope being extinguished (see: Hotspur, Tottenham).

So, it was fair to say as the second half kicked off there was a general air of trepidation among supporters up and down the land. The nerves increased nine minutes into the second half when Wigan boss Paul Jewell brought on Nigerian striker Julius Aghahowa for midfielder Kevin Kilbane, and prepared to go three up front and generally cause massive panic in the West Ham defence, something we all knew wasn't too hard to achieve. In the 56th minute, Wigan won a corner and we all held our breath, waiting for the siege to begin.

What followed was, in my opinion, the best team goal we scored all season, and one of the best and most important breakaway goals I've ever seen West Ham score.

The corner was scrambled clear as far as Tevez. The Argentinian powered past two challenges and fed the overlapping George McCartney. George was motoring down the left-hand side as quickly as I'd ever seen him move before (or since), and as one of the Wigan centre-backs came across to try and deal with him, he passed inside to Zamora. The forward took one touch and then, with his back to goal, slid the ball to the on-rushing Benayoun, who clean through on goal took one touch, a second, then rolled the ball past Filan and into the net via the inside of the post. Within 45 seconds of

Wigan's corner and expected siege beginning, we were 2-0 in front.

To say the fans were delirious would be an understatement. Finally now, there wasn't just hope, there was belief. This was the level of performance and domination we expected to see at the start of the season, back when I thought we were going to be challenging at the top of the league with our new Argentinian superstars. It had been a long, long time coming but finally one of those days had arrived, just before time ran out.

The rest of the game was spent with us pummelling Jewell's men; Tevez turned their defence inside and out and crashed a shot against the post, with the rebound being slightly scuffed by Reo-Coker and scrambled off the line by Leighton Baines.

Then with eight minutes to go, the bulldozer-like Argentine was at it again, holding off a couple of challenges before feeding Reo-Coker once more; the skipper's pass found Boa Morte, clean through on goal with not a defender anywhere near him. The midfielder chose what the kids call the 'sweaty' option rather than try and score his second of the afternoon. He squared the ball to Harewood and allowed the marvellous one the simplest of tap-ins for the third and clinching goal.

This caused the always fun 'fire drill', where nigh on all home fans got up and left the stadium; without exaggeration there were comfortably more supporters of the claret and blue persuasion than their blue and white counterparts, and scarcely could a group of fans have deserved a moment and a day like that more. To describe our away support in the 2006/07 season as 'long suffering' would have been an understatement.

The manager was understandably buoyant after the game, not only about this win but the run in general. 'I've been heartened [by our performances] since the Spurs game. We lost that unluckily, and should have won it. But the performance that day gave me a little bit of hope that if we could reproduce that, we weren't far wrong.

'They've managed to do it in recent weeks and we're still alive. But to come here today and win 3-0 – and play the way we played – was great, and we've just got to take it into the next game. It's a great run, five wins out of seven, but we need to keep it going.'

Saturday, 28 April 2007:
Wigan 0
West Ham 3 *Boa Morte (30), Benayoun (57), Harewood (82)*

We very much needed to keep it going. For all the joy of the win and the performance at the JJB, we were still in the bottom three. Other results had largely gone our way, Fulham would be beaten 3-1 at the Emirates the following day, and Pardew saw his Charlton side beaten 4-1 at Blackburn despite their fans launching what they called 'Operation Ewood', which in reality meant that more of their fans (6,000 being fair) went to an away game than normal. Not much military strategy needed for that operation then.

The one fly in the ointment was Sheffield United beating Watford 1-0 thanks to an own goal from former Hammers and Charlton left-back Chris Powell, who was hardly doing his bit for the cause of his old clubs. This put the Blades three points clear of us with two to play and they had a superior goal difference. Only one further win was needed from their games away to Villa and at home to Wigan, regardless of what anybody else did. Their destiny was very much in their own hands.

BOTTOM 6: (29/04/2007)

	P	Pts	GD
Sheffield United	36	38	-19
Fulham	36	36	-21
Wigan	36	35	-22
WEST HAM	*36*	*35*	*-27*
Charlton	*36*	*33*	*-24*
Watford	*36*	*24*	*-32*

A sign of things to come regarding the non-points deduction came in Wigan manager Paul Jewell's post-match interview after the 3-0 beating his team had suffered, against 11 men and not just one player, let's remember. After admitting his team were thoroughly outplayed, he then railed at length against the decision made the previous day. 'I don't want this to sound like sour grapes and I don't want anyone to get relegated because of an administrative mistake.'

That's nice of you, Paul, good to know you have our backs. Oh, what's that, you're doing the football manager equivalent of someone saying, 'I'm not being horrible but …' Oh right.

'But I knew for a fact when they said they would have the hearing with two or three games to go that there wouldn't be points deducted. If it had been Wigan or Watford, or if West Ham were down already, they would have had points taken off them.'

Well yes, as I've already said, I agree that if we were down already points would have been deducted, but regarding his other opinion, as fun as it is to paint the picture of 'little Wigan' or 'little Watford' or stereotypes like that, I like to think either of those clubs could afford legal representation that would have given the Premier League exactly the same issue.

I grant you, if it turned out that Wigan Athletic, a Premier League football club who had spent £16.5m in transfer fees that season, including nearly £6m for England international striker Emile Heskey, employed Big Brian from the market as their legal counsel, yes they may have been treated differently, but working on the bold assumption that they didn't and instead had a qualified solicitor working on their payroll, then no, the issue of deducting points would have been identical, which would have led to, dare I say it, an identical result.

Later that week, Jewell's employer Dave Whelan piped back up as part of a group of teams who were 'outraged' at West Ham for the temerity of being fined and punished by an independent panel rather than automatically relegating ourselves in shame, and had decided to take legal advice on the matter. The teams, strangely enough, were Wigan, Fulham, Sheffield United and Charlton. So, the teams that could have still gone down other than us, then. God they were angry at the morality of it all, or something like that. Whelan gave the press one of the all-time great football rants, which is so ridiculous I can't resist unpacking it here.

'I think the Premier League is in turmoil at present because what has been done is not right.'

I think most of the Premier League were alright actually, Dave. That's why there were four other clubs complaining, not 19.

'I think all the officials feel it is not right, and I know every club feels it is not right. If we have to go to court then it will be a shame, but this is a very serious offence West Ham have committed.'

Dave, we committed a football-related offence, for which we were punished and fined. It wasn't genocide mate; it was over a footballer's registration. Maybe once the police have caught all the murderers, they'll get on to the really big issues like whether Carlos Tevez should have been allowed to play at Wigan.

'I've no anger directed towards West Ham or their fans, apart from the fact they told lies.'

Dave, pal, no need to get me or any of the fans involved in this. I don't think we told any lies? Well, being fair, we did often chant that there was 'only one Carlos Tevez' when in reality there were probably quite a few people with that name, so yes that is a lie, and I apologise on behalf of all of us. Can you give it a rest now? Oh, you can't?

'Whether the people who told those lies are still there or not, I don't know. But West Ham have broken the rules and they should have had a much stiffer penalty than £5.5m – a figure that is peanuts to the £35m they will get if they stay up.'

Well yes, Sherlock, 5,500,000 is indeed less than 35,000,000. Can't fault you there. But we weren't guaranteed to stay up when the fine happened, so fining us the equivalent of all the money we would get if we did stay up maybe seemed a little harsh? Again, this was the biggest fine ever handed out by an English football body. Maybe they thought that was enough? But maybe yes, it could have been more.

In the same vein, though, maybe players who have been sent off for breaking a player's leg should be banned for the same amount of time as the injury they caused, but they're not. Sometimes punishments aren't exactly what you want. It is what it is, my friend.

'They should have had what every other club would have got if they had done this, and been punished properly with a ten-point penalty.'

Sorry, what was that, Dave? What every other club would have got? Every other club? Dave, are you honestly suggesting that the Premier League, Football Association, UEFA, FIFA, CONMBEOL, CONCACAF, the International Cricket Council, the NBA, the NFL, you get the point, are *all* biased towards West Ham United? Over every other club.

What in the blue hell has ever given you that idea? The 12-point head start we got at the start of every season? The rules obligating Messi to spend half a season playing for us while also temping at Nathan's Pie and Mash? The 60,000-seat stadium paid for by taxpayers' money? Actually, forget the last example. Just a theory, Dave, but maybe if they were so in favour of us, maybe there wouldn't have been an investigation to start with.

And maybe, Davo, old buddy, old pal, we would have used all that power and influence to be you know, ever so slightly more successful over the years. But what do I know?

'Good luck to them because they've got away with it,'

Well, at least he wished us luck in the end, that was good of …

'but I hope in the end that justice prevails and they go down.'

Oh.

Dave, can I explain to you what wishing somebody luck actually means?

Whelan apart, the main distraction for Hammers fans in the lead-up to the pivotal game at home to Bolton was Tevez unsurprisingly, but not whether he would be eligible for the game. This time, it was whether he would be fit for it as reports of an ankle injury that was being treated in an oxygen tank swirled around all week. Thankfully, the talisman was passed fit the day before the game and we could go into the crunch showdown at full strength with 11 players playing well and in form, not one player doing everything while a load of idiots stood still and watched him, as would be believed later on.

The Argentine's availability meant that he was available to collect the Hammer of the Year award prior to the game, which he won by an absolute landslide; it was reported that he got nearly 85 per cent of the vote, while runner-up Bobby Zamora was a long, long way back with just over five per cent. While clearly his goals beefed the percentage up in the end, I think there's a fair chance Tevez would have won it if he'd never scored, such was the work-rate he displayed in his outings from October through February, which endeared him to the fans to such a high degree, in addition to the sympathy we all felt when he was shunted out to the wing or left on the bench with a 40-year-old man preferred to him in the team.

Through the season, to West Ham fans he had become one of us, his hard work and passion resonated with football fans young and old, plus we knew he could have left in January had he wanted to, and very few of us would have blamed him. But he stayed, he wanted to make a success of his time with us and see it through, and in an era when hardly any footballers ever did that, nor do they to this day, it gave Carlos Tevez a reverence and bond with our supporters that few players have had before or since.

Anyway, on to the game. On the face of it, this looked like a tough, tough task. Bolton were sixth in the league, just a point behind Tottenham in fifth, and were coming off the back of a fantastic 2-2 draw at Stamford Bridge, which all but handed Manchester United the league title. This would be confirmed the following day when Chelsea failed to win at Arsenal; not the worst news for us seeing as now United had nothing to play for when we visited Old Trafford on the last day, as opposed to needing a result against us to secure the league.

So, if Bolton repeated the performance in east London that they had managed on the west side of the capital, this was going to be a difficult afternoon. But the glimmer of light in that equation was the knowledge that the Chelsea display had been somewhat of a one-off for the Trotters in recent weeks. They came into this game without a win in their last four matches and having taken only eight points from their last nine games, which had seen what at one point appeared to be a potential Champions League push turn into a scramble to qualify for the UEFA Cup.

This run of form, along with other factors, had led to a change of management for the North West club the week before this fixture, with long-time manager Sam Allardyce deciding to resign his post with immediate effect, citing intentions to take a break from the game. 'Big Sam' had undoubtedly done a magnificent job at the helm, taking Bolton from a mid to lower table second tier outfit to an established Premier League club, once at our expense, don't forget, as he and Okocha danced on the pitch after they'd stayed in the league in 2002/03, causing multiple remote controls to go through televisions across households of a claret and blue persuasion.

Whatever the result earned, a game against an Allardyce-led team would always have to be earned; seldom would a win against Bolton be described as anything other than 'hard fought'. Without him, would this still be the case? His replacement was incumbent number two Sammy Lee, so clearly the plan wasn't

A positive start: Bobby Zamora is congratulated by team-mates after scoring in West Ham's 3-1 opening day win against Charlton.

The signings that shocked the world: Tevez and Mascherano pose with their new manager Alan Pardew.

Kanu gives Portsmouth the lead on the way to a 2-0 loss for West Ham: one of eight defeats in a row, seven of those without scoring a goal.

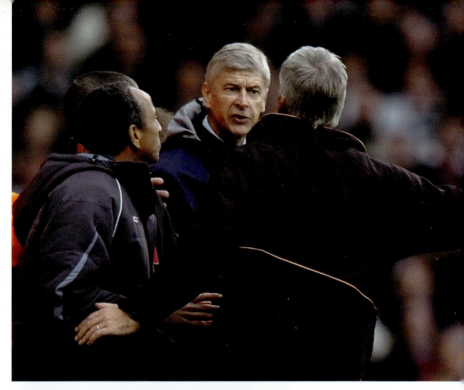

Pards and Arsene Wenger clash on the touchline following Marlon Harewood's last-minute winner against the Gunners.

Tevez is substituted in a 4-0 defeat at Bolton: Pardew would be sacked as manager two days later.

New manager and new owner: Alan Curbishley gives his first press conference having been appointed by Eggert Magnusson.

Carlos about to leap into the crowd having scored against Spurs – one of the all-time iconic goal celebrations.

Humiliation for Curbishley back at the Valley, a 4-0 defeat.

Last-minute heartbreak against Tottenham – the moment it seemed relegation was inevitable.

The performance of a lifetime: Robert Green successfully deals with one of Arsenal's 35 shots on goal in West Ham's 1-0 win at The Emirates.

A hero is born: Mark Noble celebrates scoring West Ham's third goal in a vital 3-1 win against Bolton.

Carlos Tevez scoring the winning goal at Old Trafford which secured West Ham's Premier League survival.

*The greatest escape:
completed.*

to reinvent the wheel and a difficult contest was still expected, even if their recent form and the lack of Big Sam made it look a fair bit more palatable than it may have seemed anyway.

Anyway, it was nice for me to go to the game knowing I wouldn't have to watch 90 minutes of Allardyce football at Upton Park any time soon.

So that was the good news. What of the bad? Well, we were clearly in much better form than our opponents, but if we decided to pull another Sheffield United away-esque performance, or replicated any of the 'play quite well, don't score, give away rubbish goals' matches from earlier in the season, we were sunk. A defeat for us, coupled with wins for one or two of our rivals, and we would be relegated in all but name. Needing to win at Old Trafford by four or five goals would be our best-case scenario if results went against us.

It wasn't as if many of said rivals had awful-looking games as well: Sheffield United travelled to mid-table Aston Villa knowing they only really needed a point to guarantee safety, Wigan were at home to 12th-placed Middlesbrough, themselves on a run of three defeats in four games, and Fulham hosted what was expected to be essentially a Liverpool reserve team as they were playing Milan in the Champions League Final that coming Wednesday. So, it was difficult to imagine a bad day for us would leave any second chances. It had to be today, we had to win, no ifs, buts or maybes.

Dad and I arrived at the ground expecting a tense, nervous and miserable afternoon, whatever the end result.

What we witnessed, I still cannot quite believe 13 years later.

With Tevez declared fit, we were unchanged from the win at Wigan, with the full 16 as follows:

Starting XI: Green, Neill, Collins, Ferdinand, McCartney, Benayoun, Reo-Coker, Noble, Boa Morte, Zamora, Tevez

Subs: *Spector, Davenport, Mullins, Cole, Harewood*

Bolton were largely at full strength, with big hitters Speed, Nolan, Anelka and Davies all starting. They were light at right-back and a spate of injuries in that position led to central midfielder and former Real Madrid stalwart Ivan Campo being selected to play there. This would prove to be arguably the best selection involving West Ham United all season.

Ten minutes in, Tevez picked the ball up outside the box and was brought down by Campo. The position was almost identical to the free kick he scored against Spurs, the moment even more important. The need greater.

The strike was even better.

The ball was whipped by the magnificent Argentine up and over the wall and whistled into the top corner of the net. The crowd, the players, the staff went wild. Tevez ran straight to the fitness coach who had helped him get fit to play in the first place, before he was engulfed by delirious team-mates.

A great start, but there was a long way to go. I remember worrying, had we scored too early? Would the nerves kick in and we'd start hanging on far too early and end up being punished? I'd seen it before, but I couldn't afford to see it again, not on this day.

I needn't have worried. Ten minutes later, Reo-Coker won a tackle in midfield and found Noble. Young Nobes looked to the left for a pass to Boa Morte, and no doubt would have been surprised to see that the Portuguese winger was standing all by himself. This was because Campo, fresh from giving away the free kick that put his team 1-0 down, had seemingly decided that he wasn't up for playing at right-back for the day, so had taken up his normal position in central midfield. This was all well and good for him but not really for his team-mates, as Boa was now completely unmarked and running clean through down the left flank.

The only person keeping pace with him was Tevez. Boa Morte thankfully noticed this and played the simple and obvious pass square to the Argentine, who tapped the ball in for a 2-0 lead.

This was most unexpected.

Tevez ran towards where I was sitting in the West Stand Lower, his hands cupping his ears taking in the cheers. And God believe me there were cheers. This was a roar that would have stacked up against many of the roars that greeted great moments at the Boleyn. The noise was deafening, the adulation all for one man, but the hope was there now. This really could be alright.

Cries of 'there's only one Carlos Tevez' echoed around the ground, no doubt infuriating Dave Whelan, who would have heard that our fans were telling lies again.

Eight minutes later Campo, who at this point had it not already been decided would have been in the running for the Hammer of the Year award, was dispossessed in his own half by Zamora to the soundtrack of a thunderous cheer from a crowd baying for blood. The forward found his Argentine strike partner and the noise grew even louder, with the anticipation of what the magician could create this time.

He clipped the ball to the back post, into the path of an unmarked Noble running into the area, and the future captain and West Ham icon connected perfectly, volleying the ball past Jaaskelainen and into the net.

3-0. Three nil. *Three* bloody nil.

What was going on?! This was supposed to be tense, nervous, edgy. I couldn't believe what I was seeing. None of us could; this was beyond the wildest of any of our dreams for what this afternoon could have had in store.

We were rampant. In half an hour, we were 3-0 in front and thoroughly deserved to be so. We had mastered Bolton to the level that they had battered us six months prior at the Reebok. They couldn't get near us in that first 30 minutes. It was bewildering and magnificent all at the same time.

After the third goal, the players got in a huddle in our half to refocus for the task ahead. Clearly, we knew that as healthy as the scoreline was, we were still playing a team in the top six of the league, with some serious players. This was a position that could still be squandered if we didn't do the right things and see the game out. It was the most professional moment we had displayed all season, a world away from the 'Baby Bentley' comparisons of January and February. How much of this revival was down to those comments from Curbs was questionable; in my opinion almost everything positive that had occurred was still despite those words rather than because of them, but one way or another the change had happened, and in the nick of time.

The first half ended with the 3-0 lead still intact, and their new manager, the diminutive Sammy Lee, had much to ponder, not least where he should be buying his suits from. The home fans had noticed that this one had clearly been bought from Mothercare and had let the Scouser know that we knew about this purchase several times through the 45 minutes through the medium of song.

Despite the jovial abuse, Lee sent his side out with more purpose in the second half, closer to the Bolton under his predecessor. They finally got a foothold in the game after our first-half domination, and at other points in the season, most points quite frankly, they may well have been the beneficiaries of a collapse in our defence, with it buckling under the pressure of both the match and the situation. But they weren't to be on this day, against a team playing as well as we were and with the confidence we had at this point.

Midway through the half, a mistake from Noble led to the midfielder being disposessed by Anelka. The Frenchman's pass found Gary Speed, who comfortably slotted past Green to reduce the arrears. We all shifted nervously in our chairs at the lead being reduced, but we needn't have worried. We saw the game out with relative comfort, actually having the better chances as Tevez and Harewood both saw efforts saved by future Hammers keeper Jaaskelainen. The final whistle saw cheers ring out around the ground at a priceless 3-1 victory, a third win in a row and a sixth in eight games, incredibly more than we had won in the preceding 29.

Saturday, 5 May 2007:
West Ham 3 *Tevez (10, 21), Noble (29)*
Bolton 1 *Speed (67)*

The other two results in games involving our rivals in the 3pm kick-offs that day were mixed; Fulham beat a Liverpool team that as expected featured nine changes from their starting 11 in their game away at Portsmouth the previous week. The 1-0 win meant that the Cottagers were all but mathematically safe and had lived to fight another season.

Far better news came from the JJB Stadium, where Wigan had been beaten 1-0 by Middlesbrough due to a Mark Viduka goal; it is unknown what role Tevez played in this Wigan defeat, but I'm sure according to Dave Whelan it made a huge difference and we should be punished even further.

This loss meant that if Sheffield United could get a point or better at Villa Park in the late kick-off that Saturday, the equation would be down to two teams from ourselves, Charlton and Wigan being relegated. If Charlton lost to Spurs on the coming Monday night, it would be a straight shootout between us and Wigan for one place.

To say Sheffield United froze under the pressure would be an understatement. They were beaten from pillar to post by Martin O'Neill's men; goals from Agbonlahor, Ashley Young and Patrik Berger put Villa 3-0 up within an hour, a lead they held comfortably against a team who only required a point to guarantee Premier League football yet managed to go through 90 minutes of their biggest game of the season without managing a single shot on target.

No doubt this was West Ham and Tevez's fault as well.

The Blades' defeat meant that the relegation equation was still two from four. This was the case for just over 48 hours until Tottenham ever so slightly redeemed themselves after breaking our hearts in March, as well as generally just being, you know, Tottenham, by beating Charlton 2-0 at the Valley.

The game was played in front of the Sky cameras as their *Monday Night Football* offering. I remember Spurs' first goal to this day; a mistake from their centre-half El Karkouri led to Berbatov being put clean through but still circa 40 yards from goal. The Bulgarian was a magnificent footballer, as I've already mentioned (to our cost that time), but it is fair to say he wasn't renowned for his pace.

So as he ran through on goal chased by various Charlton defenders, in my mind the visual became less of a football match and more of a horse race of sorts; I knew if Berbatov could get to the penalty area unchallenged he would score, but could he get there? I was standing in my living room shouting 'go on, go on' as the languid forward made his way to goal. Thankfully, he made it to the area, showing a surprising turn of pace to be frank, and as expected slotted the ball past Dean Kiely.

(Describing a Spurs goal in that detail and doing so with happiness makes me feel dirty, but hey, it did benefit us, so I'll let myself off on this occasion.)

Former Hammers and Charlton striker Jermain Defoe sealed the win in injury time, and in doing so confirmed the relegation of one of his former teams: thankfully not ours.

The crushing blow of the last-minute defeat at Goodison Park was one that Pardew and his men never recovered from, and the season ended for Pards as we all feared it might back in November 2006, with the team he managed being consigned to the Championship. Again, thankfully it wasn't us.

BOTTOM 6: (07/05/2007)

	P	Pts	GD
Fulham	37	39	-20
Sheffield United	37	38	-22
WEST HAM	37	38	-25
Wigan	37	35	-23
Charlton	37	33	-26
Watford	37	27	-30

The equation was now simple. If Wigan failed to beat Sheffield United at Bramall Lane, they would be relegated and we would be safe along with Warnock's side. If Wigan won, however, we would need a point in our last game. Sheffield United could only be relegated if they were beaten at home to the Latics and we got at least a draw.

Regardless of the result between our two rivals, a draw or better for us wouldn't guarantee our safety. The only issue was our last match was at Old Trafford, against the newly crowned champions.

We had passed nigh on every other test put in front of us over the previous eight games, but the toughest one was still to come.

United had won their first league championship in four years the previous week and this was to be their title-winning celebration, as at the end of the game they would lift the trophy in front of their own fans. Year in year out, teams want to do that on the back of a thumping win to show off their dominance and get the party started in the best way possible, and this would be no exception.

There is often an expectation, or possibly a hope, that these type of end-of-season games give sides at the bottom of the league more of a chance, as the more successful side has had their business completed one way or another, be it a league championship or European place confirmed, thus they have 'nothing to play for' and will turn up not caring or half-drunk or something, forget what end they are kicking towards and lose the match.

In reality, though, this very rarely happens, and in my opinion is one of the great footballing myths. This notion that a team who have been so good all season that they have successfully completed their objective with games to spare will suddenly be worse than a team on the verge of relegation is a fantasy that all supporters of said poorer teams convince themselves may happen. And then watch them easily beat your team 2-0 with a goal in each half, while you sit scratching your head at how they can run around at half pace and still be better than the side you support.

The reason for that is because they are better than the side you support. That's why they're top, or third, or even ninth or whatever, and you're third or fourth from bottom. It's because they have won a lot more games than you have, and seldom does that change simply because they've won so many the match has ceased to become as important to them.

United, as a case in point, had lost their last game once in the previous eight Premier League seasons where they had won the league. Also, it might not be a stretch to say their manager, the legendary Sir Alex Ferguson, wasn't a massive fan of losing at any time, so the hope that he was going to play a half-cut Paul Scholes in goal while singing 'Sweet Caroline' on a specially installed karaoke machine on the touchline as we went 12-0 up after 27 minutes was somewhat slim.

To put into context the challenge we were facing, whether United had anything to play for or not, they went into this game with a seven-point lead over runners-up and deposed champions Chelsea. They had lost once at home all season, 1-0 to Arsenal back in September, and were unbeaten in the 15 home games they had played since. Their previous 13 games had yielded 32 points: ten wins, two draws and just the one loss, an unlikely 2-1 reverse at Portsmouth.

Basically, it had taken them 13 matches to accrue only six less points than we had managed in our 37. They had scored comfortably over double the goals we had; in fact Cristiano Ronaldo and Wayne Rooney had only scored four fewer league goals between them than our entire team had managed. In all competitions, the attacking duo were 46-38 up.

So, it would be fair to say there wasn't a lot of hope, *but* there was some. While we were still at the bottom end of the league, we weren't playing like a team in that position. Three wins in a row, six wins out of eight, our forwards scoring, Collins and Anton at the back looking secure, Neill providing leadership, the youthful exuberance of Noble; there were positives all over the pitch, and as tall an order as this match undoubtedly was, it wasn't the complete and utter lost cause that it would have been three months prior.

It also needed to be remembered that we didn't need to win. We just needed to draw. Still bloody hard, but not as hard, for obvious reasons. And if Sheffield United could just manage not to lose at home to a Wigan outfit who had completely fallen apart and hadn't beaten anybody for eight games and two months, it would all be all right anyway. One thing was for certain; it was going to be a long afternoon.

Our team selection was the non-event it often is in any sport in which a team is winning; unchanged. It was picking itself at this point. The only change in the 16 was the security of a back-up goalkeeper being added to the bench, as Jimmy Walker replaced forward Carlton Cole.

While there wasn't much news from our team announcement, it's fair to say there were a few talking points from that of our opponents. Possibly with an eye on the FA Cup Final against Chelsea the following weekend, Ferguson left Ronaldo, Ryan Giggs, Paul Scholes and Nemanja Vidic on the bench, and Rio Ferdinand wasn't in the squad full stop.

The Reds boss had said in his pre-match press conference that he wouldn't field a weakened side, so I can only assume he deemed the 11 selected not to be a weak first team. In his defence, the team featured 11 internationals and included Edwin van der Sar, Wayne Rooney, former Hammer Michael Carrick, long-time-in-the-future Hammer, Patrice Evra, Gabriel Heinze and Darren Fletcher, all of whom could definitely be described as 'first-teamers' at the very least and world class in a few cases.

But without a doubt, the lack of Ronaldo in particular, as well as the first-choice central defensive partnership, Scholes and Giggs meant it was a far less formidable Manchester United on paper than we would have faced had they needed a result to seal the title. But it was still a team that would have been expected to beat most teams in the league, including West Ham.

The full squads for both teams were as follows:

West Ham Starting XI*: Green, Neill, Collins, Ferdinand, McCartney, Benayoun, Reo-Coker, Noble, Boa Morte, Zamora, Tevez*

Subs*: Walker, Spector, Davenport, Mullins, Harewood*

Man Utd Starting XI: *Van der Sar, O'Shea, Brown, Heinze, Evra, Solskjaer, Carrick, Fletcher, Richardson, Smith, Rooney*

Subs: *Kuszczak, Vidic, Scholes, Giggs, Ronaldo*

I watched the game at my mum's house, initially having a split screen of the two games that Sky were offering that day on *Survival Sunday*. Why be terrified watching one match when you can be terrified watching two, eh?

I certainly wasn't made to feel any less terrified in the early minutes, as on the right-hand side of my screen United swarmed all over our goal, playing like a team who still very much needed a result, and on the left-hand section I saw Wigan pretty much camped inside the Sheffield United penalty area, playing like a team who desperately needed a result – because they did.

It seemed like a matter of time until a goal went in that wouldn't benefit us, and sure enough in the 13th minute it happened. But at Bramall Lane rather than Old Trafford. A low cross from Heskey was swept into the net by Austrian midfielder Paul Scharner, a player who in my mind scored regularly but it turns out he didn't; this was only his third goal all season and one of only 14 he would score for Wigan in the five years he was at the club. Without checking the details of the other 13, I think it's safe to say it was his most important.

The strike from the Austrian took Wigan out of trouble and dropped Sheffield United into the bottom three. However, one goal for United now and we would sink below both the teams scrapping in Sheffield and back into the final relegation place. Everything was on a knife edge.

Shortly after the Wigan goal, Rooney threatened for the champions, being through on goal for a second before taking too long to decide what to do next, which let us crowd him out and clear. And breathe.

On the back of that chance, United spent what felt like about five minutes playing one-touch football on the edge of our area; our players were running after the ball in the same way my players do when I'm playing a 17-year-old whizz kid in an online game of football. The chance ended with Rooney firing wide again, but it felt more and more as if we were struggling to stem the tide.

On the half-hour mark, with us still hanging on and me having turned off the split screen in disgust having barely seen the Wigan goalkeeper such was the Latics' domination, we were forced into a change. George McCartney pulled up with an injury and needed to be replaced, so Jonathan Spector came on in his place as an emergency left-back. There was some poetry in this, I thought, which almost summed up this mad shambles of a season. At the very end, the best of the six right-backs we had tried through the season up until Neill joined finished our last game playing left-back.

Spector deserved his place due to the competence he had shown in difficult circumstances and the undoubted promise he had, but it was so deliciously West Ham-esque that after all the tribulations we'd had sorting out the right-back conundrum, we'd end up with one playing at left-back as well. Shortly after he came on, he blocked a shot from Smith, which hit him flush in the, erm, little Spectors.

In the 33rd minute, United won a corner. The set play was whipped to the near post, where striker/sometimes midfielder Alan Smith looped a header that was heading in the top-right corner, only to be brilliantly headed off the line by Benayoun, who had seemed to grow to about 6ft 10in to rise just under the bar and nod the ball clear. The header, though, only went as far as Heinze, who from ten yards drove the ball back towards the same corner. The ball was cleared off the line by the Israeli magician again! His block was pushed further out by Green and ultimately scrambled clear. Our heads were still somehow above water, but it seemed implausible that a goal could be far away now.

Three minutes later, anybody who had that thought was proved correct – but again the goal wasn't at Old Trafford, it was at Bramall Lane, and it was a goal that had West Ham fans jumping out of their chairs. Jon Stead bravely met a free kick with a diving header that saw him collide with Wigan keeper Pollitt, but more importantly nestled into the net to equalise for Warnock's men. This goal took Sheffield United back out of the bottom three and dropped Wigan back in. It also gave us precious breathing space. If the expected United goal arrived we would still be safe, as long as the Blades kept up their end of the bargain and didn't concede the lead again.

However, as Wigan went straight back to being camped in the Sheffield United half following the goal, that bargain holding up didn't look too likely.

As the half came near to a close, Green made a good save from a John O'Shea header and shortly after another

Rooney effort threatened our goal, but thankfully was again off target. At this point United had managed 12 attempts, while we had responded with erm, one. But we were still holding on. Nearly halfway there.

This game and the grim struggle to hold on reminded me a lot of a match at Old Trafford that I had attended six years prior; an FA Cup fourth-round tie against the all-conquering United team of the late 90s and early 2000s, the team that had won the Champions League 18 months earlier and were on the way to winning the league for the third consecutive season, this time by ten points, four more than the 2007 version that we were holding off on this day.

I was one of nearly 10,000 fans crammed into the away end that Sunday in January, and what an occasion it was. There was no resting of players for United that day; Gary Neville, Irwin, Stam, Giggs, Beckham, Keane, Cole – they were all there. But we held on and grafted in defence, with loan signing Hanu Tihinen spectacular and veteran defender Stuart Pearce providing a virtuoso Stuart Pearce performance. But in midfield, we had more than hard graft; we had quality. Lampard, Carrick and Cole. God, writing that even now makes me wince; so much potential, so much talent and all realised elsewhere. But we weren't to know that back in January 2001. All we saw was that we had the ability to keep the ball on the rare occasions we were afforded it.

And we stayed in the game, kept the score at 0-0. I remember what started as a running joke with my mate Jay, who was sat next to me saying '10 minutes … 20

minutes … 30 minutes' etc as time passed, became more and more important as the game ticked on. It felt like we could maybe, just maybe keep them out. And then, the 76th minute came. I will remember that detail for the rest of my life.

As a matter of fact, there aren't many goals I've ever seen that I remember as clearly as that one. I remember Kanoute getting the ball, I remember seeing Paolo make his run, I remember the ball being played to him, I remember looking immediately to the linesman and that he was running with his flag down pointing to the floor, demonstrating to all who looked over to him that the Italian was onside.

I remember thinking as clear as day, 'Oh my God, he's going to score.' Never in doubt, that. A player of Paolo's class always scored in these situations. I wasn't worried in the slightest that he would miss. He wouldn't. 'Oh my god, we are going to go 1-0 up at Old Trafford. I am going to see us score at Old Trafford. There's not long to go. Jesus Christ, I might see us beat Manchester United at Old Trafford.' It felt like I had an hour's worth of thoughts in the five seconds it took him to get the ball, go through, ignore Barthez, who was pretending he was offside, and put the ball in the corner. Never. In. Doubt.

And then, absolute pandemonium. Just the best moments you can ever have as a football fan. Anyone who ever wonders why their partners, friends, parents, grandparents, children, etc, put up with going to absolutely awful games that they moan all day are going to be terrible, and then moan all night that they were indeed as terrible as expected, why they put themselves through it. Moments like that were why. The absolute elation, the joy. Hugging people you don't know. Seeing people fall over seats and not caring. Being unaware of anything else going on in the world other than the happiness you're feeling, for a couple of glorious minutes. That's why you suffer the bad bits, because you know that one day, there will be another moment like that. And you daren't miss it.

We held on as well. Bloody did it. Won at Old Trafford. They ended up with Cole, Yorke, Solskjaer and Sheringham on the pitch, but we saw it out and won.

I vowed then I'd never go back to Old Trafford for an away game. What was the point? I, as a West Ham fan, had gone there, seen us win and not even seen them score. Why ruin that?

And I never have.

Anyway, back to the story at hand, a goal kick from Green as the half ticked into injury time seemed to have the aim to get us through to half-time unscathed, with it being launched deep into the opposition half. The long punt was won and headed back up into the air by Zamora, who had been every bit the isolated, lone frontman during the first half but was doing his best to get into the game. He had some support on this occasion as well as Tevez, who had been pretty much a fifth midfielder throughout the half due to the home side's dominance. The Argentine had managed to get up alongside him and had even won the ball from the knockdown, holding off a very end-of-season, half-hearted challenge from Carrick.

A little give-and-go with Bobby Z and all of a sudden the ball, via a deflection from Wes Brown, was looping up in the air, looking as if it would land on the corner of the six-yard box. And Tevez was getting there before anyone else. And he did get there first.

And oh my God, holy Christ Almighty, he has scored. I cannot believe what I am seeing or how has he done this. I love this man so much. Please stay with us forever and maybe marry me if you want to, Carlos.

That's roughly what I said in my mind. Out loud it came out something like 'YES OH MY GOD YOU BEAUTY, COME ON!' I shouted so loud my mum told me off, which hadn't happened since I was a child to the best of my knowledge. A strong moment for me there.

With only our second shot of the game, we'd gone 1-0 up. Whatever happened now in Sheffield, we had a buffer. We could afford a United goal now, we could be allowed one mistake, one error, one piece of bad luck, as long as there wasn't a second occurrence after it. And maybe we wouldn't even need that if Wigan didn't score again?

Our game blew for the break almost straight after Carlos' goal, so I flicked the channel over excitedly to see if the half-time whistle had gone there as well.

And as I did, I saw a close-up of their defender David Unsworth. I then saw him running up to take a penalty and celebrate with the Wigan fans having scored it. Ah.

Jagielka had inexplicably handled a cross as it came into the penalty area, a penalty was correctly given and duly smashed home by Unsworth, a defender who at this stage of his career could be best described as 'burly' and indeed had only been on the pitch for two minutes due to an injury in the Wigan defence.

So, at half-time we were safe and so were Wigan. Sheffield United needed to score to stay up, Wigan needed to stop them scoring to stay up, and we needed either Sheffield United to score, or Manchester United not to score twice to stay up. Clear? Good.

The second half started nice and calmly for us, as United had the attacking edge of a group of players who had been watching a compilation of their best bits over the season rather than being torn into by their manager for being 1-0 down. This lethargy had sadly for us been spotted by Sir Alex, who just before the hour mark made a triple change of terrifying proportions as Smith, Carrick and Evra were taken off and replaced by Giggs, Scholes and Cristiano Ronaldo. So, the final half-hour would see United with a front five of the three new subs, plus Wayne Rooney and Ole Gunnar Solskjaer. Which I wouldn't say sounds particularly understrength, but what do I know?

Meanwhile, back at a rain-sodden Bramall Lane the hosts were probing for an equaliser with the desperation you would expect from a team who had 45 minutes to save their Premier League lives. At almost the same time that Fergie was bringing on the cavalry against us, they had a golden opportunity not to need any favours from the champions as striker Danny Webber, on as a half-time sub for Nade, ran clean through on goal with only the keeper to beat. His right-footed effort did indeed go past the keeper, but clattered against the post rather than bulging the net and providing the leveller the hosts so desperately craved.

It was a glorious opportunity and one that Sheffield United had nobody to blame but themselves for not taking.

The United subs didn't take long to up the pressure on us; a header from Solskjaer forced a routine save from Green and then a scramble from a set piece led to Ferdinand hacking away a scuffed Ronaldo effort as it trickled towards the line. 'Sixty-five minutes gone. Breathe,' I remember thinking at home. I wasn't scrolling between the games now. I didn't care what Sheffield did or didn't do. We had a quarter of the game to hold out, to avoid conceding twice, and if we managed it nothing else would matter.

I remember not long before this thought the Sky TV coverage playing a part in an amusing incident. Through the game, they had been showing the 'As it stands' table with a graphic of how positions 16–19 looked after each goal. Well, the final time they showed it, we weren't in it anymore! Fulham were being beaten 3-1 at Middlesbrough and this dropped them into 16th and below us. Surely we had to be safe; according to Sky we weren't even in the equation! Not quite, sadly. There was still work to be done.

Harewood came on for the hobbling Zamora at this point. He may have been injured, or the hobble may have been to eat up a few more seconds, I don't know. I also don't know what the marvellous one's instructions were when he came on. I'm not sure if they were 'just run after the ball for the next 25 minutes', but that was all he did.

Wherever United had the ball, he popped up. He was brilliant. To this day, it's one of my favourite sub cameos of all time. I can't believe he was told to do that. I like to think he just did it because he cared.

It would end up being Harewood's last appearance for West Ham before he was sold in the summer; I didn't agree with it then and still don't. He'd had a poor season but with a change in fortune and increased confidence, he still could have been an important striker for years to come. He certainly didn't lack the commitment and passion, which he proved beyond all doubt in this outing.

Fifteen minutes to go now. Still a two-goal cushion. United corner. Swung in, Ronaldo leaping like a salmon and hanging in the air, meeting the corner with a powerful downward header. We'd seen it a few times before, we've seen it so many times since, from arguably the best player ever to play the game. (In my opinion he is, but if you think it's Messi I won't argue with you. If you think it's anybody other than those two, I damn sure will though.) And in those times before and since, that leap signals a goal is about to be scored. 'Oh no,' I said out loud. I knew.

But on this day, fortune wasn't hiding. The header hit Green more than the keeper saved it, but he fell on the ball at the second attempt and we remained in front. And we all remembered to take another breath.

Shortly after that, the future CR7 was running down the left wing, ready to cut inside and unleash an Exocet of a strike on goal. Neill did his best to hold him off but the turn inside came, as did the shot. But it wasn't in the corner as the Portuguese desired, and this allowed Green to beat the ball clear. The chance was recycled as far as Scholes on the edge of the area, whose shot was just over the bar.

This was torture.

Wigan were down to ten men now due to a red card for midfielder Lee McCulloch. Could Sheffield United not just score and end this misery?

Eight minutes to go now, the ball found John O'Shea, who was being far more of a nuisance than would have been expected prior to the game. The Irishman drove into the area and was about to shoot before being brought down by Boa Morte from behind as Green came out to meet him. Nailed-on penalty. At Old Trafford, where they get penalties if you sneeze five yards from a player when they're losing at home in the last ten minutes. And yet, referee Martin Atkinson said no.

Martin, in the unlikely event you are reading this, thank you. I don't know why you didn't give it, maybe you didn't see it, maybe you thought he got the ball, maybe it was because you couldn't be bothered spending the last seven minutes of your season refereeing a proper dramatic contest and just wanted your summer break to come, I don't know. But whatever reason it was, thank you.

Just after that Tevez was replaced by Mullins. He clapped the Hammers fans in the corner, left the pitch, put his coat on and sat on the bench. And that was it for Carlos Tevez as a West Ham United player. It wouldn't be it for Carlos Tevez at Old Trafford though, as we all know.

And that, besides a shot from Giggs that went just over the bar, was that. United had thrown nigh on everything at us, but as the minutes ticked down, thoughts drifted to their trophy presentation and league-winning afterparty, and we held out relatively comfortably.

We won. We won at Old Trafford, 1-0. And we had done it.

We had stayed up.

Sunday, 13 May 2007:
Man Utd 0
West Ham 1 *Tevez (45)*

The players embraced on the Old Trafford pitch, joined by the jubilant coaching staff and players who had been sitting on the sidelines. The fans in attendance were going insane, quite justifiably. They'd witnessed the culmination of a sporting miracle. Several supporters were shown on TV shedding tears of joy and I'm sure there were many, many more than that.

I was sat indoors nigh on open-mouthed at what I'd witnessed. I'd given it up two months ago, and always had a hunch that in the end it would be the hope that killed me, and despite the surge in form we would meet the same result at the end anyway. But I was wrong and rarely in my life had I ever been happier to be so.

Nine games, seven wins, 21 points earned. Every one of them needed. We'd beaten United home and away. We beat Arsenal home and away as well. 1-0 in all four games.

We played six of the top seven in those nine games and beat five of them.

For what needed to be done, and who it needed to be done against, it was the greatest escape from relegation in English top-flight history. We more than doubled our points tally from 29 games in the final nine.

To put this into context, the following season Derby, who ended the season with one win and only 11 points, and who were statistically the worst team ever to play in the Premier League, would have been relegated by only five points if they had replicated our run in the final nine games. That was the level that we had managed.

BOTTOM 6: (07/05/2007)

	P	Pts	GD
WEST HAM	38	41	-24
Fulham	38	39	-22
Wigan	38	39	-22
Sheffield United	38	38	-23
Charlton	38	34	-26
Watford	38	28	-30

I went for an excited, celebratory drink with my dad after the game. We basically sat there in a state of semi-shock; rarely had either of us had so little to say about anything to do with football, let alone something of this magnitude. We were both in genuine disbelief at what had been accomplished. There was hardly any conversation about the future or the following season. The fact that we were even able to contemplate an upcoming Premier League season was almost beyond our wildest dreams.

I managed to get over the shock somewhat as the night went on; seeing some old secondary school friends walk into the pub we were in helped. I'll spare you the details but you can probably imagine what took place that led to a quiet drink with my dad ending up with me being shouted to 'get in the bloody house' by my mum at around midnight, with yours truly staggering drunk down the road singing 'there's only one Carlos Tevez' at the top of my voice. One hundred per cent true story.

So, if we were the winners of the relegation battle, what of the losers? Sheffield United lost 2-1 at home to ten-man Wigan and were relegated. Wigan celebrated their first win in two months and nine games, which guaranteed their survival at the Blades' expense.

So, whose fault was it, according to manager Neil Warnock, that his side were relegated on the final day? Was it theirs for not getting a point at home against the most out-of-form team in the league? Was it due to a poor mentality, having only needed a point from the final two games, or five from their last five games after they'd beaten us 3-0? Was it his strikers, who failed to score more than once against ten men and an overall defence that conceded the joint-second most goals in the league?

No, it was Alex Ferguson's.

He began with a subtle barb that 'what goes around comes around and maybe Chelsea will win the FA Cup and AC Milan the Champions League', referencing not only United's team selection but also that of Liverpool, who made wholesale changes to their team before their loss at Fulham the week prior.

As we did with our good friend Dave at Wigan, let's look at his comments and see how valid his issues are.

'I was disappointed at United's team,' he continued. 'You would have hoped and thought that, last game of the season, Cristiano Ronaldo, Nemanja Vidic and probably two or three more might have played. I think Sir Alex sold me a dummy in midweek when he said he would field a strong team.'

Well, Ronaldo played the last half an hour but yes, I can see why that is annoying. Vidic, however, hadn't played for six weeks due to injury and I dare say would have come on in the second half for a run-out had we not had the cheek to be 1-0 up. Would Warnock have been happy then if the defender had come on and his match fitness prioritised over an attacking change to chase an equaliser? I assume not.

'He [Ferguson] has his own reasons, though. Maybe the FA Cup Final next week is more important to him.'

I'll assume it was, yes Neil. As you get a trophy for winning that, there isn't a 'beating West Ham in the last game of the season' Cup that he was playing for. He's the manager of Manchester United and the following week Manchester United could win the FA Cup. I've never spoken to Alex Ferguson but I dare say that would be more important to him than picking all his best players just in case Sheffield United can't get a point at home to Wigan.

'At least I knew the players that were playing. I didn't even know two of those that played for Liverpool at Fulham last week.'

I grant you, he may not have heard of young full-backs Emiliano Insua and Gabriel Paletta. And Liverpool's team selection was without a doubt annoying to anybody involved in the relegation battle; I was angry at it myself. But Benitez wasn't picking fans or competition winners; they were contracted professional footballers registered to Liverpool Football Club and he was perfectly allowed to do it.

'I'd never heard of them but when you are a foreign manager like Rafa Benitez, you probably don't give two hoots about what Sheffield United think.'

Hard Brexit opinions aside Neil, you're correct, I'm sure he doesn't. And nor should he.

In the same way you didn't give two hoots about Chelsea when you made five unforced changes to the team that beat us 3-0 when you yourselves visited Old Trafford in April. Maybe your full-strength 11 could have given them a game and nicked a point, which would have helped United's title rivals chase them down? But you didn't, you picked contracted professional footballers registered to Sheffield United Football Club, which again you are perfectly allowed to do.

Just don't complain when somebody else does it.

On that note regarding how 'weak' the United team was when they played us, let's look at the starting XI and used subs Ferguson picked when they played Sheffield United at home:

(Different players in bold)

Starting XI: *Kuszczak*, Heinze, Brown, Carrick, Evra, *Ronaldo*, *Scholes*, Fletcher, *Giggs*, Rooney, Smith

Subs used: Richardson, Solskjaer

Four changes. That's all. Fewer changes to that United side than Warnock himself deemed necessary to make. Also, of those four changes, three of them still played in our game for half an hour and one was their back-up goalkeeper. Edwin van der Sar, one of the world's premier goalkeepers, lined up against us. They also didn't have Michael Carrick playing at centre-half when we came to town.

So maybe, just maybe, it was roughly the side United had been picking most weeks, then?

If they had picked this 11, however, I may have had more sympathy with Warnock's cause for indignation:

(Different players in bold)

Starting XI: *Kuszczak*, Fletcher, Brown, O'Shea, Heinze, *Eagles*, Smith, Richardson, *Lee*, *Fangzhuo*, Solskjaer

That team played at Stamford Bridge four days before our game at Old Trafford. And drew 0-0. United in this era didn't have bad players, they just had great players and very good players. Whatever starting 11 that was picked was monumentally difficult to beat.

For final argument's sake, below listed is the Wigan team that beat Sheffield United that day:

Starting XI: *Pollitt, Taylor, De Zeeuw, Boyce, Baines, Valencia, Scharner, Landzaat, Kilbane, Heskey, McCulloch*

Subs used: *Unsworth, Skoko, Folan*

Yep, we definitely had the easier task that day.

Warnock would later recount in his autobiography that Ferguson rang him in the days after to apologise. 'He [Ferguson] said he was sorry about what had happened at Old Trafford. "We battered them, Neil," he said. "We had 25 shots. And the stats would back me up on that. The team was good enough to win."

'"I know, Alex," I said. "It's just the psychological boost the other team gets when they see all those names not on your team sheet."

'"I can't tell you how sorry I am," he said. He was quoted the next day saying everything was all right between us. But it's still difficult for me to digest what happened.'

Nice of Ferguson to apologise, but I'm not sure it was an admission of guilt, as Warnock seems to suggest. More just that he was, you know, sorry they'd got relegated. He was good friends with Curbishley as well. I'm sure if we'd gone down, he would have expressed sorrow to Alan for playing a part in that happening. Pretty sure he wasn't admitting guilt for any of it, more just that he was sad it happened. But whatever helps you sleep at night, I guess.

The final words on the day, and the escape of all escapes, go to the manager who oversaw the miracle run, Alan Curbishley. 'The players have got to take great credit. The run we've had – seven wins out of nine – against top Premiership opposition has been fantastic.

'Nine or ten that started today were players who were here before I got to the club, so great credit to them. We've had a real topsy-turvy season; we went eight games without winning before I took over, then after I took over we had a bad ten-game spell as well.

'So when you consider that for half the season we've not won any games, and that we've had to pick up all our points in the remaining half – fantastic.'

Couldn't agree more, Curbs. He also had some special words for the man of the hour.

'Tevez's goal? It was a great finish. We felt that Man United would commit and push people forward as that's the way they play, and that we may have a chance on the break. We fashioned a couple of chances but we needed to take one of them. Carlos took it, and it gave us something to defend.

'He's been inspirational in the last two months, along with a number of other players. It's been a settled team and there's been some fantastic performances, as you saw today.'

And finally, he had some words of hope for the future.

'If you said to me nine games ago, we were going to win seven of them and get ourselves out of it, it was a big ask. But it just shows you what can happen in football.

'I just hope we don't have to go through anything like this again.'

And we never did.

For three years.

Epilogue

THE FINAL part of this season encapsulates why it really was one of the most insane seasons any professional football team can have ever experienced; as it was decided in a courtroom 16 months after the 2006/07 Premier League campaign came to a close. In the days after the win at Old Trafford, which kept us in the Premier League at Sheffield United's expense, the so-called 'gang of four' made up of themselves, Charlton, Wigan and Fulham were discussing legal action against the Premier League, West Ham and pretty much anybody else.

'Charlton, Sheffield United, Wigan, Fulham and Middlesbrough are all determined that we should get justice,' ranted Dave Whelan, again.

'West Ham should have been deducted points. It has to be done quickly because the longer this goes on, the less likelihood [there is] of the league reviewing it at all. We are going to fight and support Sheffield United – and we will fight with them to the end.'

Sheffield United chairman Kevin McCabe was also in full-on attack mode in an interview with BBC

Sport. 'I think most of the Premier League clubs and other football clubs support us over this injustice that has come about this season. I think there is a consensus most clubs support an injustice, so I hope we will get the vast majority of clubs in the Premier League supporting our case.' Spoiler for you here: they didn't.

He went on with equal fury, 'If there is any justice we will be in the Premiership next season, but I can see the Premier League will try and hide behind the Commission's rule-making process. I am prepared to go as far as is needed to protect the interests of Sheffield United – probably even into Europe to the Human Rights Commission.'

OK. As I said earlier when Dave-o was moaning, this wasn't mass murder. I'm not sure the Human Rights Commission was set up to decide football issues, but maybe I'm wrong and the dubious goals panel is done from there or something.

Also, during all this ranting – and there was plenty, plenty more that I won't subject you to – it was never clear who exactly they wanted justice from? Was it the Premier League for deciding the punishment, the arbitration panel that provided the ruling, or West Ham for the rule-breaking, or having the temerity to stay up, or not automatically demoting ourselves to League Two in shame?

As we know in the end the clubs, and Sheffield United, settled on West Ham as the ones that should be rounded on rather than the Premier League. The ones who actually decided the punishment that they were all so furious about. This may have been due to a letter sent from the Premier League to all member clubs in the wake of the Tevez furore, which detailed the reason for the judgment and clearly stated the league's position.

'At no point were West Ham United charged with playing an ineligible player,' the letter stated.

'Both Tevez and Mascherano were registered on 31 August 2006. All the required documentation was received. At no time has Mr Tevez's registration been revoked or terminated and at all times he has been eligible to play for West Ham. Tevez has been properly registered to play for West Ham United since 31 August 2006. He continues to be registered with West Ham United.'

This was a point I made continually at the time, and still do now and then today: We never fielded an ineligible player. Tevez, and Mascherano while he was at the club, were never ineligible. They were registered by the club to the Premier League and this was done legally.

The issue was that when registering them we didn't disclose the third-party part; now I know and acknowledged earlier the argument that if we had disclosed this part, they wouldn't have been allowed to be registered etc, so thus yes, they were ineligible, but this is also covered in the letter.

'The media, and of course those aggrieved by the decision, have analysed the seven reasons given by the independent commission for not deducting points and concentrated on those that to them seem the least convincing.

'However, there are others that have a less convenient truth, particularly the one that says "had the club in time made disclosure of the third-party contracts to the FAPL, then, in all probability, contracts could have been entered into which would not have offended the rules.'"

Well, there you go. Had we disclosed the agreement in full, in all probability we would have been able to make alterations so the players could have signed for us anyway.

We didn't do that, though, so we were punished accordingly with the largest fine ever administered by an English football governing body. And as I have said before, I believe we would have been deducted points had we not rallied and given ourselves a chance of staying up. The fact that we weren't was not the fault of West Ham United. It was the fault of the Premier League. But they'd made it clear that it wasn't their fault and they weren't about to change their minds, so it fell on us to be the baddies who needed punishing. More than we'd already been.

Sheffield United pressed ahead for another arbitration hearing under the argument that the first panel's ruling was 'irrational and perverse', literally ignoring the rules they'd helped create as a Premier League club at the start of the season, which stated that any disciplinary issues would be handled by an independent panel and then the ruling adhered to. It didn't say you could just keep asking for hearings until you got the result you wanted.

The arbitration hearing was held in mid-June, with some Blades fans led by Sean Bean, who I can assume must have been having a quiet period in his acting career, protesting outside the court during the hearing, with their cringeworthy 'campaign for fairness' in full swing.

Obviously, fairness didn't mean accepting relegation because 17 other teams got more points than you, or that you should stick to the rules you helped decide. Or even that if you have an issue with a punishment, you should take it up with the people who decided upon the punishment rather than the ones who accepted both guilt and the punishment handed down.

The hearing was concluded in early July with the second panel upholding the decision of the first; they rejected the Yorkshire club's claim that the findings were 'irrational or perverse' and ruled that the decision didn't need to be changed. They did, however, massively overstep their mark and state that 'this tribunal would, in all probability, have reached a different conclusion and docked points from West Ham'. Which was in no way, shape or form what they were asked to rule on. The arbitration was there to decide whether the ruling was completely wrong; it wasn't there to decide if it was marginally wrong or offer opinions on what they would have done differently had it been their decision, because it wasn't.

It was the equivalent of a criminal conviction being upheld on appeal but the judge saying, 'Oh, but by the way if you'd presented that bit of evidence better, I definitely would have found them not guilty.' It would never happen, of course, and nor should anything resembling that have happened in this case. All it did was give Sheffield United's lawyers, who I imagine by this point had been given so much money by the club it probably equated to a controlling share of the business, yet another avenue to pursue.

This time, it would be in the form of a lawsuit against West Ham for them not being able to draw at home to Wigan; sorry, I mean cheating them out of a Premier League place. The compensation figure was either plucked out of thin air or meticulously worked out, depending on which side of the fence you were on, to be in the region of £30m and £50m. One of the legal team filing the suit spoke of the need to 'restore the integrity of English football, which has been tarnished by this affair', which gives a pretty good indication of the hyperbolic rhetoric going on at the time. This 'fight for justice' would continue into the hearing.

And incredibly, on 23 September 2008, this paid off. An independent tribunal, at the third time of asking, gave Sheffield United what they wanted. We were ordered to pay compensation in the region of £30m in instalments to the Blades due to the 'Tevez affair', the final payment being made in 2013.

There were two main reasons given for the verdict. The first one read, 'We have no doubt that West Ham would have secured at least three fewer points over the 2006/07 season if Carlos Tevez had not been playing for the club. Indeed, we think it more likely than not on the evidence we heard that even over the final two games of the season West Ham would have achieved at least three points less overall without Mr Tevez. He played outstandingly well in the two wins West Ham secured in those last two games.'

To this day, I shake my head in disbelief when I read that justification. It is ill informed, insulting, and just plain wrong. To look at the 'two games' comment first. Yes, of course Tevez was brilliant in those two games, no arguments there, three goals and an assist. But against Bolton, the whole team were magnificent, from 1–11. Tevez got the goals but he was a striker, that's what they tend to do, particularly when playing in a team performing as well as we did that day. His second goal was laid on a plate due to fantastic play by Noble and Boa Morte; any striker playing professional football would have expected to score it. His 'assist' was without doubt a lovely chipped pass to Noble, but the goal was far more because of the quality of the then-young midfielder's volley as opposed to the pass.

I genuinely believe that the performance of the other ten players that day would have meant had Harewood, or Cole, or even Sheringham been up front instead of the Argentine, we would have won the game.

But, of course, I can't say that for definite.

And at Manchester United, he did indeed score the winner. But we didn't concede a goal. And that was what we needed to do that day. We didn't need to win, we just needed to draw. And not conceding a goal means you at least draw. That's a fact, my friends.

Take the Tevez goal out, we draw 0-0 and we stay up anyway. Unless, of course, you've decided that Tevez was not only a great forward, he was also the finest defender to ever play the game, a mixture of Moore, Beckenbauer, Nesta and Malky Mackay rolled into one, and single-handedly kept Rooney, Ronaldo, Giggs, Scholes, Solskjaer et al out that afternoon.

Except he didn't, did he? It was a fantastic defensive display from the whole team, with Green, Neill, Collins and Ferdinand playing magnificently, as they had done in every single one of the games we won in the late run.

To say the result at Old Trafford was nothing to do with them is downright insulting, as well as moronic.

People might say 'the goal gave them something to hold on to'. Which is utter rubbish. We already had something to hold on to, which was our place in the Premier League. A clean sheet that day kept us up whether we scored none, one or 30.

If anything, it could be argued that the goal may have worked against us, as without that Vidic would have come on rather than one of the three offensive players, and United may have eased off a lot earlier than they did, rather than continuing to attack us due to not wanting to lose the game.

But again, of course, I can't say any of that for definite. *Because how can you say for definite in a game with 22 people in it, what difference one person not being there would have made?*

Case in point, Tevez was a big part of the Bolton win. But so was Ivan Campo being asked to play at right-back. If he wasn't there, would the goals have happened? If we'd swapped ends and attacked the Bobby Moore Stand in the first half, would we have won the game? If Lucas Neill had worn different boots that day and one of his passes had gone off for a throw rather than to a team-mate, would the move that led to the third goal 14 minutes later have taken place? Nobody knows. So how can you award £30m to someone based on a guess?

And as for there being 'no doubt that West Ham would have secured at least three fewer points over the 2006/07 season if Carlos Tevez had not been playing for the club', really? To make that judgement over the whole season is incredible. As let's not forget, for all his good play, Tevez didn't score his first goal until March.

The first seven games he started for us, we lost six and scored one goal. In the first nine games he started, we scored one goal with him on the pitch. Now I am not saying this meant the Argentine was awful in those games, he wasn't. But the whole team were playing poorly, sometimes terribly, and he was a part of that. He also, while being very, very good, wasn't good enough to take an entire team on and beat them by himself.

He must have learnt that trick after the Tottenham game then.

West Ham with Tevez starting up to Tottenham (H):

Played: 9

Won: 1

Drew: 1

Lost: 7

Points: 4

Goals with Tevez on the pitch: 1

Goals with Tevez off the pitch: 4

He also made six sub appearances in this time, in which we drew one game and lost the other five.

So, in the 15 games he appeared in prior to the Tottenham game, we won five points. Overall, in 25 league appearances for the club, West Ham got 26 points. Just over a point a game, which would equate to roughly relegation form, which is exactly where we were in the league.

Can it really be argued that there was no doubt at all we would have got three points fewer without him?

The other reason was that there was doubt as to whether we really had amended the terms of Tevez's agreement after the initial Premier League ruling.

The document recorded in testimony from Joorabchian's solicitor, Graham Shear said, 'Admittedly, on that same day, 27 April, and also again at the meeting the following week at which I was present, [West Ham] made clear that they intended to and would, notwithstanding the 27 April letter, perform their obligations under the Private Agreement. This has, at least in private and behind the scenes, always remained [West Ham's] position.'

In another passage, tribunal chairman Lord Griffiths asked Shear for clarification. 'The impression that your evidence has left with me is that Mr Duxbury was saying to you, "Don't worry, we are not going to depart from the terms we had agreed." Shear replied, "Broadly, yes."

'West Ham were desperate to ensure that Mr Tevez played for the club in the critical last few games of the season. Whilst having no choice but to adhere to the Premier League's requirements, West Ham wanted to do everything possible to attempt to placate the rights owners.'

Now this may well be true. The fact that by the time the hearing took place Tevez was playing for Manchester United indicates as such. But there was no actual hard evidence of it, aside from somebody reporting conversations.

Which typically isn't enough to pass judgement, except in this case it was.

I'm not going to offer opinion on that part of the ruling as I don't know the truth and unlike Lord Griffiths, who was judging the importance of one player to a football team over a season, I do not want to speculate.

But to me, this comes back to an issue I mentioned earlier, which was that the Premier League shouldn't have allowed Tevez to play the last three games of the season. That single ruling caused more damage and indignation than anything else. Had we won enough points from those three games and stayed up without the Argentine's help, none of this would have taken place.

As I have already said, we were right to try to keep Tevez available. But we should have been told no and the fact that we weren't is the fault of the Premier League and not West Ham United.

But in the end, we carried the can and were punished excessively for the crime of being arguably punished too leniently in the first place.

In a way, the whole mess of the binding arbitration, followed by another binding arbitration followed by another binding arbitration, summed up the entire shambles that was West Ham United in the 2006/07 season.

From signing seven quite good players when we only needed two very good ones, to losing our best forward to a career-ending injury three days before the season's start only to then sign two of the best young players in the world, which would, of course, lead to us not scoring a goal for two months.

Add to that a manager who got us into Europe being sacked six months after being two minutes from winning the FA Cup, to be replaced by a bloke whose 'new manager' bounce lasted one match, before then not winning a league game for another three months, all the while signing six more players, three of whom would hardly ever play for the club again when the campaign was done.

And then the most improbable, the most ridiculous, the most controversial 'Great Escape' of them all. Two managers, 29 players, six right-backs, two Argentinian superstars, three court cases and 38 games after it began, the craziest season in West Ham United's history was over.

I dare say it will never be topped. But don't ever rule out this club's ability to try and beat it.

Squad of 2006/07: What Happened Next?

1: ROY Carroll: 'Roy the Boy' left the club the following summer to join Rangers. He made just the one appearance for them in six months before leaving to play in goal for the Derby side that is to this day the lowest-point-scoring team in Premier League history. After that, his career took several random turns, with spells in Denmark and Greece yielding somewhat limited success, although he did end up playing at Old Trafford in the Champions League for Olympiakos, as you do.

His last English club was a two-year stint with Notts County from 2014–16 and he ended his career with Linfield back in his native Northern Ireland.

2(a): Tyrone Mears: By the end of this season, Mears was already at Derby on loan; he turned that into a permanent move, making 48 appearances for the Rams over two years. A very odd loan move to Marseille followed, after which five seasons were spent back in his native North West, where he played 82 times for Burnley, including one ever-present season in the

Premier League, and then three injury-plagued seasons with Bolton. The MLS came calling for Mears after that with spells at Seattle, Atlanta and Minnesota, before he finished his career in 2019 with a brief ten-game stint at West Brom.

2(b): Lucas Neill: 'Number two the captain, Lucas Neill' I remember him as, for it was the only way I ever heard his name read out at Upton Park. He had a successful two and a half years with us, playing 79 times before deciding not to renew his contract at the end of the 2008/09 season and joining Everton on a free transfer. A season at Goodison Park was followed by one in Turkey with Galatasaray and then not much else. A couple of appearances for teams in the UAE, Sydney FC, Japanese side Omiya Ardija and, weirdly, one game for Watford and four for Doncaster in 2014 was all Neill managed after he left the Turkish side, as he disappeared from view at great pace. He reportedly now lives an extremely private life back in Australia.

3: Paul Konchesky: Another player who left that summer, 'Konch' moved across London to Fulham for a reported fee of £3.25m. Three very successful seasons for the left-back culminated in him playing an important role in the Cottagers' 2009/10 Europa League run, which took them all the way to the final against Atletico Madrid.

This led to then-Fulham manager Roy Hodgson taking his player with him to Anfield, where he made 15 appearances for the Reds in a spell that is still fairly or unfairly mocked periodically to this day. He was quickly shipped off to Leicester, with whom he spent four successful years, before the poor sod was loaned to QPR for the season by new manager Claudio Ranieri, and thus missed all the Foxes' miraculous title-winning campaign. His career wound down at Gillingham and a couple of seasons in non-league football before he retired in 2019.

4: Danny Gabbidon: The groin problem that ruled the centre-half out for the season in January sadly persisted for the rest of his career, which limited him to only 25 appearances in the following three years, including none whatsoever in the 2008/09 season. He played a fuller role in his final season with the Hammers, which saw him making 26 starts in the season in which we came bottom of the Premier League.

Gabbidon was released at the end of that season and joined QPR for a year, which saw him turn out 17 times for the R's in the top division. One final Premier League season came after that as part of a two-year spell at Crystal Palace, before he finished his career back at hometown club Cardiff. The popular Welshman now works in the media.

5: Anton Ferdinand: After five seasons and 163 appearances for the Hammers, Anton headed a long way north to Sunderland in an £8m deal in August 2008 as part of a double signing that would see Curbishley resign as manager due to not being consulted on the deal. There were hopes that the defender could kick his career on in the North East and join big brother Rio as an England international. This sadly didn't happen and three underwhelming years on Wearside followed before he moved back to London with QPR in 2011; on his debut he reprised his once-successful partnership with Gabbidon at the centre of defence in a 0-0 draw with Newcastle.

The only thing memorable about his 18 months at Loftus Road was the 'John Terry affair' involving alleged racial abuse by the former England captain, and the talented centre-back moved to Turkish side Bursaspor in January 2013. Stints back in Britain with Reading, Southend and St Mirren followed, and Ferdinand retired from the game at the end of the 2018/19 season.

6: George McCartney: McCartney was the other player who moved to Sunderland in 2008 with Anton. For George, this was rejoining the club he had left to move to east London at the start of the 2006/07 campaign. The move was initially successful as he was the first-choice left-back under Roy Keane's charge, but after Steve Bruce came in as manager the Northern Irishman fell down the pecking order and wasn't even allocated a squad number for the 2010/11 season due to injuries and a loss of form.

This led to a season-long loan spell at Leeds before the following season George trod the path between Wearside and east London again as he rejoined us on loan for one season, when he played a full part in the promotion-winning campaign of 2011/12 (winning the players' player of the year award no less) before signing on a permanent deal the following summer. McCartney was with the club for three more years in total, making another 82 appearances, which took him to 147 in total in the claret and blue.

7: Christian Dailly: The oddly regular right-back during the 2006/07 season, who as we know by trade was actually an uncomplicated and committed central defender, didn't make another appearance for the club after the end of the campaign before joining Rangers in January 2008 after 191 games in over six years with the Hammers. He played 36 times in his 18 months at Ibrox before returning to London and joining Charlton on a free transfer. He played for the Addicks for two seasons, winning the club's player of the year award in his first season at the age of 36. He retired in 2012.

8: Teddy Sheringham: The vastly experienced forward was also released at the end of the 2006/07 season shortly after signing for Colchester, where during his season with the U's he became the oldest outfield player in the English football league at 42. He retired in 2008 and six years later returned to Upton Park as an 'attacking coach', a job he held for a year before becoming manager of Stevenage. He was sacked after a nine-month spell as manager with the club fighting relegation.

Outside football, Sheringham is an accomplished poker player who has competed at professional tournaments, and recently appeared on the ITV show *The Masked Singer*, on which he sung 'Evergreen' by Will Young dressed as a tree.

Which is the oddest sentence I will ever type.

9: Dean Ashton: As covered earlier in this book, Ashton retired in late 2009 due to the ankle injury suffered in 2006 never fully healing. He played the majority of the 2007/08 season, scoring 11 goals in 35 games, but did so in great pain and after four matches (and two more goals) the following season, he called it a day. He did at least win the England cap he deserved, playing for the Three Lions in a friendly against Trinidad & Tobago in the summer of 2008.

Ashton now has a successful career in the media, and at the time of writing is still only 36 years old. What could have been.

10: Marlon Harewood: As I mentioned earlier, the marvellous one was another player who left at the end of the 2006/07 campaign, joining Aston Villa for a reported fee of £4m. After an OK first season in which he scored six goals having mainly been deployed as a substitute, the arrival of Emile Heskey pushed Harewood down the pecking order and he joined then-Championship leaders Newcastle on loan having not made a start for the Villans in the 2008/09 season. He scored five goals in 16 games for the Geordies before injury struck and his loan was cancelled. Harewood was subsequently released by Villa.

Somewhat surprisingly, Marlon was back in the Premier League the following season as he signed for newly promoted Blackpool. Five goals in 16 appearances followed before he fell out of favour with Ian Holloway and ended up moving to Barnsley on loan.

The following five years saw the striker play for Guangzhou in China, boyhood club Nottingham Forest, Barnsley again, Bristol City, Hartlepool and Nuneaton before he retired in 2016. Harewood now works back at West Ham as a club ambassador and co-owns a business selling high-end bespoke cars.

11: Matthew Etherington: Matty stayed with the Hammers until January 2009, when he was sold by then-manager Gianfranco Zola to Stoke City for a fee of around £2m. Etherington made 195 appearances for the club in his five-and-a-half-year spell, scoring 18 times.

He was with Stoke for a similar amount of time, and also with a great deal of success, playing 177 times for the Potters with a further 16 goals, including another losing FA Cup Final appearance in 2011 against Manchester City.

Etherington retired in 2014 due to a back injury and now works as manager for Peterborough's under-18 team. He has spoken at length in the media about the gambling issues he had throughout his career and revealed that at times while a West Ham player he lost his entire weekly wages (estimated to be £20,000) in card games on the team coach after matches. The games were outlawed by then-manager Alan Pardew.

12: Carlton Cole: One of three long-term successes for the club from this group of players, something I doubt anybody would have expected at the end of the 2006/07 campaign. Due to an injury crisis in attack the following season, Cole found himself in the starting 11 come October and rarely lost this spot over the next six years. He got into double figures of goals in all competitions for three straight Premier League seasons, and top-scored for us in the promotion campaign of 2011/12 with 15 goals, his career personal best.

The following season was his least successful for the club as he was primarily used as a sub or back-up for first-choice forward Andy Carroll, and with his contract expiring at the end of that season he was released by West Ham in July 2013.

He signed for West Ham in October 2013.

In possibly the most West Ham thing of all time, we signed Carlton Cole to replace Carlton Cole.

In his 'second spell' with the club, he made 56 appearances (mostly off the bench) and scored another nine goals before leaving the club for definite (sort of) at the end of the 2014/15 season after a nine-year spell at Upton Park. All in all, he turned out in the claret and blue 293 times and scored 68 goals. He also made seven appearances for England, all as a sub. He has at the time of writing made the second highest number of appearances for West Ham in the Premier League (216) and scored the third highest number of goals (41).

A brief spell with Celtic and then the brilliantly named Indonesian club Persib Bandung followed before Cole officially retired in 2018.

He now works back at the club (of course he does) as an ambassador, as well as coaching some of the club's young players.

13: Luis Boa Morte: 'Boa' would be a regular starter for the club over the following two seasons, in which he played 64 times in all competitions with, shall we say, mixed reviews from supporters. He also over those two seasons scored no goals. None. An attacking midfielder who we signed to score goals from midfield managed one goal (the one at Wigan) in his first 80 games for the club. Yet another 'classic West Ham thing'.

Before the start of the 2009/10 season, Boa Morte sustained a severe cruciate ligament injury in a pre-season friendly against Tottenham and missed all but the entire campaign. He made his one and only appearance in the final game of the season against Manchester City. In which he scored. Of course he did.

This goal got him a two-year contract extension, which ended up only lasting for one season as he played 28 times in the West Ham team that came bottom of the league and were relegated. He scored no further goals.

The Portuguese played one further year in Greece and one in South Africa before retiring from the game. Most recently, he was assistant manager at Everton to Marco Silva before being sacked along with the manager in December 2019.

14: John Pantsil: The Ghanaian defender may as well have been on the missing persons list for most of the 2006/07 season, but rebounded the following year to gain cult hero status amongst fans with an excellent display in central midfield alongside fellow right-back Jonathan Spector as we beat Manchester United at Upton Park (that sentence gets stranger by the word), playing a large part in that, as well as part-weird, part-endearing solo laps of honour around the pitch after games. Pantsil departed the following summer to join Konchesky at Fulham, where he was a first-team regular for two seasons and ended up making 75 appearances over three years. Pantstil left Craven Cottage for a spell at Leicester that only ended up lasting a year and just seven games before spells in Israel back with former club Hapoel Tel Aviv and South

Africa with Santos and Maritzburg United wound down his career.

15: Yossi Benayoun: The Israeli playmaker left West Ham in controversial circumstances at the end of this season as he seemingly reneged on an agreement to sign a four-year contract extension with the club and instead expressed a desire to join Liverpool, a wish that was granted with a £5m fee agreed between the two clubs.

Yossi spent three seasons on Merseyside to great acclaim; making 134 appearances in all competitions and scoring 29 goals, including notably netting the winning goal as Liverpool beat Real Madrid in the Bernabeu in 2009.

He also became a pub quiz question answer while playing for Liverpool as he became the first player to score a hat-trick for the same club in the Premier League, Champions League and FA Cup, against Burnley, Besiktas and Havant & Waterlooville respectively. (Harry Kane and Sergio Aguero have done it since.)

Benayoun left Anfield in 2010 to sign for Chelsea for a fee of around £5.5m. Unfortunately, he ruptured his Achilles in a League Cup tie at Newcastle and by the time he returned to fitness had fallen out of favour at the Bridge.

A season-long loan spell at Arsenal followed in 2011/12, when he played 25 times and scored six goals, and the following year he returned to Upton Park on another year-long loan. Sadly, injury curtailed the move after only two months and six games, but it was nice to see the playmaker pull on the claret and blue again, even if only for a short spell.

A season with QPR in the Championship followed as Yossi continued a seemingly odd mission to play for every club in London one year after another, before he played for a further five years back in Israel and retired in 2019.

In his club career, the attacking midfielder played 746 times and scored 185 goals, as well as winning 102 caps for his beloved Israel from 1998 to 2017, netting another 24 times.

16: Javier Mascherano: After leaving us in January for Liverpool, Javier spent over three years at Anfield, playing in a Champions League Final loss to AC Milan and overall making 139 appearances for the Reds.

He left England in August 2010, joining Barcelona for €24m, and it was there that Mascherano truly realised the potential he had back when first signing for us. Playing either as a defensive midfielder or at centre-half, the Argentine played 334 times over eight trophy-laden years for the Catalan giants, in which they won La Liga and the Copa del Rey five times each, the Champions League twice, the World Club Cup twice and the Super Cup twice.

Not bad.

In terms of international recognition, Mascherano retired after the 2018 World Cup having made 147 appearances for his country, scoring three goals. He played in the 2014 World Cup Final, in which Argentina were beaten 1-0 by Germany. The midfielder was nominated for the Golden Ball award at that tournament.

Mascherano wound down his career with two years in China and at the time of writing is playing back in his native Argentina for Estudiantes.

Without a doubt, he lived up to the billing when he first joined the club, and has gone on to be one of the premier defensive players of the last 20 years.

17: Hayden Mullins: The defensive midfielder remained at Upton Park for another 18 months after the end of the season, whereupon he joined Portsmouth for an undisclosed fee, ending a five-year association with us during which he appeared 213 times in all competitions.

Mullins stayed at Fratton Park until the end of the 2011/12 season, a highlight for him being an appearance in the 2010 FA Cup Final, in which Pompey were beaten 1-0 by Chelsea; redemption for the midfielder with him having missed the 2006 final due to suspension.

Spells with Reading, Birmingham and Notts County followed before Mullins retired at the end of the 2014/15 campaign. He currently works as an under-23 coach at Watford.

18: Jonathan Spector: Spector remained with the club for another four seasons after 2006/07, mostly in the full-back positions, although the most famous of his 115 appearances for the club was in a central midfield role, where he scored twice against Manchester United in a League Cup tie in 2011, when we somehow beat the future champions of that season 4-0.

The American left after the club were relegated in 2010/11 and joined Birmingham. He would stay at St Andrew's for six years and play 179 games in all competitions for the Blues before returning to his native America to spend two seasons in the MLS with Orlando City, where he played with the Brazilian icon Kaka in one of those years and no doubt taught him a thing or two ...

He currently works for Atlanta United in a recruitment role.

19: James Collins: My fellow 'ginge' missed almost the entirety of the following season due to a knee injury. He returned and played 24 more times for the Hammers before departing for Aston Villa in August 2009, primarily due to the club being in financial difficulties at the time and needing money from the sale.

Collins turned out 108 times over three seasons at Villa Park before returning to east London after we were promoted in 2011/12.

Six seasons and a further 149 appearances followed for the Welshman, who gained hero status among the fans for his committed and whole-hearted displays. He left the club at the end of the 2017/18 season and save for a short spell at Ipswich pretty much ended his career with West Ham.

All in all, he played 214 times for us and scored nine goals across two spells, and would be widely considered as one of the most universally popular players among West Ham fans in the past 15 years.

20: Nigel Reo-Coker: The club captain over the 2006/07 season handed in a transfer request over the summer, citing a breakdown in relations and being 'hung out to dry' by the club management and supporters over the 'Baby Bentley' comments, as well as various rumours and accusations over a poor attitude in training and the dressing room.

He moved to Aston Villa for a reported £8.5m fee and would play 123 times for the Villans over four years, many of the appearances at right-back under Martin O'Neill before a disagreement with the Northern Irishman saw Reo-Coker ostracised for several months. He was restored to the team in the 2010/11 season by then-manager Gerard Houllier and eventually made club captain before leaving the club when his contract expired at the end of that season. Reo-Coker moved to Bolton and spent a virtually ever-present season there, but was unable to save them from relegation from the Premier League, whereupon he chose to leave the club.

And that, save for a short spell at Ipswich, was that for Reo-Coker's career in England at only 29 years old. He played in the MLS from 2013 to 2015 for Vancouver, Chivas and Montreal, and now works in the media as a football pundit.

21: Robert Green: 'England's number six', as he was affectionately known by West Ham fans, spent five further years at Upton Park as very much West Ham's number one. He missed just one game in the next four Premier League seasons and was a reliable and immensely popular player amongst the Hammers faithful. He won Hammer of the Year in 2007/08 and was runner-up for the award in the relegation season of 2010/11, as well as adding 11 more caps for England during his time at the club, in addition to the one he received while at Norwich.

He should have won many more than that such was his quality. While we all remember the horrible error he made against the USA in the 2010 World Cup, I believe that had he been the established number one for the previous two years, rather than going into the tournament still looking to establish himself over David James, that error wouldn't have taken place. Green left West Ham for QPR after helping the club win promotion in 2011/12 and stayed at Loftus Road for four years. He helped them gain promotion in 2014 as well, although they were relegated back to the Championship the following season.

A one-year spell at Leeds followed before non-playing seasons at Huddersfield and Chelsea finished up his career. Green's last act as a footballer was a memorable one as he lifted the Europa League trophy for Chelsea, despite not even being on the bench for the game.

Green's career saw him play 658 times in all competitions, with 241 of those coming for West Ham. I personally think he was the best goalkeeper that I have seen play for the club.

24: Mark Noble: No memory of what happened to this young player, I presume he drifted away from West Ham not long after …? I joke, of course. The 2006/07 season was just the start for the future 'Mr West Ham', as he is now known, his ten-match run in the team at the tail-end of the campaign setting the stage for what is now without question one of the most legendary careers in the history of the club.

I could write a separate book on Noble's time with the Hammers but to sum up as briefly as I can, he is, as I write, in his 13th season as a first-team regular since the 'Great Escape' season and has been club captain for just over half of that time. He led the team out in our last match at Upton Park and first match at the London Stadium, cementing his place in West Ham folklore. He has won our player of the year award twice and in late 2019 was voted by the fans as West Ham's player of the decade.

At the time of writing, Noble had scored the fourth highest number of penalties in Premier League history, and overall has scored over 60 goals in over 500 appearances in the claret and blue. He has played with them all over the past nearly 15 years in east London, from Tevez, Parker and Payet to Kovac, Zaza and Roberto, and has been the one constant through that entire time.

In 2007, we all had high hopes for what the midfielder could be for the club, and he has far surpassed all of those hopes in his career. I would like to write about his international career to finish this piece, but as all West Ham fans know, he is 'too good for England'.

25: Bobby Zamora: 'Bobby Z' stayed with the club for the following season but sadly saw the campaign blighted by injury as issues with knee tendonitis saw him miss over five months of the season and slide down the pecking order.

This led to Zamora swapping east London for west London the following summer as he signed for Fulham for a fee of just under £5m. His first season saw him score just twice in 35 Premier League games, which suggested the forward may have been a spent force as a top-division striker, only for his second season to be an absolute revelation. Out of nowhere, Zamora scored 19 goals, including eight in Fulham's run to the Europa League Final. The most memorable game of this run saw the forward take the legendary defender Fabio Cannavaro to the cleaners in a 30-minute spell in which Zamora scored and the Italian was sent off as Fulham casually beat Juventus 4-1 at home and knocked them out of the tournament.

Performances like this throughout the season saw the striker find international recognition and win two England caps across 2010 and 2011, and he may have played more if not for a broken leg suffered in the 2010/11 season that caused him to miss six months of action.

In early 2012, Zamora signed for QPR for a fee of £4m and spent just over three years at Loftus Road, most notably scoring the last-minute goal that took Rangers back to the Premier League in the 2013/14 play-off final against Derby, the second winning goal he had scored in that fixture following his strike for us against Preston. My brother Callum believes that these two goals make Zamora the biggest money-generating player of all time in English football, which is an interesting argument.

After a brief spell back at Brighton, Zamora retired in 2016 after a career that saw him score 190 times in all competitions in 570 first-team games.

27: Calum Davenport: The tall defender barely played for West Ham again after the 2006/07 season, with a handful of appearances at the start of 2008/09 being the sum total of the rest of his Hammers career. Loan spells at Watford and Sunderland barely provided him with first-team football before his contract was cancelled in 2010 after an incident led to him being stabbed multiple times in his legs. Davenport retired not long after and is now a college football coach in Plymouth, as well as working closely with his local church on fundraising projects.

29: Lee Bowyer: The midfielder spent another 18 months at Upton Park before departing for Birmingham, having made a total of 71 appearances during his two spells with the club, scoring five goals.

He enjoyed a stellar season in 2009/10 at St Andrew's, scoring six times as the Blues achieved their highest Premier League finish of ninth, and the following year won his first major trophy as a player as Birmingham beat Arsenal 2-1 to win the League Cup.

Bowyer retired in 2012 and at the time of writing is manager of his boyhood club Charlton Athletic, who he guided to promotion via the play-offs from League One in 2019.

33: Nigel Quashie: Quashie somehow stayed under contract with West Ham until 2010 despite never playing another match after the 2006/07 season. He was injured for the entire 2007/08 campaign, and then spent the next two years out on loan at Birmingham, Wolves, MK Dons and QPR.

After being released in January 2010, he played for a few years in Iceland before retiring in 2015.

35: Matthew Upson: The central defender remained at Upton Park until his contract expired at the end of the 2010/11 season, when the club were relegated. During his time with the club, he played 145 times in all competitions, scoring four goals. While at West Ham, he also played 14 times for England, including three matches at the 2010 World Cup, where he scored England's goal in their 4-1 second-round loss to Germany. He played 21 times in total for the national team.

Upson joined Stoke after leaving us, staying there for 18 months and making 27 appearances. Another 18 months in the Championship with Brighton followed before he finished his career with short spells at Leicester and MK Dons. He retired in 2016, and now does regular punditry work for the BBC.

37: Kepa Blanco: Kepa joined Getafe after his loan spell with ourselves expired, scoring twice in three seasons. He also played for Recreativo and Guadalajara before retiring in 2013.

Eggert Magnusson / Bjorgolfur Gudmundsson: Eggert stepped down as executive chairman and left West Ham early into the 2007/08 season. He sold his five per cent stake to 'BG' later that year.

Gudmundsson was financially decimated by the 2008 global banking crisis and declared personal bankruptcy in 2009, owing almost $750m.

In the single most West Ham thing of all time, our 'billionaire takeover' recorded the biggest personal bankruptcy in financial history under three years after he had taken over the club.

He released the club in June 2009 to asset management company CB Holding, which subsequently sold West Ham to David Gold and David Sullivan in January 2010.

And last, but not least …

32: Carlos Tevez: After a protracted 'transfer saga' in the summer of 2007, Tevez eventually joined Manchester

United on a two-year loan deal from … nobody. He played 99 times for the Red Devils in all competitions, scoring 34 goals. He won the Premier League in both seasons, as well as the Champions League in 2007/08, scoring the first penalty in the shootout win over Chelsea. (Tevez was one of *five* former West Ham players who started the match that night, along with Rio Ferdinand, Michael Carrick, Joe Cole and Frank Lampard.)

Memorably for West Ham fans, Tevez's first return to Upton Park, which resulted in a 2-1 win for the Hammers, saw him salute all corners of the ground with the 'crossed hammers' arm salute; when he was substituted he applauded the home fans with far more gusto than his own team's supporters, something he continued to do every time he returned to the Boleyn.

The Argentine was widely expected to stay at Old Trafford but sprang a surprise in the summer of 2009 by deciding to sign for 'noisy neighbours' Manchester City. He would stay there for four seasons, scoring 73 times in 148 games and winning the FA Cup in 2010/11 and the Premier League in 2011/12. He missed a fair part of the title-winning season, however, after he was ostracised for five months for refusing to come on as a substitute in City's Champions League game at Bayern Munich.

After a 0-0 draw at Upton Park that saw Tevez repeat the 'crossed hammers' salute, he was asked about the gesture after the match and explained, 'I have always had a fantastic relationship with the West Ham supporters. They were singing my name before the game and that's why I did that, in tribute to them. I've always felt really at home there.'

The striker departed for Juventus in June 2013 for a reported fee of £12m. He had what some people might say was a reasonable two years in Italy, scoring 50 times in 99 matches, winning Serie A twice and the Coppa Italia once, as well as playing in another Champions League Final, this time on the losing side as Juve were beaten 3-1 by Barcelona. Tevez also won the Italian giants' player of the year award in his first season, and Serie A player of the year in his second.

Spells with Boca Juniors, where he won two further league titles, and Shanghai Shenhua followed before Tevez returned to the Argentine side whom at the time of writing he still plays for, and where he will seemingly finish his career.

The dream that he may return to east London for one final stint has never died, however, and the player himself has stated that were he ever to return to Europe to play, it would only be for West Ham.

If that ever did happen, he would do well to make it more memorable or more talked-about than the first time.

Also available at all good book stores

9781785317309

9781785316906

9781785316883

9781785316845

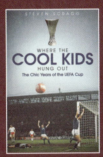

9781785316838

9781785316814

9781785316708

9781785316531

9781785316463

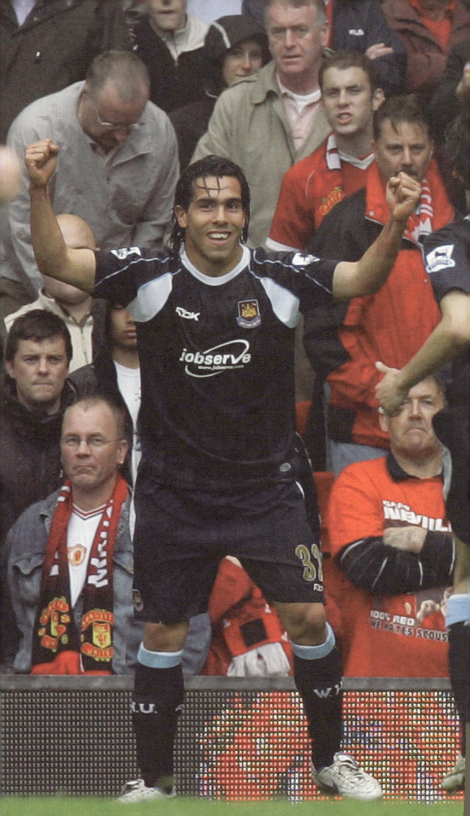